Joe ☑ P9-BIG-337

Omit ch. 2
    Appendix to ch. 3
    Appendices 1 & 2

Managing Pension Assets

Pension Finance and Corporate Financial Goals

Walter R. Good
President
Mellon Universe Management Group

Douglas A. Love
Managing Director
Matrix Capital Management

McGraw-Hill Publishing Company
New York   St. Louis   San Francisco   Auckland   Bogotá
Caracas   Hamburg   Lisbon   London   Madrid   Mexico
Milan   Montreal   New Delhi   Oklahoma City
Paris   San Juan   São Paulo   Singapore
Sydney   Tokyo   Toronto

Library of Congress Catalog Card Number: 89-39779

1234567890   DOC/DOC   89432109

ISBN 0-07-023729-8

*The editors for this book were Barbara B. Toniolo and Winifred M. Davis, the
designer was Naomi Auerbach, and the production supervisor was Suzanne W.
Babeuf. This book was set in Baskerville. It was composed by the McGraw-Hill
Publishing Company Professional and Reference Division composition unit.*

Printed and bound by R. R. Donnelley & Sons Company.

The authors are not engaged in rendering legal, tax, accounting,
or similar professional services. While legal, tax, and accounting
issues covered in this book have been checked with sources
believed to be reliable, some material may be affected by changes
in the laws or in the interpretations of such laws since the
manuscript for this book was completed. For that reason the
accuracy and completeness of such information and the opinions
based thereon are not guaranteed. In addition, state or local tax
laws or procedural rules may have a material impact on the
general recommendations made by the authors, and the
strategies outlined in this book may not be suitable for every
company or individual. If legal, accounting, tax, investment, or
other expert advice is required, obtain the services of a
competent practitioner.

*For more information about other McGraw-Hill materials,
call 1-800-2-MCGRAW in the United States. In other
countries, call your nearest McGraw-Hill office.*

Contents

About the Authors

Walter R. Good, CFA, and Douglas A. Love are highly respected authorities in the field of fund asset management and have written and lectured widely on investment subjects.

Good, a member of the New York Society of Security Analysts and the Institute of Chartered Financial Analysts, is president of Mellon Universe Management Group. He has managed pension assets from the vantage point of both plan sponsor and external investment manager, having served as chairman of the pension investment committee for the Continental Group, Inc., director of research for Brown Brothers Harriman & Co., and chief investment officer of Lionel D. Edie & Co. He holds undergraduate and M.B.A. degrees from the University of Chicago.

Love, managing director of Matrix Capital Management, was vice president/research of BEA Associates, founder and former chairman of Buck Pension Fund Services, and former chairman of D. A. Love & Associates. He also served as project manager for the Council of Economic Advisors to the President. He holds a B.M.E. in engineering from Cornell, an M.B.A. in finance and investments from New York University, and a Ph.D. in economics from Columbia University.

Preface

This book addresses—from the plan sponsor's point of view—the economic and investment fundamentals underlying pension asset management. To this end, it looks behind the actuarial assumptions, the accounting conventions, and the sometimes conflicting concepts involved in pension law. The resulting conclusion is critical to the management of pension assets. Pension finance is identified as a component of corporate finance, providing a framework for developing the pension investment objectives that best serve the plan sponsor's shareholders.

Equally important is the treatment of the investment process itself. The book explains how to organize, evaluate, and control pension investment activity to implement the plan sponsor's investment objectives. It distinguishes between investment policy and investment strategy—and shows how these two contrary approaches can be managed so that they complement each other. The management structure outlined here is supported by a review of how the investment markets work and by the formulation of an unambiguous method for measuring investment performance and determining accountability.

The need for a fresh look at pension asset management as the 1980s draw to a close is underscored by changes in several important areas.

Federal Regulation

Although Congress revised federal regulation of pension asset management with the passage of the Employee Retirement Income Security Act (ERISA) in 1974, the full implications are only gradually taking hold. Confusion during the years since passage of the legislation reflects not only the persistence of previously established concepts but also the conflicting assumptions indicated in various parts of the law itself.

Accounting

Accounting practice is still struggling to adapt to the redefinition of the rights of beneficiaries and the obligations of plan sponsor decisions incorporated in ERISA. The issuance in 1985 by the Financial Accounting Standards Board of FAS 87 was an important step in the right direction. This standard, however, represents a number of compromises that tend to obscure the underlying economic relationships.

Advancing Investment Technology

Progress has been achieved both in investment theory and in the development of new market instruments and new quantitative tools to implement investment decisions. The body of investment knowledge has benefited from research during the past generation in much the same way as has progress in other fields. Many of the old principles still hold true, but others are in doubt. Some have been displaced by new insights based on persuasive evidence. In this rapidly evolving environment, investment management must necessarily achieve increasing professionalization in order not to fall behind.

Corporate Mergers and Restructurings

Corporate mergers and restructurings, having put pension assets "in play," underscore their importance as a corporate finance vehicle. The role of pension assets in the corporate framework has been enlarged by their growing market values, most recently as a result of the bull markets in both bonds and stocks during much of the 1980s.

Acknowledgments

The authors gratefully acknowledge many valuable suggestions that have been provided by a number of sources. These sources include Jack R. Meyer, treasurer and chief investment officer of The Rockefeller Foundation; Jack L. Treynor, president, Treynor Capital Management, Inc.; Bryan F. Smith, senior councillor, Towers Perrin, and formerly, chief financial officer of Texas Instruments; Laura L. Fraley, CFA, vice president and director, Trust Financial Services, Ralston Purina Company; Robert E. Shultz, vice president, Pension Investments, RJR Nabisco; Charles R. Morris, partner, Devonshire Associates; Philip Silver, chairman of the board, Silgan Corporation, and formerly, chief financial officer of The Continental Group, Inc.; Leonard S. Chaikind, administrator, Shell-Provident Pension Trust/Fund; Paul H. Fullum, consultant, Rogers, Casey Associates; and associates at Mellon Universe Management Group and BEA Associates.

WALTER R. GOOD
DOUGLAS A. LOVE

Introduction: The Trillion-Dollar Opportunity

Growing Opportunities—and Risks

In recent years, pension funds have become an increasingly important issue in the management of corporate finance. Consider a few statistics. By the beginning of 1989, private pension funds representing defined benefit plans amounted to about $838 billion. (This estimate, provided by the Employee Benefit Research Institute [EBRI], does not include either defined contribution or insured plans.) At the same time, the current value of common shares trading in public markets approximated $2.7 trillion. While they do not deal with precisely the same population of companies, the two sets of figures are broadly comparable. They indicate that assets in corporate defined benefit plans, now approaching $1 trillion, may already average about 30 percent of the value of the common equity of the sponsoring corporation.

Higher Exposure for Many Companies

For a number of companies, pension assets constitute an even higher proportion of the market value of the plan sponsor's common equity than is indicated by the industry average. In certain cases, the ratio is increased by the use of ultraconservative actuarial assumptions, which overstate pension liabilities and encourage more rapid buildup of pension assets. While actuarial assumptions may be modified (within limits)

1

at the discretion of the plan sponsor, other—more basic—factors also tend to raise the ratio of pension assets to the plan sponsor's common equity and are more difficult to change. These basic factors include:

1. High labor content of the company's products
2. An older work force averaging long service
3. Slow growth, which implies relatively large liability for past service benefits
4. A low value placed by the market on the company's common stock (because of such factors as poor earnings record, low current profit margins, and either increasing competition or shrinking demand for the company's products)

When a plan sponsor with several of these characteristics faces an extended period of hard times, the market value of the pension fund may suddenly loom very large in any assessment of the company's financial health. For such companies, the pension fund is not only highly significant to future operating results but may also be critical to the company's survival.

Impact of Pension Fund on Plan Sponsor Profits

Successful management of pension assets will ultimately add to the level of the company's profits and cashflow, since incremental investment returns permit reduction both in cash contributions and in pension expenses as recorded by accountants. A dollar is invested in the pension fund today with the expectation that it will provide for certain retirement benefits to be paid in the future. If the investment return turns out to be greater than required to meet these anticipated retirement payments, the company's shareholders will benefit accordingly. An unanticipated gain in pension assets relative to pension liabilities will ultimately make possible an offsetting reduction in the company's cash contribution to the pension fund. (Adjustment for the effect on the company's tax liability will depend on the company's marginal tax bracket.)

In a perfectly efficient equity market, the market value of the company's common stock would immediately adjust for the future benefit to profits and cashflow, net of tax savings, from an unanticipated increase in pension assets. In reality, securities markets are not perfectly efficient and such precise, immediate adjustments almost certainly do not take place. Yet, evidence is accumulating that market prices of the plan sponsor's common stock reflect in large measure the changing relationship between the company's pension assets and liabilities. The market value of pension assets in relation to the market value of the sponsor's common equity is therefore a measure of the opportunity associated with pension financial management.

Further Opportunities to Enhance
Plan Sponsor Value

A pension plan may also provide opportunities to enhance the value of the plan sponsor's operations in at least two other ways. First, the size of a company's plan liabilities signals the importance of the plan in managing the firm's labor costs. If there were no pension plan, a company would be forced to pay compensation in an alternative form, such as higher wages or profit sharing. During recent years, the pension plan, with the aid of such devices as early retirement incentives, has even been used to manage the size and composition of the work force. Second, at the same time, a pension plan, within the range of its minimum and maximum funding standards, provides a means of managing the timing of tax payments.

Cumulative Impact of Incremental
Fund Returns

The most dynamic influence on the value of corporate equity is the return that the company obtains from its pension assets. The cumulative effect of very small increments in investment return on pension assets is often overlooked. Raising the total investment return by one-tenth of one percentage point adds only $1 million to a $1 billion fund during a single year. Compounded over a decade, however, a one-tenth of one point increase in annual return from 11.9 to 12 percent would amount to $28 million. The benefit of such incremental returns to the value of the company's common stock would be reduced to the extent that tax savings are associated with company contributions to the pension fund.

For a more extreme example, suppose that market values for both pension assets and the common stock of the plan sponsor amount to $1 billion and that tax savings, because of the particular tax situation of the company, do not apply to company contributions to the pension fund. Under these circumstances, an addition of two percentage points to the average rate of return over a 10-year time horizon, resulting in an increase in the average compound rate of return from 10 to 12 percent, would amount to $512 million. To the extent this increment is reflected

in the market value of the plan sponsor's common stock, it could add
about 50 percent relative to the value at the beginning of the period.
Thus, if the market price of the common stock would have increased
100 percent over the decade without the incremental return on the pension fund, it could rise 150 percent with the addition of the incremental
return. Suppose, on the other hand, that the company sponsoring the
pension plan encounters a difficult operating environment over a 10-
year period, which—in the absence of unexpected gains or losses for the
pension fund—would result in a 50 percent decline in the market value
of the common shares. Under these circumstances, the incremental return on the pension fund could mean the difference between a 10-year
decline in market value of 50 percent and holding even.

Increase in Risk since the
1973–1974 Bear Market

The other side of opportunity is risk. If the increase in the market value
of the plan sponsor's common equity should lag behind that of the pension fund assets, the market price of the plan sponsor's shares would
become increasingly vulnerable to poor results for the pension fund. As
a result of the 1973–1974 bear market, pension contributions as a percentage of payroll for many companies increased during the subsequent
5 years by multiples of 2, 3, or even more. The shortfall in investment
returns over that 2-year period resulted in levels of pension assets about
half of what had been expected. Repetition of such negative investment
returns in the early 1990s would be even more troublesome, in view of
the general increase since the mid-1970s in pension assets relative to the
market value of the plan sponsor's common equity.

Confusion in the Executive Suite

Despite the magnitude of pension assets—and even where they are un-
usually large relative to corporate net worth—pension financial management continues to be subject to controversy, if not confusion, in the
executive suite as well as in the boardroom. The increasing importance
of pension issues in the management of corporate finances is signaled
by their role in the financial maneuvers involved in takeovers, acquisitions, leveraged buy-outs, spin-offs, and corporate restructurings. Pension plans have clearly been put into play in the life and death struggles
of corporations. Yet, confusion is widespread with regard to their workings and their relation to the operating company and, specifically, to

stockholders. At the very least, plan sponsors are confronted with multiple, conflicting interpretations of their role. Much of the opposition to new financial accounting and disclosure rules, which aim to reduce the confusion, can be attributed to misunderstandings about the role of pension finances within the framework of the total corporation.

Fundamental Flaw in ERISA

A large part of the current confusion can be explained in terms of the history of pension legislation. Before 1974, pension assets and liabilities were contractually separate from corporate affairs. Pension contracts universally contained provisions assuring that the security of pension liabilities was limited exclusively to the assets in the pension trust. Pension liabilities could not reach through pension assets to constitute claims on corporate assets. Because of perceived abuses of plan participants resulting from such provisions, Congress passed the Employee Retirement Income Security Act (ERISA) in 1974.

The ERISA goal of overturning these provisions resulted in a major legal error that interfered with accurate interpretation of the role of pension finance. Congress, relying on a staff inexperienced in corporate finance and securities law, presumed incorrectly that the traditional disciplines of trust law, accounting, and actuarial methods were sufficient to the aims of the new legislation. (See Chap. 3, Appendix.) Consequently, ERISA retained a trust-law framework which in fact is in conflict with the basic intent of the legislation. Trust law provides that the liabilities of a trust cannot exceed the assets in the trust and, furthermore, excludes an IOU as a permissible trust investment. In actual fact, a major asset of the pension fund is the IOU of the plan sponsor to provide necessary future funding of liabilities.

Traditional accounting in the pre-ERISA world correctly relegated pension finances to footnotes to the financial statements. This approach was based on the then-correct premise that pension liabilities were not corporate liabilities and pension assets were not corporate assets. In the second decade after the passage of ERISA, changes in accounting disclosure rules have finally recognized the new financial and legal reality created by the 1974 legislation.

Who's in Charge?

Who in the plan sponsor organization is responsible for pension financial management? Since responsibility goes with authority, the person ultimately responsible for pension financial management is the same person who is responsible for product development, manufacturing, marketing, and finance. It is the chief executive officer (CEO). The CEO can delegate responsibility (typically to the chief financial officer), along with the commensurate authority, but he or she remains account-able for the net impact of pension management on the total company operations. With pension funds now averaging close to 30 percent of the market value of the plan sponsor's equity, the CEO must be satisfied that pension finances are being managed in a manner consistent not only with the fiduciary responsibility to plan participants but also with overall company goals.

While it may be comforting to assume that pension financial manage-ment can be delegated to well-qualified outside experts—benefits con-sultants, actuaries, accountants, investment consultants, and money managers—plan sponsors increasingly recognize that critical policy de-cisions must be made in house. These policy decisions, while leaving im-plementation to specialists, affect benefits, funding, and investments.

What Does the CEO Have to Know?

What does the CEO have to know in order to meet his or her respon-sibility for pension financial management? Surely a CEO does not have to focus on the detailed provisions of benefit arrangements, actuarial funding methods, or day-to-day decisions involving the purchase and sale of pension assets. Rather, the CEO should direct attention to the broad policy questions. The CEO, even though able to devote only a very small amount of time to pension issues, still needs to develop the working knowledge necessary to address the three key pension policy decisions:

1. *Benefits Policy.*   What kind of benefits and how large should they be?
2. *Funding Policy.*   How much to contribute to plan assets and when?
3. *Investment Policy.*   How to invest plan assets?

Who Should Read This Book

Because of the crucial role of the policies of top management in the area of pension finances, we address this book, first of all, to the CEO. This specific focus automatically broadens the interest in the book to the myriad other staff, both inside and outside the company, who have a role in shaping and implementing pension investment policy. Ulti-mately, what interests the CEO, as head of the team concerned with management of pension assets and liabilities, is likely to become compelling to all other members of the team and to those outside professionals hired to implement their policies. We target the book particularly to those ambitious segments of the team, such as the pension officer of the plan sponsor whose goal is to achieve an increased role in pension asset management or the external investment manager who plans to build a book of business with plan sponsors. We also expect that it will prove useful to specialists in mergers and acquisitions who must be concerned with the contribution of pension assets and liabilities to the value of the corporation and its parts. In recognition of varying reader backgrounds, discussions throughout will be sufficiently clear to anyone with a business background.

Need for Various Specialists to Understand Policy

The scope of the book is defined by the policy issues that dominate investment performance. This policy orientation reinforces the significance of the book to various specialists, including actuaries, accountants, and investment managers, who are first concerned with understanding the policy framework in which they work, and, second, must be prepared to participate in the formulation of policy recommendations, as requested by management of the plan sponsor.

Without clearly defined policies, the various professionals involved in management of a pension plan may unwittingly work against the investment program that would most effectively support corporate goals within the framework of fiduciary obligations to plan participants. Actuaries, if permitted, may favor an ultraconservative approach to investments and funding, since conservatism minimizes risk of embarrassment resulting from underfunding of pension liabilities. Accountants may too often be inclined to emphasize decisions implied by numbers in accounting statements rather than by economic consequences. Financial executives may mistakenly view pension fund management as a demonstration of special skill in forecasting interest rates and stock prices—and perhaps also prospects for other financial markets. Individual portfolio managers, who manage a portion of fund assets in isolation from other fund assets, plan liabilities, and the business of the plan sponsor, are not in a position to resolve the key issues relating to pension fund management.

Central Policy Role of Top Management

A sufficiently qualified pension officer who is a member of senior management is in a position to bring the key issues together so that they can be properly resolved by top management. The pension officer, however, does not always have the necessary qualifications or may not be in a position to exert much influence. As a result, the key issues may not be addressed in a way that is most effective in supporting corporate interests within the framework of fiduciary obligations to plan participants.

The premise of this book is that pension asset management, at least for most corporations, has become an increasingly important issue in recent years—and therefore requires corresponding attention to a well-considered policy framework. The CEO, although delegating the responsibilities in this area to the various specialists, is well advised to identify the appropriate issues and to insist that they be resolved within the policy framework defined for the total corporation. The attention of the CEO on the few key issues related to pension fund management, as indicated here, can do more than anything else to influence, focus, and direct the way the other members of the pension management team address their assignments.

How This Book Is Organized

Pension asset management may be considered at three levels. Viewed narrowly, it is the management of a portfolio of securities, with little allowance from one fund to another for either the differing patterns of pension liabilities or the differing circumstances of the sponsoring corporation. A second and broader view focuses on the management of pension assets in relation to pension liabilities. This emphasis on the management of pension surplus—within the pension plan itself—represents a step forward, but it still ignores the larger corporate context. The third alternative looks at management of the pension assets, together with pension liabilities, in the context of total corporate assets and liabilities. It recognizes that management of the pension fund, while meeting all fiduciary obligations to plan participants, also operates with wide latitude in support of corporate goals.

Since our view is described by this third alternative, the discussion that follows is organized accordingly. Chapters 1 through 5 examine the role of the pension plan within the framework of federal regulation but as part of total corporate operations. This initial section uses several current examples to show how the goals for pension fund management can be advantageously integrated with those for the total corporation. The middle portion of the book, Chaps. 6 and 7, brings a view of the financial markets and focuses on the development of pension investment policy. Chapters 8 through 11 are concerned with key issues confronted by the plan sponsor in delegating responsibility for various segments of the fund to individual investment managers. These issues include evaluation of the decision process, its application to active asset allocation, measurement of investment performance, and selection and supervision of the people who manage money. Chapter 12, in summary, provides an overview of the three critical issues involved in pension asset management and how these issues have been resolved in the earlier pages of the book. Appendix 1 summarizes Financial Accounting Standards no. 87, which deals with accounting for pensions. Appendix 2 addresses a recently proposed standard which concerns accounting for postretirement benefits other than pensions.

1
Pension Plans and Corporation Finance

A primary objective of this book is to legitimize pension finance in general, and the management of pension assets in particular, as an important, ongoing function in corporate finance. The essence of employee benefits, whether retirement income or postretirement medical benefits, is the exchange of future dollars or services for reduced wages. As such, retirement benefits are the financial equivalent of privately placed bonds. Top management must understand the cost, funding, tax, and investment consequences of these transactions.

Pension financial policies can be usefully broken down into three areas:

Benefits Policy. What kind of benefits, how much, and for whom? For starters, management must take care that employees value benefits fully. Stockholders should not provide more than a dollar's worth of benefits (present value) for a dollar's worth of labor (Chap. 1).

Funding Policy. How much to contribute, when? The purpose of funding for employee benefits (Chap. 2), its nature (Chap. 3), and its relation to pension cost (Chap. 4), are widely misunderstood. Moreover, because of the complexities and professional terminology surrounding actuarial funding methods, companies have tended to cede excessive control of corporate cashflows to their actuary. An overview and general approach to funding, which management can use to reclaim control, is outlined in Chap. 2.

Investment Policy. How to invest plan assets, longer term? We demonstrate that asset allocation as between stocks, bonds, and cash, conditions stockholder risk and returns and alters the firm's capital structure (Chap. 5). This view provides the background for the subject of investment management that begins with Chap. 6.

The Exchange of Values

Private pension plans could not exist in our competitive, free-market economy without benefit to both stockholders and employees. Liabilities for private defined benefit pension plans, as well as associated plan assets, are in the area of $1 trillion, and they amount to more than $2 trillion once postretirement medical obligations are added. Commitments of this huge size are not adequately explained by such simple answers as "because employees like them" or "all our competitors have them." More penetrating answers and understanding are required to serve as a guide to the design and management of these programs in the interests of corporate stockholders.

The fact is that pension and other employee benefit plans are a corporate-finance vehicle. Financial Accounting Standards Board standard no. 87 (FAS-87) radically overhauled pension accounting. (Its major provisions are excerpted in App. 1.) While we regard the accounting changes as a major step forward, we develop several criticisms of it in later chapters. Its principal contribution is to promote pension liabilities to the balance sheet. Before the new accounting standards, these plans were an off–balance-sheet liability. Second only to home ownership, private-sector pensions are middle-income America's premier tax shelter. The ability to save pretax dollars and to shift income to later years—when the tax bracket is lower—is an important inducement for employees to forego a portion of current wages in return for pension benefits. While this trade-off may not be apparent to outsiders, it is well understood, particularly by employees and employers in heavily unionized industries, and is explicitly visible to negotiators dealing with company–union wage settlements. Pension and other deferred compensation plans create current cashflows through reduced current compensation in return for promised future cashflows. This is a financing transaction.

Concept of Total Wages

In our modern financial society, firms compete in the labor market on the basis of total employee compensation (and equivalent stockholder cost) comprised of two components:

$$\frac{\text{Total}}{\text{compensation}} = \frac{\text{current}}{\text{wages}} + \frac{\text{increase in present value}}{\text{of deferred compensation}}$$

Corporations sponsor pension plans because they enhance stockholder value. Otherwise, they would offer employees current wages only. Total compensation costs can be lowered by the introduction of a pension plan, since a compensation package of current wages only is tax-inefficient. The employee would require more total compensation to be as well-off in terms of present values after tax. To provide the same income in retirement from after-tax savings, as opposed to savings out of pretax income as provided by a company-sponsored pension plan, is expensive. Thus, in substance, a corporate pension plan constitutes a continuous placement of corporate bonds with employees. The corporation receives the proceeds from the "sale" of the bonds in the form of lower current wages than would otherwise prevail.

Essence of Corporation Finance

The exchange of values is the essence of corporation finance. Stripped to its barest essentials, all corporate finance is the exchange by investors of value today in return for larger promised values in the future (interest, dividends, pension benefit payments, or medical services). Pension liabilities meet this test. The "proceeds" of the pension bond issue consist of the offsetting reduction in current wages. These cashflow savings merge with other sources of funds and become part of the pool out of which dividend payments to stockholders and the purchase of corporate and pension assets are made. Stockholders gain to the extent that, in combination, assets purchased by the corporation provide a higher return than the firm's debt, including pension liabilities. Pension assets in excess of pension liabilities earn a pretax rate of return after taxes, and also provide the firm with certain tax options because, to a degree, plan contributions can be timed to a firm's current-year tax situation.

Benefits Policy:
Defined Benefit versus
Defined Contribution Plans

A defined benefit plan promises future benefits for and places investment risks with stockholders. Conversely, a defined contribution plan places investment risk with employees. This critical difference has several ramifications for corporate finance.

1. *Defined contribution plans generate fewer benefits.* Compared with the same investment in a defined benefit plan, a dollar of defined contribution is likely to produce less final wealth for the employee. On the average, individual employees are much less sophisticated investors, and necessarily have shorter term investment horizons, than professionally managed institutions. It is not unusual for the asset mix of a defined contribution plan to be roughly 80 percent guaranteed investment contracts and other low-risk investments. In contrast, at least for most larger plans, defined benefit plans invest 60 percent in stocks. Although sustaining higher short-term volatility, the higher equity commitment will produce a higher long-term return. Consequently, the lower-risk investment choices made by individuals for their defined contribution plans will produce lower long-run investment returns and, consequently, support fewer benefits.

On the other hand, the portability and earlier vesting associated with defined contribution plans are of considerable value to employees (and of corresponding cost to stockholders). Moreover, there is something tangible about a defined contribution plan statement that most company defined benefit communications have so far failed to achieve.

2. *Defined contribution plans don't raise funds.* Defined contribution plans, unlike defined benefit plans, do not raise corporate capital. The liability accrual and the cash outflow occur simultaneously and are not separated by any meaningful period of time. As a consequence, there are no funds for the company to invest and no possible excess plan assets earning tax-sheltered returns.

3. *Defined contribution plans don't have a tax-timing option.* Because the contribution to a defined contribution plan is automatic, these plans yield no ability to manage plan cashflows to tax advantage. In contrast, defined benefit plan contributions, and hence tax timing, can be managed within some limits.

4. *There is a hidden put in defined contribution plans.* In a major decline of the securities markets, a whole class of retiring workers will find that the market value of their defined contribution assets will purchase fewer retirement benefits than they had planned. As a result, there will be considerable pressure, both privately and publicly, to seek redress from employers. Congress and the courts will be under nationwide political pressure, to the surprise and consternation of stockholders, to create value for these hidden plan *puts* associated with defined contribution plans. Many companies, in fact, did provide such special benefits outside of the terms of the plan to newly retiring employees in 1974 in response to the 1973–1974 bear market.

5. *Defined contribution plans are not necessarily cheaper.*   It is not at all clear that defined contribution plans are cheaper per dollar of ultimate benefits provided. Defined benefit and defined contribution plans have very different risks and rewards for stockholders and employees. They have different consequences for corporate finance and taxation. The shift of investment risk from stockholders to employees is a cost to employees. Lower investment returns on plan assets and the absence of tax sheltering and tax-timing options are important handicaps in the competition between defined benefit and defined contribution plans. In all, a shift to defined contribution plans is not the free lunch that many have made it out to be.

Pensions and Stockholder Value

As a source of capital, pension plans increase stockholder value as long as company projects and pension assets can be found to produce higher rates of return than the return on pension promises—i.e., the rate on long-term bonds. (A discussion of the appropriate discounting methods for appraising the present value of pension liabilities is the subject of Chaps. 3 and 4.) If employees implicitly give up less than a dollar of current wages in return for a dollar in present value of benefits, the firm's cost of capital is higher. Hence, if pension plans are going to benefit stockholders, employees must "purchase" or value them at or near par value.

Traditionally, the corporate finance dimension of pensions has not been explicitly treated. Vague generalities on the importance of communicating the value of employee benefits to employees have not focused on the economics of their capital-raising function. Unfortunately, there is survey evidence that the majority of employees may not appraise pension or postretirement medical benefits at their full value or at the cost necessary to purchase them in the open market. As a consequence, defined benefit plans can constitute a source of corporate funds with excessively high cost. Postretirement medical plans are proving even more dangerous in this regard.

Plan Design Issues

The corporate-finance and employee-management dimensions of pensions suggest that employee benefit designs adhere to several key financial principles.

1. *Employee Compensation Budget.*   All benefits should be "purchased" from a budget by each individual employee along the lines of a

salary reduction plan—an approach recently associated only with defined contribution plans. If employees are asked to pay explicit prices for benefits, they will make better decisions for themselves—and for stockholders, too.

2. *Flexible Benefits.* The mix of benefits should be at each employee's choice, subject, perhaps, to certain minimums. By optimizing his or her respective compensation portfolios of benefits, each employee will obtain the highest value of all available benefits.

3. *Risk Bearing and Disclosure.* Whether the employee bears investment risk (as in all defined contribution plans) or stockholders bear the investment risk (as in all defined benefit plans) must be absolutely clear to both parties. The idea that defined contribution plans are cheaper because they shift investment risk from stockholders to employees fails to allow for the employee response to the greater risk. If employees are to bear investment risk, they must demand either higher contributions or higher current wages to be as well-off on a risk-adjusted basis. It is for this reason that the big, well-counseled auto and steel unions have fought against the substitution of defined contribution for defined benefit plans by management. As with financial markets more generally, there is no free lunch available from shifting economic risk from one party to another. Individuals may not demonstrate such economic acumen. However, because errors in judgment tend to be offsetting, economic acumen is demonstrated by large groups, particularly over the longer term.

Financial Disclosure

Relative to operating assets, pension assets and pension liability accruals are very significant for most corporations. If the ultimate users of corporate financial statements—outside investors—are to fairly appraise company values, liabilities, and expenses, the size of pensions must receive explicit treatment on a consistent basis. So far, the corporate community has been reluctant to have the FASB adopt an accrual accounting standard for the financial reporting of pension obligations and expenses. The economic realities of pension finance, although ongoing, have had executive visibility primarily only in conjunction with mergers and acquisitions and with plan terminations and asset reversions.

Postretirement Medical Plans

Recently, postretirement medical plans have been much in the news, and as this is being written the FASB is in the final stages of promulgating pension-like accounting standards for these liabilities. In a narrow sense, the subject is beyond the scope of this book, which is addressed to the management of pension finances. The corporate-finance dimensions of postretirement medical benefits are just surfacing and receiving attention corresponding to their impact on corporate expenses and profits. Consequently, we summarize here the broad financial features of postretirement medical plans. We also highlight and comment on selected excerpts from the FASB's Exposure Draft on its proposed accounting standards for this subject in App. 2.

To the surprise of many top executives, company buy-outs, spin-offs, and restructurings have unearthed large liabilities for medical benefits. Costs have escalated rapidly as more employees have become eligible and as medical-cost inflation has exceeded general inflation by two or more percentage points. Unlike defined benefit pension plans, these are liabilities to provide real services and are therefore linked to inflation. They do not promise a predetermined amount of nominal dollars. Moreover, while a person can only use so many television sets or automobiles, there is no such diminishing marginal utility for medical services. Their consumption has no such satiation bounds. Medical technology can create cures whose high cost presents society with severe ethical problems over whose life will or won't be spared.

The good news about corporate involvement in this service industry is that it interposes between the medical profession and consumers a professional economic interest in the quality and cost of care. The bad news is that it is tantamount to management writing a naked call on inflation.

Benefits Policy

Companies offering postretirement medical benefits have done so largely as an extrapolation of their medical-cost coverage of active employees. However, their deferred nature, combined with the pattern of medical claims experience by age, and their complete indexation to inflation were bound to result in runaway costs. There can be no assurance that stockholders obtain a dollar's worth of labor for a dollar's worth of future medical benefit promises unless (1) postretirement medical plans contain a means of putting a cap on inflation and (2) employees "spend" for them out of a current compensation budget, such as that described above.

Recent court cases have found these promises irrevocable to existing retirees. In the celebrated LTV Corporation bankruptcy case, Congress rushed through special legislation to force LTV to reinstate postretirement medical benefit payments. Having appraised the potential cost buildup in these plans, some companies have gone so far as to eliminate these benefits for future retirees. To be sure, the value of these plans to employees is great. However, increased clarity in their design, legal status, and the projectability of the cashflows they will entail in the future are required before stockholders can be assured that these plans economize on total employment costs.

In response to these problems, companies have taken a range of steps to control or curtail benefits. First dollar coverage is being abandoned in favor of significant and growing deductibles. Dollar caps are being introduced. Some firms have eliminated benefits for all new hires, and some have eliminated them even for existing employees not currently eligible to receive benefits. In return for the elimination of benefits, employees have been given mixtures of additional pension benefits, newly created Employee Stock Option Plans (ESOPs), joint defined contribution plans for the payment of medical insurance premiums, and guaranteed insurance coverage with private carriers contracted by the company.

Funding Policy

The ability to contribute to prefunding postretirement benefits has been severely limited by budget problems of the federal government. Tax deductibility has been severely constrained and limited to a maximum specified as a proportion of contributions to defined benefit pension plans. For fully funded or overfunded pension plans, this means no deductibility at all for funding postretirement medical benefits. Congress has expressly and repeatedly turned aside proposals by the Department of Labor and the administration to allow companies with overfunded pension plans to use some portion of surplus to begin prefunding postretirement medical obligations.

Some companies have bitten the bullet by initiating funding with taxable funds. Public utilities and defense contractors have more incentive to proceed with taxable funding because of their ability to incorporate such expenses into their product pricing. Ameritech, a major supplier of telephone services in the midwestern states, has been one of the very first companies to prefund postretirement medical benefits.

Investment Policy

The approach to the investment policy issues surrounding the investment of pension assets, as detailed in subsequent chapters, also applies to the investment of assets held to secure postretirement medical plans. Very few companies have thus far initiated funding of postretirement health care plans, and this book does not specifically address investing for this purpose. As spelled out later, however, we support policies that go well beyond the piecemeal matching of individual corporate liabilities with individual corporate assets, or *immunization* (except for benefit plans imminently to be terminated).

Our position concerning pension plans applies with even greater emphasis to postretirement medical plans. Our analysis of the FASB's Exposure Draft on accounting for postretirement medical liabilities in App. 2 makes clear that the daunting assumptions underlying the necessary actuarial projections of benefit payments cannot be usefully matched by an immunizing bond portfolio. Perhaps the biggest risk in these plans is medical-cost inflation, against which fixed-income securities cannot be a good hedge. In fact, the inability to settle these claims through defeasance via an arrangement with an insurance company is testimony to the fact that fixed-income investing is not a reasonable replication of the economics of postretirement medical obligations. If insurance companies have not found a low-risk way to secure such promises for their clients, companies sponsoring these plans should not expect to, either.

Skip

2

The Nature of
Pension Funding

When it comes to pension funding and investment, senior corporate management has been handicapped by impressions gleaned from the actuarial, legal, and accounting professions that do not gibe with economics or with real-life corporate treatment of pensions. This handicap has had the result that many companies have ceded too much management prerogative to their actuaries. In order to control pension finances in the interest of stockholders, management must first achieve a shared clear perception of the corporate finance dimensions of pensions.

Confusion about the Role of Pension Funding

Confusion about the role of pension funding is underscored by confusing it with pension cost (the subject of Chap. 4) and, more fundamentally, by several purposes erroneously attributed to it.

The Purpose of Funding Is Not to Pay Benefits. The common belief that the purpose of stockholder pension contributions is to pay benefits is an incomplete one. Over the life cycle of a pension plan, contributions *exceed* benefit payments until full funding is achieved.

The Purpose of Funding Is Not to Reduce Pension Costs. Nor is funding a means of reducing cost. This misperception ignores the basic financial principle of present value: that the present value of all future pension contributions is the same whether they are made soon or late.

It's always pay now or pay more later. Contributing early and earning investment returns reduces future contribution needs, but it does not reduce current period costs.

The Purpose of Funding Is Not to Achieve Equity between Generations of Stockholders. Nor is it the purpose of funding to enforce "intergenerational" stockholder equity: to ensure that pension claims incurred by a generation of owners is paid by that generation. This view ignores the economics of the pricing of securities in competitive securities markets. As long as pension obligations are properly accrued and disclosed, the markets will appropriately dock stock values for pension costs whether or not they are funded currently. Consequently, the current generation of stockholders pays the same for its pension promises whether they fund or not.

The Purpose of Funding: To Secure
Benefit Payments

The real purpose of funding is to secure benefit payments against the contingency that the sponsoring company becomes unable to make benefit payments at some point in the future. A plan for which assets are "book reserved" (accrued on the balance sheet but not funded with cash) does not provide anything like the security of a funded plan.

Key Financial Attributes of a
Funded Plan

A funded plan has three key financial attributes that a "book-reserved" plan does not:

1. Pension assets are *trusteed* such that beneficiaries have first and exclusive claim in bankruptcy.
2. Pension assets are *diversified*. Claims against the undiversified operating assets of a troubled company provide much less security.
3. Pension assets are *liquid*. Annuities can be purchased with plan assets with little loss of market value.

In short, only pension funding provides employees (or the Pension Benefit Guaranty Corporation, on their behalf) with means independent of the future success of the sponsor's operating business.

Managing Funding Policy

The Quest for "Constant" Contributions

In the actuarial community there is a maxim that says a good actuary is one who does not surprise clients with changes in plan contribution requirements. Consequently, there is a continual search for a magic combination of funding method and assumptions that will produce a contribution stream that is constant as a percentage of total payroll. Many corporate executives and actuaries evaluate funding schemes according to the constancy of the contributions produced—most practically, as a constant percentage of payroll. Presumably, "good" funding methods do not lull management into profligate ways by producing a pattern of contributions that is higher later than initially. The models frequently used to test for constancy are based on simplistic demographics—an individual life or a static group (constant average age and other real-world factors held constant). In fact, changing demographic dynamics and reasonable differences in assumptions can reverse the time pattern produced by any two funding methods.

In a very fundamental sense, there can be no such thing as constant funding. Assets must be built up whose future returns will be sufficient to preclude the need for further contributions (*full funding*). Contributions must exceed benefit payments until adequate funding is built up and then they decline, possibly to zero. By way of analogy, the driver of a car must step harder on the gas to climb a hill (to reach full funding) than to keep going once the top is reached.

In the end, management should seek a 3- to 5-year plan of its own design. Although the plan must conform to legal constraints, management should retain enough control to tailor contributions to current-year tax status or to support other varying short-term needs.

"Steady State" Funding.[1] An excellent way to gain insight into the dynamic process of pension funding is to investigate what engineers describe as the system's "steady state" properties—the behavior when a process settles down into a repetitive pattern. A pension plan reaches such a long-run pattern, or full maturity, when two key conditions are met:

1. All retirees and active employees are covered by the same plan provisions. This means that the latest plan amendments must be at least

---

[1]These concepts were taught by James J. Cryan, retired director of Buck Consulting Actuaries, Inc., New York, N.Y.

10 years old so that the predominance of employees are under the same plan terms. In general, a constant state cannot exist unless the plan terms governing all participants are the same.

2. The ratio of the number of retirees to active employees, and the average age of both groups, has stabilized (become constant).

Under these conditions, pension liabilities and benefit payments will grow at the same rate as wages and salaries (say, 7 percent per year). The ratio of both benefit payments and liabilities to payroll will then also be constant. (Assume benefit payments are 12 percent of the total payroll.) A constant funding ratio of assets to liabilities (say, 1.2 to allow a cushion for declines in asset market values) means that assets, after benefit payments and contributions, are also growing at the same rate as total payroll. A 3:1 ratio of liabilities to payroll means that benefit payments are $[12 \text{ percent}/(3 \times 1.2)] = 3.33$ percent of assets. If investments are assumed to return 9 percent, then, *without contributions,* asset growth would be 1.33 percent short of the necessary 7 percent required to keep the funding ratio from deteriorating. Contributions must be 1.33 percent of assets to close the gap. (Note that if a funding ratio of 2:0 were maintained, contributions required to sustain it would be zero.)

The Equilibrium Balance.   Out of these simple calculations comes the following balancing requirement:

Sources			Uses (pension cost)		
Investment returns	+	contributions	= benefit payments	+	growth in liabilities
9%	+	1.33%	= 3.33%	+	7%

For an immature plan, liabilities are growing faster than payroll because (1) the average ages for both active and retired employees is still increasing, (2) newer and presumably higher benefit amendments are becoming effective, and (3) the ratio of retirees to actives is still growing. Contributions as a percentage of payroll must be increasing for an immature plan and must be significant as a percentage of plan assets.

"Back of the Envelope" Pension Funding

Management can make use of these very simple relationships to do calculations on minimal actuarial data for establishing approximate pension fund policy. The process involves the following steps.

1. *Project benefit payments and liabilities forward.* Using management's wage and salary growth assumptions and long-term interest rates, have the actuary project benefit payments and pension liabilities forward.

2. *Select target horizon date and funding ratio.* Select a future date (say, 7 years) and a target funding ratio as of that date. This yields a target level of assets.

3. *Project assets forward with no contributions.* Project *existing* assets forward gross of assumed investment returns and net of projected benefit payments.

4. *Piece in the required contributions.* Evaluate the assets required to close the gap between projected "existing" assets and required assets. This increment must be produced by contributions and investment returns on these contributions. The pattern can be one that grows at the same rate as payroll, which then dictates what the initial contribution must be.

Actuarial Funding Methods

Some executives invest considerable effort in understanding the nuances of different actuarial funding methods and of different actuarial assumptions. However, these technicalities cannot overcome or supersede the consequences of the back of the envelope approach. Each of the accepted actuarial methods represents a coherent internal logic, none of which can lay claim to superiority over the others. Moreover, under different demographic conditions and assumptions, one method can produce results much like another. Consequently, management can within reason (related to funding levels some years hence) decide on an accommodating projected contribution stream. It then becomes the actuary's job to use a selection of methods and assumptions to produce that result. Within limits, this approach is the reverse of current practice, where the actuary unilaterally determines the pattern of the contribution stream for management.

All actuarial methods begin with the same computations, concluding with the difference between two values: actuarial liability (the funding target) and the (actuarial) value of plan assets.

Actuarial Liability. The actuary's liability measure was never intended to represent any legal or financial liability. It is better thought of as a very conservative (i.e., large) funding target. The actuary's definition of liabilities allows for projected wages, projected service, and, possibly, liabilities to be accrued in the future for employees not yet even hired (open group projections). Traditionally, actuarial funding methods employ the same assumed rate for both (1) discounting (present valuing) projected benefits and (2) projecting future investment returns on plan assets. This dual purpose number is often below current long-term market interest rates. In combination, these factors produce a large target liability. Under the actuary's definition of liability, full funding implies that all present and future liabilities under the existing terms of the plan require no further contributions.

Actuarial Value of Plan Assets. To help in smoothing contributions, the actuary will frequently apply a moving average of asset market values, or at least a method of smoothing the difference between assets at cost and at market.

Unfunded Actuarial Liability. The difference between these values for assets and liabilities is then funded according to two components: (1) a *normal cost* defined by the funding method and (2) the amortization of the remaining actuarial unfunded liability defined to be

Unfunded actuarial liability	=	actuarial pension liability	−	actuarial value of plan assets	−	present value of future normal costs

In this formulation, the present value of future normal costs is counted as an asset, even though these contributions have yet to be made.

Actuarial Liability Not a Liability. To anyone other than an actuary, the value of a plan's unfunded actuarial liability is potentially misleading for several reasons:

- The value is net of a large IOU in the form of future contributions identified as "normal costs" whose value is determined by the logic of the chosen funding method. It is *not* the difference between liabilities and assets (unless one is willing to accept contributions not yet made in the form of the present value of future normal costs as an asset).

- The gross liability measure does not, and is not intended to, correspond to any concept of financial liability.

- Neither the liability nor the asset measure is marked to market but is governed by subjective assumptions and to past as well as current values.

Projection Studies

Traditional funding determinations are the outcome of a classic actuarial valuation study, which, importantly, does not produce along the way any explicit projections of benefits, liabilities, or assets in future years. Increasingly, management is turning to studies with the advantage that future values for assets, liabilities, benefit payments, and contributions are explicit. In addition, greater realism in asset return and wage volatility is incorporated. Originally intended to study present and future funding, these studies are now employed to explore the consequences of different investment policies or of asset mixes between stock, bonds, and cash.

These studies are valuable in pulling together a common understanding among the several management interests involved—human relations, treasury, investment management, and actuarial interests. They reinforce the need to settle on an explicit investment policy with respect to average long-term asset allocation across asset classes. It is well to renew these studies about every 3 years, or on occasions when significant change in operations impact company demographics.

3
The Economic Nature of Pension Claims

In order to measure pension costs realistically, as well as to fund pension liabilities and invest pension assets wisely, it is necessary first to come to grips with the real economic nature of pension claims. This is a challenge, because much conventional wisdom is derived from misinterpretations of, or mistaken premises relating to, past and present accounting methods, actuarial funding methods, federal regulations, and tax law. To clarify our position, we focus on four key principles about pension plans and their financing:

1. *Pension claims* are more real (denominated in goods and services) than nominal (denominated in dollars).

   CONSEQUENCE: Long-term, *fixed*-coupon bonds (e.g., not index-linked) are not an adequate proxy for pension liabilities.

2. *Pension plans* are designed to replace a targeted fraction of the real standard of living after an employee achieves retirement age.

   CONSEQUENCE: In the long run, the support of real living standards requires ownership of real assets or productive capital (such as real estate and common stocks).

3. *Pension liabilities* are corporate liabilities. They are part of the capital (debt) structure of the firm.

   CONSEQUENCE: There is no reason to single out pension liabilities for hedging to the exclusion of other corporate *liabilities*.

4. *Pension assets* are corporate assets. They are part of the asset pool that gives rise to stockholder risk and return.
CONSEQUENCE: There is no reason to single out pension assets for hedging pension liabilities to the exclusion of other corporate *assets*.

Pension Claims, Nominal or Real?

Should pension claims be considered claims on future dollars (*nominal claims*) or claims on future goods and services or a standard of living (*real claims*)? The difference between the two is crucial for estimating the exposure of future claims to changes in inflation and interest rates and, hence, for appraising their present value and their balance sheet volatility.

The answer to this question can be pursued by restating the question in another form: To what extent are pension claims indexed for inflation, either explicitly by plan provisions that relate benefits either to wages and/or inflation or implicitly by company policies implemented over time? The answer is as follows.

For Retirees. Pension history indicates that the average corporation makes up something like one-half of inflation's impact every 3 years to retirees. Many plans contain explicit provisions for partial indexation in retirement—COLAs (cost-of-living adjustments). Management will typically provide for some ad hoc adjustments from time to time.

For Actives. A long-standing actuarial insight is that all pension plans, ultimately, are "final pay" plans. A true final pay plan might provide something like 1 to 2 percent of the final year salary for every year of service with the company. Some use a *final average* of pay—typically the final 5 years. Others may use *career average*. Union plans are typically *flat dollar* plans—so many cents per hour of work. But, sooner or later, with lags of differing length, all respond to changing levels of pay. Over long enough periods of time, all produce more or less complete indexation for inflation during an employee's active years by virtue of the link between wages and salaries and inflation. At a minimum, then, it might be considered to produce perhaps 30 percent real (or indexed) benefits for retirees and 80 percent to 100 percent indexed benefits for active employees. Thus, benefits might be considered to be 30 percent real (or indexed) for retirees and 80 to 100 percent indexed for employees while active. By holding the gap between wage growth and interest rates constant, the actuary is assuming a parallel impact of inflation on wages and interest rates, and thereby full indexation, at least for active employees. In reality, wages respond to realized (recent past) inflation and interest rates respond to expected (future) inflation.

Hence, the actual gap between wage growth and interest rates fluctuates, but these fluctuations tend to average out in the longer term.

The consequences for pension finances of the relationship between pension claims and inflation and interest rates are pivotal in appraising liabilities, their balance sheet volatility, and the construction of long- or short-term hedges.

Interest Rate Exposure
(Liability Volatility)

"Duration." If the coupon and principal on a bond are both fully indexed to prevailing interest rates, the bond's price will be completely unresponsive to changes in interest rates. It will have an interest rate exposure of zero. A standard 5-year, zero-coupon bond will, on the other hand, decline (or increase) in price by 5 percent for every 1 percent change in interest rates. It is said to have an interest rate exposure, or *duration*, of 5 years—the ratio of its percent change in price to a 1 percent change in interest rates. The interest rate exposure, or duration, for a zero-coupon bond, is equal to its maturity. This is not the case for a coupon-paying bond or for a stream of cashflow. The duration of a coupon-paying bond is always less than the time to the last payment. A 20-year U.S. treasury bond, for example, has a duration (depending upon the current level of interest rates) of about 10 years. The duration measure, then, is a device for converting the interest rate sensitivity or exposure of any bond or cashflow stream into that of a zero-coupon bond having the same interest rate risk exposure.

Financial analysts considering the sensitivity of pension liabilities to interest rate fluctuations will find that retiree liabilities currently have a duration of about 7 years, and active liabilities have about 14 years. A total plan will have a combined interest rate exposure of from 10 to 12 years—typically 11 years. Under these conditions, a 1 percent rise (or fall) in interest rates will cause an 11 percent fall (or rise) in the marked-to-market value of pension liabilities. This is the appearance given by the new (1985) accounting standard (FAS-87). By requiring that a market-determined interest rate be used for the present valuation of pension liabilities, the FASB has cast pension liabilities as long-term (fixed-coupon) bonds with interest rate sensitivity comparable to a 30-year treasury bond. *The FASB's approach to the valuation of pension liabilities is appropriate, provided projected wages are also adjusted for changes in expected inflation imbedded in market interest rate changes.* By ignoring this link, financial analysts and executives seeking to hedge interest rate risk in their liabilities are induced to misapply the FAS-87 framework.

Interest Rate Hedge. A simplistic view of interest rate exposure has led many corporations, frequently supported by the advice of their investment banker, to substantially increase their allocation to bonds at the expense of stocks and/or to lengthen the maturities of bonds held as pension assets. This strategy aims to hedge the interest rate risk in plan liabilities with long bond pension assets to neutralize balance sheet volatility. For an ongoing pension plan, this approach to pension investment policy has serious flaws because it violates all four of the principles outlined at the beginning of this chapter.

This strategy assumes that there is no indexing of pension liabilities to inflation. Assuming that pension liabilities are predominantly real (indexed) leads to the opposite hedging strategy. Following sound actuarial precedent, projected wage and salary growth rates should be tied to a long-term bond market rate. This has the effect of cutting liability volatility by more than half.

For example, suppose long-term interest rates increase by 1 percent. Other things equal, the rise in interest rates, as indicated previously, would result in an 11 percent decline in the present value of pension liabilities having a duration of 11 years. But other things are not equal, because the same increase in expected inflation that caused long rates to rise will sooner or later result in an increase in future wages and have the impact of *increasing* pension liabilities, partially offsetting the interest rate–induced decline.

Consider the data shown in Table 3-1. The approach taken by corporate executives, bankers, and investment managers is an overly simplistic interpretation of pension liabilities based on accounting convention. *If* pensions were not at all indexed to wages and/or inflation, the volatility of pension liabilities in response to 1 percent interest rate changes can be seen by reading the numbers vertically. A better version of fi-

Table 3-1. Pension Liability Volatility: Interest Rates, Inflation, and Wages
Projected Benefit Obligation (dollars in millions)

Interest rate	Projected wage growth		
	5%	6%	7%
8%	$106	$111	$116
9%	95	100	105
10%	85	90	95

nancial reality recognizes that the major source of changes in interest rates is changes in *expected* future inflation. Wages, on the other hand, respond to experienced inflation. Because the bond market is a very good forecaster of inflation, over periods of sufficient length, wages and interest rates will move in tandem. If investment policies are sufficiently long term, at least 3 to 5 years, the upper left to lower right diagonal is a better representation of the actual state of affairs. Note, in Table 3-1, that the range of volatility on the diagonal (from $106 to $95 million), when both *wages as well as interest rates* are incorporated in the analysis, is only half that of interest-rate-driven volatility on the vertical (from $111 to $90 million).

Because aggregate stock dividends tend to respond to inflation experienced over time, statistical (as opposed to theoretical) measures of the sensitivity of stock prices to long interest rates suggest a duration of only 3 to 5 years. Total bond market indices, like the aggregate corporate/government universe, have a duration of 4.5 to 5 years. Hence, if the objective is to hedge pension liabilities *to the exclusion of other corporate liabilities and assets,* any asset mix, as between stocks and bonds representative of the entire corporate/government bond market, will have an approximate, appropriate interest rate sensitivity for hedging ongoing, aggregate pension liabilities.

In the very short run, interest rates change and wage rates don't. In the long term, interest rates and the rate of change in wages move together. This has the following Rip Van Winkle effect.[1]

Bonds. Consider a pension plan 100 percent funded, all in long bonds (11-year duration) with frozen contributions. In the short run, since only interest rates are changing, plan liabilities are fully hedged (assuming that projected wages either are ignored, as in accumulated benefit obligation [ABO] measures of pension liabilities, or are held constant). In the short run, the probability of being underfunded is small. However, as actives become retirees and as inflation and real wage gains are realized, the probability of an underfunded plan increases. If one naps for 7 years or so, liabilities then will be dominated by benefits driven by wages and inflation accrued in the interim. If inflation surges, bonds collapse in value at the very instant when prospective pension payments are accelerating.

Stocks. Suppose on the other hand that the plan were invested 100 percent in common stocks. Owing to their greater volatility, the probability of an underfunded position is significant because of the sheer vol-

---

[1]This allegory was originally used by Jeremy Gold of Morgan Stanley & Co., New York, N.Y.

atility of stocks. However, several longer-term characteristics of stocks work in the plan's favor. First, dividends are likely to keep up with wages. Second, higher *average* total returns will cumulatively put some distance between assets and liabilities. Over the longer term, stock prices tend to rise with dividends, and total investment return includes both dividends and capital appreciation. Finally, if future living standards are very high, it is because the economy has very productive capital in place, from which the stock market should have benefited while this capital demonstrated its value.

Coping with Balance Sheet Volatility

Under accounting rule FAS-87 companies may be intimidated by the consequences for short-run balance sheet volatility of the adoption of a market-determined interest rate for present valuing pension liabilities. Without the counteraction of a matching (immunizing) bond portfolio, the fear is that the difference between assets and liabilities may fluctuate wildly. A more realistic fix is to employ a wage and salary projected growth rate equal to long-term interest rates minus some fixed amount (say, 3 percent).

If the goal is to match the interest exposure of pension assets and liabilities—a goal that we do not support *for ongoing companies*—management has a choice. Management may either (1) match a fiction (that pensions are nominal, or not substantially indexed) with poorly hedging assets (long bonds) or (2) match an approximate truth (that pensions are real, or substantially indexed) with productive (real) assets such as stocks. While these two options may represent extreme positions, the long-bond syndrome has greater long-term danger at the enticement of short-term stability.

Plan Terminations and Spin-Offs

Of course, anything that truncates the management horizon of a plan, such as an imminent termination or spin-off in conjunction with the sale of an operating company, signals an immediate need to convert pension assets into a liability matching bond portfolio. It is because of this that FAS-87 has been characterized as a termination construction, not an ongoing view. For a healthy company with ongoing operations, the goal of simply matching the (interest rate) risk of pension liabilities with pension assets overlooks the broader goals of pension finance in relation to corporation finance.

Pension Plans as Provision for Real Living Standards

Pension plans are targeted to some explicit "replacement ratio" of income in retirement to income just prior to retirement. Hence, they are indexed to total wages and not just to inflation. The ultimate pension plan objective is the provision of a standard of living relative to one's working years and to one's peers. This difference between inflation and wages is far from trivial for an individual employee when increases related to promotion are added in. The wage data reported by the financial media imply that wages increase with inflation plus some measure of aggregate productivity. However, the demographic dynamics of group measures suppress the real wage increases posted by *individual* employees when promotions are considered. Thus, the living standards of an employee aged 65 is much higher than a 45-year history of inflation and, say, a 1 percent annual real wage gain would suggest. Changes in real living standards over time, then, are of considerable importance to understanding pension claims.

If future living standards are much higher, it is because much of the right kind of capital has been accumulated, from which the stock market must have benefited in the interim. Consequently, the best hedge against big rises in future living standards is to participate via the stock market in what makes those high living standards possible.

Pension Liabilities as Corporate Liabilities

In pre-ERISA days, pension plans contained explicit covenants that limited pension liabilities to the assets segregated in trust for the purpose. Liabilities then were liabilities of the trust, not of the sponsoring corporation. However, a couple of renowned bankruptcies (Horn & Hardart and Studebaker-Worthington) left numerous employees without pension promises. These incidents produced a media-amplified constituency that Congress had to respond to. The response was an inadequately drafted law, the Employee Retirement Income Security Act of 1974. Since the law was written by staff and counsel familiar with pensions and not with securities law, the drafters were too quick to presume that trust law was the appropriate legal model. From this model comes the admonition that assets are to be employed for the "exclusive benefit" of the (pension) beneficiaries. However, in order to accelerate the security of benefits, the law's Title IV provided that pension liabilities could reach through plan assets to attach corporate assets, should plan assets prove insufficient in a termination. Moreover, the newly created Pension Benefit Guaranty Corporation (PBGC) was given the power to force plan terminations, should it deem that continuance posed an undue threat to the insurance facilities of the corporation.

Individually and collectively, these provisions blew away the relevance of trust law. The liabilities of a trust are defined by the assets in the trust. A trust cannot have an IOU as an asset. Liabilities in a trust cannot exceed or reach through the assets in the trust, nor can it have an "unfunded" liability. Consequently, contrary to conventional wisdom and the formative basis of ERISA, a pension plan cannot be a trust. Federal legislation will remain problematic until it is recognized that the appropriate legal model is bankruptcy law.

An unfunded liability signifies that somebody has a liability and hence is a beneficial owner of the assets in the trust because if the assets do well, that liability is reduced. Since the employees presumably are to receive their claims regardless of asset performance, they are not in the position of beneficiaries of a trust. By allowing the PBGC to reach through pension assets on behalf of employees, these assets become merely a first line of defense. The ultimate liability is shifted to stockholders.

As a corporate liability, pension debt is part of the firm's capital structure and leverage, just as is other corporate debt. Hence, any risk management strategy that singles out pension liabilities to the exclusion of other corporate liabilities is a special form of myopia. This myopia will dissipate when someday the FASB calls for marking all corporate debt to market.

Pension Assets as Stockholder Assets

The act of making pension liabilities de facto corporate liabilities also made pension assets stockholder assets. Good or bad investment performance reduces or increases the need for future contributions by raising or lowering the value of pension assets. This difference in required future contributions translates into either the ability to pay dividends currently or the firm's break-up value. Hence, stockholders bear the investment risk of pension assets in a direct manner—and *risk bearing is the hallmark of ownership*.

Short of a termination for which plan assets are not sufficient to cover benefits in excess of PBGC maximum insurance guarantees, employees are not at risk for pension assets. Two modifications to this segregation of the beneficial ownership of asset risk and return need be mentioned.

First, to the extent that a plan is underfunded, the PBGC is at risk that it will have an underfunded plan "put" to it. In other words, the risk of plan assets is partially underwritten by a free put against the PBGC. Second, some have made much of the fact that an underfunded plan affords management a stronger bargaining position with labor over pension benefits. But this position is likely to be transitory. In general, total compensation is effectively set by industry and, in the longer term, by the national labor market, not by an individual company.

Our four economic principles are fundamental and differ importantly from conventional wisdom. Given the principles we have enunciated, much current practice is suspect.

Appendix $SKI\textup{\textrightarrow}$
Employee Retirement Income Security Act of 1974

Conflicting points in law incorporated in ERISA are documented in the following pages by reference to excerpts from the act as published in its updated and consolidated form by Prentice Hall Information Services.[2] Titles and paragraph numbers as well as text are as reported in the Act.

By way of introduction, the first section (2) excerpts the purpose of the legislation. The next section (403) specifies that pension assets be held in trust for the "exclusive benefit" of plan participants. The conflicts in law arise from the exceptions—sections 4042, 4044, and 4062. These provisions are explicitly contrary to trust law and directly oppose the purpose of section 403 and the concept of exclusive benefit. Section 4042 gives the Pension Guaranty Corporation unilateral rights to terminate pension plans. Section 4044 credits the plan sponsor with reversion rights to assets in excess of plan liabilities. Section 4062 establishes liability against the net worth of specific persons should pension assets prove insufficient, and section 4068 establishes the priority of that liability as equal to that of a federal tax lien.

Title I—PROTECTION OF EMPLOYEE BENEFIT RIGHTS

Subtitle A—General Provisions

2. *Findings and declaration of policy*

SEC. 2. (a) The Congress finds that the growth in size, scope, and

---

[2]David C. Areson, ed., *Employee Retirement Income Act of 1974 (Updated through September 1, 1986)*, Prentice Hall Information Services, Paramus, N.J., 1986 (reprinted with permission from the Prentice Hall Information Services).

numbers of employee benefit plans in recent years has been rapid and substantial; that the operational scope and economic impact of such plans is increasingly interstate; that the continued well-being and security of millions of employees and their dependents are directly affected by these plans; that they are affected with a national public interest; . . . that they substantially affect the revenues of the United States because they are afforded preferential Federal tax treatment; that despite the enormous growth in such plans many employees with long years of employment are losing anticipated retirement benefits owing to the lack of vesting provisions in such plans; that owing to the inadequacy of current minimum standards, the soundness and stability of plans with respect to adequate funds to pay promised benefits may be endangered; that owing to the termination of plans before requisite funds have been accumulated, employees and their beneficiaries have been deprived of anticipated benefits; and that it is therefore desirable in the interests of employees and their beneficiaries, for the protection of the revenue of the United States, and to provide for the free flow of commerce, that minimum standards be provided assuring the equitable character of such plans and their financial soundness.

(b) It is hereby declared to be the policy of this Act to protect interstate commerce and the interests of participants in employee benefit plans and their beneficiaries, by requiring the disclosure and reporting to participants and beneficiaries of financial and other information with respect thereto, by establishing standards of conduct, responsibility, and obligation for fiduciaries of employee benefit plans, and by providing for appropriate remedies, sanctions, and ready access to the Federal courts.

(c) It is hereby further declared to be the policy of this Act to protect interstate commerce, the Federal taxing power, and the interests of participants in private pension plans and their beneficiaries by improving the equitable character and the soundness of such plans by requiring them to vest the accrued benefits of employees with significant periods of service, to meet minimum standards of funding, and by requiring plan termination insurance.

Subtitle B—Regulatory Provisions

Part Four—Fiduciary Responsibility

Establishment of Trust

SEC. 403. (a) . . . All assets of an employee benefit plan shall be held in trust by one or more trustees. Such trustee or trustees shall . . . have exclusive authority and discretion to manage and control the assets of the plan, except to the extent that—

(2) authority to manage, acquire, or dispose of assets of the plan is delegated to one or more investment managers. . . .

(c)(1) *Except as provided* in paragraph (2), (3), or (4) or subsec-

tion (d), or under section 4042 and 4044 (relating to termination of insured plans), *the assets of a plan shall
never inure to the benefit of any employer and shall be
held for the exclusive purposes of providing benefits to
participants in the plan and their beneficiaries and de-
fraying reasonable expenses of administering the plan.*

. . .

TITLE IV—PLAN TERMINATION INSURANCE

Subtitle C—Terminations

Institution of Termination Proceedings by the Corporation

SEC. 4042. (a) The corporation may institute proceedings under
this section to terminate a plan whenever it determines that—
  (1) the plan has not met the minimum funding standard re-
      quired under section 412 of the Internal Revenue Code of
      1954, or has been notified by the Secretary of the Treasury
      that a notice of deficiency under section 6212 of such Code
      has been mailed with respect to the tax imposed under sec-
      tion 4971(a) of such Code,
  (2) the plan *will be* unable to pay benefits when due,
  (3) the reportable event described in section 4048(b)(7) has oc-
      curred, or
  (4) the possible long-run loss of the corporation with respect to
      the plan may reasonably be expected to increase unreason-
      ably if the plan is not terminated.
*The corporation shall as soon as practicable institute proceedings
under this section to terminate a single-employer plan whenever
the corporation determines that the plan does not have assets available to pay benefits, which are currently due under the terms of the
plan.*

Allocation of Assets

SEC. 4044. (a) In the case of the termination of a single-employer
plan, the plan administrator shall allocate the assets of the plan
(available to provide benefits) among the participants and beneficiaries of the plan in the following order:
  (d) (1) Any residual assets of a single-employer plan may be
          distributed to the employer if—
          (A) all liabilities of the plan to participants and their
              beneficiaries have been satisfied,
          (B) the distribution does not contravene any provision
              of law, and
          (C) the plan provides for such a distribution in these
              circumstances.
      (2) Notwithstanding the provisions of paragraph (1), if any
          assets of the plan attributable to employee contributions
          remain after all liabilities of the plan to participants and
          their beneficiaries have been satisfied, such assets shall
          be equitably distributed to the employees who made

such contributions (or their beneficiaries) in accordance with their rate of contributions.

Subtitle D—Liability

Liability for Termination of Single-Employer Plans Under a Distress Termination or a Termination by the Corporation

SEC. 4062 (a) In General—In any case in which a single employer plan is terminated in a distress termination under section 4041(c) or a termination otherwise instituted by the corporation under section 4042, any person who is, on the termination date, a contributing sponsor of the plan or a member of such a contributing sponsor's controlled group shall incur liability under this section. The liability under this section of all such persons shall be joint and several. The liability under this section consists of—

(e) Definitions—

    (1) Collective net worth of persons subject to liability—

        (A) In general—The collective net worth of persons subject to liability in connection with a plan termination consists of the sum of the individual net worths of all persons who—

            (i) have individual net worths which are greater than zero, and

            (ii) are (as of the termination date) contributing sponsors of the terminated plan or members of their controlled groups.

        (B) Determination of net worth—For purposes of this paragraph, the net worth of a person is—

            (i) determined on whatever basis best reflects, in the determination of the corporation, the current status of the person's operations and prospects at the time chosen for determining the net worth of the person, and

            (ii) increased by the amount of any transfers of assets made by the person which are determined by the corporation to be improper under the circumstances, including any such transfers which would be inappropriate under title 11, United States Code, if the person were a debtor in a case under chapter 7 of such title.

        (C) Timing of determination—For purposes of this paragraph, determinations of net worth shall be made as of a day chosen by the corporation (during the 120-day period ending with the termination date) and shall be computed without regard to any liability under this section.

Lien for Liability

SEC. 4068 (a) If any *person* liable to the corporation under section 4062, 4063, or 4064 *neglects or refuses* to pay, after demand, the amount of such liability *to the extent of an amount equal to the unpaid amount described in section 4062(b)(1)(A)(i)* (including interest), there shall be a lien in favor of the corporation *to the extent of an amount equal to the unpaid amount described in section 4062(b)(1)(A)(i)* upon all property and rights to property, whether real or personal, belonging to such *person.*

(b) The lien imposed by subsection (a) arises on the date of termination of a plan, and continues until the liability imposed under section 4062, 4063, or 4064 is satisfied or becomes unenforceable by reason of lapse of time.

(c) (1) *Except as otherwise provided under this section, the priority of a lien imposed under subsection (a) shall be determined in the same manner as under section 6323 of the Internal Revenue Code of 1954 (as in effect on the date of the enactment of the Single-Employer Pension Plan Amendments Act of 1986). . . .*

(d) (1) In any case where there has been a refusal or neglect to pay the liability imposed under section 4062, 4063, or 4064, the corporation may bring civil action in a district court of the United States to enforce the lien of the corporation under this section with respect to such liability or to subject any property, of whatever nature, of the *liable person,* or in which he has any right, title, or interest to the payment of such liability.

(2) The liability imposed by section 4062, 4063, or 4064 may be collected by a proceeding in court if the proceeding is commenced within 6 years after the date upon which the plan was terminated or prior to the expiration of any period for collection agreed upon in writing by the corporation and the *liable person* before the expiration of such 6-year period.

4

What Does a Pension Plan Cost? Decoding FAS-87

The object of this chapter is to unravel the complexity of pension cost by discriminating between employee pension income (stockholder expense) and the returns on pension assets (stockholder income).

The Need to Discard Conventional Wisdom

Accounting and actuarial conventions are indifferent to much of the real economic content of pension plans. Hence, if corporate management is to make informed decisions on pension finance, it is important to see its fundamental economic dimensions clearly—particularly as related to expense. Present measures of pension expense are dominated by either actuarial practice or budgeting and funding considerations. Federal tax legislation has reinforced this approach. As a matter of enlightened public policy, Congress purposefully promoted plan funding by making contributions (cash) deductible for tax purposes rather than some measure of pension expense (accruals). Because something is tax deductible does not mean it must constitute an appropriate measure of expense.

Financial Accounting Standards Board—Standard FAS-87

Prior to the issuance of FAS-87 (see App. 1), Accounting Principle Board APB-8 reigned for many years. APB-8 confined pension disclosures to balance sheet footnotes and used actuarial assumed interest rates and other actuarial assumptions. Actuarially required contributions were accepted as the appropriate measure of pension expense and thereby led to the acceptance of very different funding methods. The wide latitude in contributions and disclosure was supported by management, actuaries, and accountants as a necessary reflection of "differing circumstances as between companies and plans."

With time, two criticisms of APB-8 began to overwhelm the status quo. First, it became clear that companies in similar circumstances were able to report widely differing pension expense. This gave rise to the charge, brought to the attention of Congress, that companies were using APB-8 to manipulate earnings. Moreover, plan terminations and merger and acquisition activity made it clear that APB-8 provided little guidance as to the real price effects of pensions on company purchases and sales. Second, the size and significance of pension finances for many companies became obviously too large to confine to financial statement footnotes. Management, actuaries, and accountants continued to argue, despite the dictates of ERISA's Title IV, that the pension "trust" had no place on the balance sheet. Stirred by criticisms in the popular financial press, and by pressure from the SEC and Congress, the FASB was motivated to overhaul APB-8.

The new standard broke much ground, but it included key weaknesses, some left over from the past and some newly introduced to contain balance sheet volatility and to smooth the transition. The principal features and accomplishments of the new standard are as follows.

1. *Promotion.* Pension finances were given *almost* full balance sheet recognition. The "almost" comes from the fact that unfunded, but not surplus-funded status, is recorded.

2. *Model.* A single consistent methodology was adopted as a consequence of the application of fundamental accounting principles. The computations happen to coincide with one of several actuarial funding methods (*unit credit*). As a consequence, there is to this day a generally held, incorrect, criticism that the FASB had arbitrarily selected one of several equally "good" actuarial methods.

3. *Liabilities.* Pension liabilities are marked to market by the application of a market-determined interest rate for present-valuing projected benefits.

4. *Liability measure.* The liability measure for determining cost is the projected benefit obligation (PBO), which includes the accumulated benefit obligation (ABO) plus the impact of projected future wages for active employees. The smaller ABO was given balance sheet status as a measure of "minimum liability." Hence, balance sheet and income statement related liabilities are not the same!

Accumulated benefit obligation (ABO) = liability computed considering service to date and current wages.

Projected benefit obligation (PBO) = liability computed based on service to date and a projection of future wages to retirement age.

5. *Assets.* Pension assets are disclosed at fair market value. Their performance contributes to negative pension expense, and only after significant smoothing. The liability offset role accorded pension assets is the FASB's reading of ERISA's "exclusive benefit" rule.

6. *Cashflows.* While the FASB's "Preliminary Views" document and public hearings promised relevant cashflow data (benefit payments, contributions, and dividend and interest income on assets), these disclosures were withheld at the eleventh hour on grounds of "excessive disclosure." In defense, the board pointed out that these numbers could be derived from the required disclosures. However, doing so has generally proven to be impossible in practice.

7. *Smoothings and amortizations.* These accounting adjustments give great latitude for smoothing fluctuations in assets and, to a lesser extent, in liabilities. Pension surpluses are leached into earnings by amortization over many years. This accounting anomaly produces a significant reserve, contributing to earnings for years to come as a result of conservative funding and buoyant securities markets for many past years.

While FAS-87 correctly sought to uncouple a measure of accounting expense from funding (and hence taxation), it is still predominantly a funding formulation. Moreover, its results are dominated by heavy-handed smoothings and amortizations.

Criteria for Proper Cost Measures

FAS-87 does not meet simple economic criteria for financial cost. A proper cost measure should meet several elementary criteria not met by existing measures. These criteria reflect important economic principles of ownership and the symmetry of income and expense measures with assets and liabilities.

1. Income and expense measures must logically reconcile (articulate) with changes in measures of asset and liability values, respectively. (*Articulation* is a term used to recognize the principle that income and expense items must reconcile with changes in asset and liability—balance sheet—items.)

The FAS-87 measure of expense articulates with a projected measure of pension liabilities, which includes future wage increases (the PBO). The FAS-87 balance sheet liability, however, is determined by an accrued pension liability recognizing only wages earned to date (the ABO). Thus FAS-87 does not meet a straightforward articulation test.

2. A corporation is not a person, but a collection of constituencies. Hence, for a corporation, every expense is somebody else's income, and every liability is somebody's asset. (This important articulation principle in economics is not consistently observed by accounting.)

The FAS-87 measure of pension expense is nobody's income. If correctly measured, it should be an unambiguous component of employee income reflecting changes in pension wealth.

3. The only logical source of reduction in pension expense has to be a reduction in promised benefit payments. How can the cost of a pension plan be reduced without reducing pension benefits? The ultimate cost of a pension plan is solely determined by the benefits it promises to make. Therefore, pension expense must "articulate" only with changes in pension liabilities.

The FAS-87 measure of pension expense is "reduced" by the return on pension assets.

4. How pension assets figure into a corporation's income and expense as between employees and stockholders must reflect the substance of the pension contract and, in particular, the stockholder's de facto ownership of pension assets. While higher investment returns mean lower stockholder contributions, neither investment returns nor contributions have anything to do with pension cost. Because investment returns have everything to do with stockholder risk, however, they are a component of stockholder income. As a consequence, then, stockholder contributions are not an expense but, like plant and equipment, a stockholder purchase of assets.

FAS-87 treats investment returns on pension assets as negative pension expense. With sufficient plan assets, good returns frequently produce a negative total pension expense number.

5. Finally, the financial essence of pensions is the issuance of privately placed (indexed) bonds with employees. Consequently, pension

cost and the cost of bond issues, sooner or later, must have similar accounting treatment.

FAS-87 marks pension liabilities to market, but corporate bonds continue to be carried on the balance sheet at face value.

FAS-87 is careful to employ current market interest rates in present-valuing projected benefit payments, but it avoids addressing the issue of how the projected benefit payments themselves should be altered on a basis consistent with the expectations about future inflation imbedded in interest rates. In practice, substantial changes in long interest rates over extended horizons are partially offset by parallel changes in wage growth.

Pension Contributions Not an Expense

Just as the purchase of plant and equipment produces future returns to stockholders, so, too, does the purchase of pension assets. Returns on plan assets diminish the need for stockholder contributions in the future. Correspondingly, stockholder contributions—which are then used to purchase pension assets—are no more an expense than is the purchase of new plant or equipment. Returns on plan assets are an element of stockholder income. Pension contributions are a (tax-deductible) acquisition of stockholder assets (used as collateral for accrued pension claims), not an expense.

Investment Returns Not a Component of Pension Expense

Consistent with the recognition that plan contributions are not a cost is the recognition that the cost of a pension plan is independent of the existence of plan assets. Whether or not a plan is funded has no bearing on what it costs stockholders. Funding and associated investment returns do not change *the present value* of all required contributions but merely redistribute contributions over time. This is so even though such redistribution has consequences for the time pattern of cashflows and possibly tax timing. It is the promise to pay benefits that is the source of all costs. How these costs are financed or met does not alter them. When a company buys a machine, its price is fixed. If it pays cash or borrows and defers ultimate payment, the present value of the payment is the same although the timing of the flows differs. The price of the machine does not change. Its cost is unaltered by how or when it is paid for.

Pension Liabilities and Pension Cost

Stockholders have assumed the liability to pay accrued, vested pensions. This stockholder liability is an employee asset. Employee pension income, and therefore stockholder pension expense, articulate (reconcile) with changes in pension liabilities. Anything that increases pension liabilities increases employee wealth and constitutes a cost to stockholders. An appropriate measure of pension cost is the sum of (1) the change in the value of pension liabilities between the beginning and end of the year and (2) benefit payments made during the year.

Each year a number of events take place that alter the present value of these liabilities and, symmetrically, represent components of employee income and stockholder expense.

The Components of Pension Cost

Interest Cost. The interest due on a pension liability is the same cost element as on any debt obligation. It represents the increase in present value of future benefits because they are 1 year closer to being received. This increase in value is referred to in the jargon of the bond market as "rolling down the yield curve." It is equivalent to the income investors earn on zero-coupon bonds. This element, adjusted for currently received benefit payments, is also a component of current retiree income.

Service Cost. Over the course of the year, employees have earned additional benefits because they have accumulated another year of service and have generally achieved higher pay. Every pay increase then has an associated pension cost.

Plan Amendments. Pension plans are frequently revised to grant additional benefits based upon service already rendered in the past (prior service). These increases may include additional cost-of-living adjustments (COLAs) for retirees.

Actuarial Losses (Gains). Changes in demographics and estimated utilization of different benefit elections also affect pension liabilities and, hence, employee wealth. An actuarial gain is a reduction in cost to stockholders and a reduction in the expected present value of employee income.

Capital Gains (Losses). Current interest rates reflect the cost to stockholders of the defeasance of pension liabilities. A decline in rates results in an increase in the present value (defeasance cost) of pension liabilities

L reflects a change

and constitutes a capital loss to stockholders and a capital gain to employees. In part, these wealth transfers reflect changes in market expectations about future inflation. A decline in rates reflects the market's belief that the real purchasing power of promised future cashflows is higher and that future pension dollar claims will be more valuable. The gain or loss is computed by taking the difference between (1) closing plan liabilities based on year-end interest rates, (2) the value of the same liabilities based on interest rates as of the opening date, and (3) an inflation adjustment recognized by computing the closing liability at opening and closing projected wages.

Inflation Adjustment. We take the view (see Chap. 3) that pension promises are substantially indexed (real). Hence, a reduction in interest rates today reflects in large part a reduction in inflation expectations in future years and, therefore, also a reduction in projected benefit payments. The same holds in reverse, of course. Thus, changes in interest rates in their impact on liability values are partially offset by prospective wage changes and, hence, projected benefit payments. If there is no indication of adjustments to projected pension liabilities for changes in expected inflation when interest rates change, we instigate an adjustment using an estimated duration measure. As a rough estimate, we employ an interest rate exposure (duration) measure of 5 years rather than the 11 or so years that financial analysts find when measuring the sensitivity of pension present values to changes in interest rates only.

Together, these six preceding components capture all the elements of pension cost. Actuarial and accounting statements group these pension cost (stockholder cost/employee income) elements differently and require manipulation of data to tease out the separate pieces. However, financial analysis is best understood in terms of these six component pieces. Henceforth, we reserve the word *cost* for our measure and the word *expense* for accounting using FAS-87–derived numbers.

Computing Pension Cost

The following tables present pension financial data according to the economic principles just outlined. Table 4-1 reconciles changes in pension liabilities over the year for two companies, one small (West Company) and one large (General Motors). Table 4-2 shows the identity between two routes to computing pension cost. The first method adds together the elements of pension cost described earlier in this chapter. The second method simply adjusts the change in pension liabilities for benefit payments made during the year—a simple and direct measure of how much better off employees are at the end of the year than at the

Table 4-1. Analysis of Pension Cost*

	West Company (dollars in thousands)	General Motors (dollars in millions)
Opening interest rate	@ 9%	@ 10.9%
Opening pension liability (12/31/1985)	$38,731	$25,012
Interest	3,400	2,599
Service cost	1,395	640
Benefit payments	−1,845E†	−2,080E
Amendments	—	—
Gains/(losses)		
Actuarial	—	—
Capital	6,447	7,627
Closing pension liability (12/31/1986)	$48,128	$33,799
Closing interest rate	@ 8%	@ 8.5%

*Sums may differ by 1 or 2 digits, due to rounding.
†E = estimated value because this data is not shown, nor normally disclosed, in annual reports.

Table 4-2. Pension Cost Identity*

	West Company (dollars in thousands)	General Motors (dollars in millions)
Method One		
Interest cost	$ 3,400	$ 2,599
Service cost	1,395	640
Capital gains	6,447	7,627
Pension cost	$11,242	$10,866
Method Two		
Closing liability	$48,128	$33,799
−Opening liability	38,731	25,012
Change in liabilities	$ 9,397	$ 8,787
Benefit payments	1,845	2,080
Pension cost	$11,242	$10,867

*Sums may differ by 1 or 2 digits, due to rounding.

Table 4-3. Adjustment to Pension Capital Gains for Changes in Expected Inflation*

	West Company (dollars in thousands)	General Motors (dollars in millions)
Change in interest rate†	−1.0	−2.4%
"Real" duration	5 yrs.	5 yrs.
Percent "real" capital gain	5.0%	12.0%
Closing liability	$48,128	$33,799
"Real" capital gain	$ 2,406	$ 4,056
Reported gain	6,447	7,627
Adjustment for change in expected inflation	($ 4,041)	($ 3,571)

*Sums may differ by 1 or 2 digits, due to rounding.
†Change in interest rate × "real" duration = percent "real" capital gain. Percent "real" capital gain × closing liability = "real" capital gain. "Real" capital gain − reported gain = adjustment for change in expected inflation.

beginning. Table 4-3 shows the adjustments that we make to accommodate the consequences of eventual indexation of benefits to inflation by way of their link to wages and salaries. This table incorporates a "duration" calculation can be used to estimate the capital value changes for pension liabilities (employee wealth) as the result of changes in interest rates (as described in Chap. 3).

Stockholder Income

Corporate restructuring transactions of the 1980s have clearly demonstrated that pension assets are "in play." Acquisitions, leveraged buyouts, and other deals have been quick to look to pension plan surpluses to help finance paying off debt. Plan terminations and asset reversions have been ratified by the courts. Clearly, then, by usage and by the content of ERISA itself, plan assets are stockholder assets.

As the economic owners of pension assets, stockholders derive income from cumulative investment in past years in pension assets. Consistent with the economic definition, total return—the sum of dividends, interest payments, and all realized and unrealized capital gains—constitutes stockholder income. This calculation is shown in Table 4-4.

Table 4-4. Analysis of Income from Pension Assets*

	West Company (dollars in thousands)	General Motors (dollars in millions)
Opening pension assets (12/31/85)	$ 52,277	$ 27,069
Plan contributions	1,176	1,641E†
Benefit payments	−1,845	− 2,080E
Investment returns: Dividends & interest Capital gains (losses) Fund expenses	7,620	6,865
Closing pension assets (12/31/86)	$ 59,229	$ 33,496
Opening pension assets (12/31/85)	−52,277	−27,069
Benefit payments	1,845	2,080E
Plan contributions	−1,176	− 1,641E
Stockholder investment income	$ 7,620	$ 6,865

*Sums may differ by 1 or 2 digits, due to rounding.
†E = estimated value because this data is not shown, nor normally disclosed, in annual reports.

Pension Surplus as a Termination View

Interest Rate Exposure

On a termination basis, it is the pension surplus or deficit that stockholders own, not gross pension assets. FAS-87 reinforces this view. Stockholders are exposed to the risk of interest rate declines, which can greatly increase termination (defeasance) costs of pension liabilities (and the corporation's other outstanding bonds as well). Asset/liability matching tactics appropriate in a termination (imminent defeasance) are important, but should not be confused with management objectives for pension assets for ongoing plans.

Focusing on Pension Surplus

Pension financial decisions, including investment policy (Chap. 7), are increasingly made on the basis of a surplus in pension assets net of pension liabilities. It is important, therefore, to analyze changes in pension surplus in appraising break-up values. This is done in Table

Table 4-5. Changes in Pension Surplus*

	Stockholder assets	Employee assets	Surplus
West Company (dollars in thousands)			
Opening balances (12/31/85)	$52,277	$38,731	$ 13,546
Pension cost		11,242	−11,242
Benefit payments	−1,845	−1,845	
Contributions	1,176		1,176
Investment returns	7,620		7,620
Closing balances (12/31/86)	$59,228	$48,128	$ 11,100
Change	$ 6,952	$ 9,397	$ −2,445
General Motors (dollars in millions)			
Opening balances (12/31/85)	$27,069	$25,012	$ 2,057
Pension cost		10,866	−10,866
Benefit payments	−2,080E†	−2,080E	
Contributions	1,641E		1,641E
Investment returns	6,865		6,865
Closing balances (12/31/86)	$33,496	$33,799	$ −302
Change	$ 6,427	$ 8,787	$ −2,360

*Sums may differ by 1 or 2 digits, due to rounding.
†E = estimated value because this data is not shown, nor normally disclosed, in annual reports.

4-5 for the same two companies. When an inflation adjustment is appropriate, its purpose is to approximate the effect that revisions in expected inflation related to projected wages would have on pension liabilities.

Articulating changes in pension surplus, or their contribution to the restructuring value of the firm, gives a very clear definition of net pension cost—that which reduces pension surplus, the marked-to-market asset reversion value of pension assets, is a net pension cost.

The FAS-87 Expense Measure

Although the above data give a complete picture of pension-related employee and stockholder income for the year, it has not been politically possible to translate this format into accounting practice. The Financial Accounting Standards Board has been reluctant to impose the consequences of pensions onto the face of corporate balance sheets all at once. Furthermore, accounting convention does not permit elements on the balance sheet that have not come through the income statement. Hence, the FASB ruled that the pension surplus (or deficit) would be amortized through the income statement over the average remaining working life of the firm's active employees (typically about 16 years).

Next, because of concern for financial statement volatility, and the absence of consistent precedent for recording events at market value, the FASB ruled also that investment returns and certain other fluctuations could be averaged (subject to falling within a very wide dollar corridor). In all, three techniques were introduced to dampen expense volatility:

1. Averaging of asset market value changes over up to 5 years

2. Use of expected, rather than actual, investment returns

3. Expensing of asset-value changes and actuarial gains/losses only if the amounts exceed 10 percent of the larger of assets or projected liabilities

Because the question "When is a pension actually earned?" has no generally accepted answer, a straight amortization of plan amendments is equally satisfactory over any reasonable period. Consider the introduction of a new plan itself. On the first day, there is frequently a substantial liability (and no assets) as new plans or amendments grant credit for some "past service." However, if employees give up a portion of their future wages, stockholder net wealth need not be diminished. In fact, no employee benefits should be introduced unless stockholder wealth is increased. As discussed in Chap. 1, the financial benefit to stockholders of a pension plan is the reduction in current wages that it permits. If wages are reduced by less than the amount of benefits earned, stockholders are well advised to abandon the plan and grant more current wages instead. Stockholders would be better off and employees no worse off.

In most cases, amortization serves principally to muddy current financial results with prior period results. If the purpose is to attempt to present some notion of long-term income and costs, no concept of what constitutes the long run is offered by the FASB. In fact, the accounting profession has never fully settled on whether reported earnings are intended to be exclusively a current period concept or some measure of permanent or sustainable income.

Table 4-6 reconciles the key elements of pension cost (finance) with pension expense (accounting)—before any inflation adjustments.

To focus on the relative magnitudes involved, it is useful to compare

Table 4-6. Pension Cost and Expense

	West Company (dollars in thousands)	General Motors (dollars in millions)	
Interest cost	$ 3,400	$ 2,599	
Service cost	1,395	640	
Capital gain/loss	6,447	7,627	
Pension cost (finance)	$11,242	$10,866	Employee income
Investment returns	−7,620	−6,865	Stockholder income
Deferrals	−3,742	−3,307	Smoothing/goodwill
Pension expense (accounting)	$ −120	$ 694	FAS-87 disclosure

the cost and expense numbers for General Motors in Table 4-6. Pension cost (employee income) amounted to $10,866 million. It consist of three parts. The interest cost of $2,599 million represents the increase in the present value of liabilities as the result of the accrual of interest (at the opening rate) for the year. Service cost of $640 million reflects the additional benefits for the year earned by active employees. The gain of $7,627 million was primarily the consequence of the capital gain, owing to the decline in interest rates over the year—an upward revision in the present value of promised future benefit payments. However, it should also be expected that lower expected inflation will be incorporated in future wage assumptions and cause future benefit payments to be lower. Our duration adjustment indicates that the rise in pension liabilities has been overstated by $3,571.

In sharp contrast, the pension expense number displayed by accountants is only $694 million. This differs from the pension cost described above because of two items. Investment returns of $6,865 million, which should be treated as stockholder income, is used as negative pension expense. Smoothing and deferrals of $3,307 million is the remaining adjustment, leaving a reported pension expense amounting to less than 7 percent of pension cost.

Note also that the amount of amortizations and deferrals was some $3,307 million, or about five times the amount of reported pension expense—a mere $694 million. This 5:1 ratio is commonplace among current corporate disclosures. The resulting accounting expense number is indeed a very arbitrary residual. Because it is the difference between two very large numbers, pension liabilities and assets, this number is overwhelmed as a consequence of smoothing levels and changes either or both.

Conclusion

Accounting (expense) conventions are misleading when they leave the impression that financial cost can be altered by changing funding methods or assumptions, or by successful or unsuccessful investing. It is fair to present financial results to outsiders within the boundaries of accepted accounting practice. But the economic weaknesses of accounting conventions must not cause top management to be misled. The newly established pension accounting conventions were motivated in part by criticism that preexisting practice fostered manipulation because companies under similar circumstances reported widely differing results. Although the new standard permits less room to maneuver, accounting should not be confused with finance.

5

Putting It All Together: Augmented Financial Statements

In order to define the role of pension assets in the total corporate finance scheme, we adopt an augmented representation of corporate financial statements. The statements developed here differ significantly from convention in two important respects.

1. Pension assets and liabilities are separately consolidated with, respectively, other operating assets and other liabilities. The new accounting rules, by way of comparison, employ a single net figure—the difference between plan assets and liabilities to represent the total plan. Further, the accounting standards are inexplicably asymmetric—they show pension plan deficits but not surpluses on the face of the balance sheet.

2. All asset and liability values are stated in terms of observable or implied market values. Current accounting practice uses a mix of market values and depreciated historical cost measures—an apples and oranges approach.

The financially oriented statements we develop here, as opposed to conventional accounting statements, make clear that funding decisions are a capital budgeting decision: what form to hold assets in—plant and equipment, net working capital, or pension assets? These new statements also make clear that the pension-fund asset-allocation decision is part of the total corporate financial leverage or debt/equity ratio of the company's capital structure.

The Argument for Augmentation

The augmented financial statements consolidate pension financial data with the company's operating finances. Our analysis of pension finances relates income and costs with changes in assets and liabilities and differentiates between accruals and cashflows. An economic view of the firm requires that the assets and liabilities, and, therefore, income and expense, be identified separately for different corporate constituencies— employees, bondholders, and stockholders. Each group needs to identify the amount of company value net of more senior claims that supports their claims. These principles, together with the arguments we have made about the nature of pension liabilities and the ownership of pension assets, lead to the conclusion that pension assets and pension liabilities be consolidated separately with the company's business finances.

Accounting Reflects the Contradictory Provisions of ERISA

The separate consolidation of pension assets and liabilities differs from accounting procedure that nets pension assets against liabilities. The accounting rationale in support of this net position is based on the exclusive benefit rule of ERISA—that pension assets are to be used "for the exclusive benefit" of plan participants.

Thus, accounting contradicts the fact, which we pointed out earlier, that trust law has no room for any concept such as deficits and surpluses. In fact, Title IV of ERISA overrides the exclusive benefit rule by, on the one hand, allowing liabilities to reach through to corporate assets and, on the other hand, recognizing that surplus assets may be realized by stockholders in a plan termination.

Insurance Company Analogy

In the search for a model for financial disclosure, some, including a number of actuaries, have likened pension finances to an insurance company subsidiary. However, no insulation from liability is appropriate here under ERISA, and all constituents are employees of the company. There is no substantive reason not to consolidate. Hence, we reject both the accounting/trust view and the unconsolidated insurance company subsidiary models of financial disclosure. The appropriate construction simply identifies pension liabilities as privately placed bonds and identifies pension assets with stockholder risk and welfare.

Implications of Augmentation

Augmentation of financial statements to include pension assets and liabilities clarifies several key issues:

- Plan contributions are a purchase of assets, not an expense.
- Benefit payments are ultimately made by stockholders, not an intermediary fiction called "the plan."
- Pension expenses, just like the cost of all forms of indebtedness, articulate (reconcile) only with changes in liabilities.
- Pension assets are corporate assets. They appear on the left-hand side of the balance sheet at market value.

Priority of Claims. What is the priority of pension (PBGC) claims in bankruptcy? The financial disclosure of corporate liabilities has evolved over the years to reflect the priority of claims. The right-hand side of the balance sheet discloses senior claims listed ahead of those more junior. One of the major unresolved—and underappreciated—issues in pension finance is the priority of pension (PBGC) claims in bankruptcy. Much of the turmoil surrounding the solvency of the PBGC will remain until this issue is resolved by a rationalization of ERISA with bankruptcy law. For our purposes, we shall consider pension claims to rank behind the general creditor but ahead of preferred stockholders.

Marking to Market. Under the new FAS-87 accounting rules, pension liabilities (pension bonds) are effectively marked to market. The present value of these benefit payments at going interest rates determines the cost of purchasing annuities (defeasance). According to current accounting precepts, in contrast, other corporate debt is noncomparably carried at face value even though current market values may be much higher or lower. On the augmented balance sheet, all corporate liabilities are marked to market.

Tax Adjustment. Valuation of pension assets and liabilities on the augmented balance sheet takes into account potential tax adjustments. Pension liabilities are equal to the present value of all contributions, which, if managed properly, are tax deductible. Similarly, contributions reflect the after-tax cost of replacement of pension assets. Finally, assets can only be reverted subject to an excise tax.

To allow for the tax implications under differing circumstances, we make separate adjustments for a plan in deficit and a plan in surplus. For a plan in deficit, we establish an asset on the balance sheet equal to the tax savings on the present value of required future contributions—the projected benefit obligation (PBO) net of existing assets. For a plan in surplus, we show a liability in the amount of taxes that would be paid, currently at a 15 percent rate, if surplus assets were reverted. The latter tax adjustment is based on the accumulated benefit obligation (ABO). It reflects the principle that, on termination, the plan sponsor is responsible only for the benefits accrued to date.

Toward a Market-Valued Balance Sheet

This book seeks a more realistic economic representation of pension financial data rather than a review of accounting issues per se. Economic logic supports the conclusion that there are no decisions by management or investors for which depreciated, historical cost data is relevant (except for tax management). For investors or claimholders, the security of promised payments lies only in market values, and these are established by, or inferred from, securities markets or asset market prices.[1]

One principal difference between book value and market value statements is the identity of the residual or "plugged" item. The market value of the net worth of a public corporation is observable based on the market price of the shares outstanding. The market value of net working capital can be taken as stated, while preferred stock and publicly traded debt can be valued at market prices. The residual, balancing value is the aggregate of fixed operating assets, which can be determined by simple arithmetic.

Augmented Financial Statements in Operation: The Ralston Purina Company

The concepts underlying our recommended approach are developed using data taken from the financial statements of the Ralston Purina

---

[1]Early work on such financial representation is credited to Jack L. Treynor: Walter Bagehot [Jack L. Treynor], "Risk and Reward in Corporate Pension Funds," *Financial Analysts Journal*: January–February 1972.

Company. A detailed discussion, along with more complete data displayed in the accompanying tables, is provided in the appendix at the end of this chapter. Because of certain deficiencies in current accounting practices, important data items are not available in published statements. Those items marked with a bracketed asterisk [*] were kindly provided by the company for this book. Items marked E are estimates of numbers not available as of the publication of this book.

Accounting Balance Sheet

Table 5-1 shows an abbreviated version of Ralston Purina's accounting statement as presented in its annual report for the fiscal year ending September 30, 1987.

Augmented Corporate Valuation

Valuing a company requires reference to market or break-up values of assets and company securities. Depreciated historical cost bears little relation either to replacement values or to break-up values that drive mergers, acquisitions, and spin-offs—the real facts of management and stockholder life. The approach here takes the market's valuation of corporate liabilities as its starting point. Assets such as working capital and market-valued pension or other marketable assets are valued directly by observing securities market prices. The result is that the value placed by the markets on operating assets is then deduced or imputed.

For Ralston Purina, both assets and liabilities are marked to market in Table 5-2. The market value of corporate liabilities, including bonds ($1,603 million), pension liabilities ($541 million), and common stock

Table 5-1. Ralston Purina Company, Consolidated Balance Sheet, September 30, 1987 (dollars in millions)*

Assets		Liabilities	
Net working capital	$ 295	$1,403	Long-term debt
Investments & other	681	962	Stockholders equity
Net plant & equipment	1,732	342	Deferred taxes & other[†]
Total assets	$2,708	$2,708	Total liabilities

SOURCE: Data supplied by Ralston Purina. Used with permission.
*Sums may differ by 1 or 2 digits, due to rounding.
†Deferred taxes considered as equity.

Table 5-2. Ralston Purina Company, Company Valuation, September 30, 1987 (dollars in millions)*

Assets			Liabilities
Net working capital†		$ 502	
Fixed assets (imputed value)		6,589	$1,603	Bondholders†
Pension assets:			
Cash	65E‡		
Bonds	197E		
Stock	525E		
Total	787		541	Employees' pension liability (PBO)
(Less tax liability @ 15% of reversion after ABO)	−58	729	
			5,675	Stockholders
Total assets		$7,820	$7,820	Corporate valuation

*Sums may differ by 1 or 2 digits, due to rounding.
†Adjusted for $206 million of long-term debt due within 1 year.
‡E = estimated asset allocation.

($5,675 million), is $7,820 million. Somewhat higher interest rates than those that prevailed at the time of issue have resulted in a bit smaller market value for the corporation's bonds. Since total liabilities are by definition equal to the market value of Ralston Purina's assets, the value of operating assets is imputed by backing out the value of net working capital ($501 million) and pension assets ($788 million) net of a potential tax liability ($58 million) that would be triggered should surplus pension assets be reverted to stockholders.

Capital Structure and Stockholder Risk

Using the additive properties of market risk, "beta,"[2] we explore the sources of market systematic risk for Ralston Purina's stockholders. As shown in Table 5-3, the market risk (beta) of Ralston Purina common shares (0.81) is higher than that for either operating assets or pension assets because of leverage in the capital structure. The general framework attributes the sources of stockholder risk to that stemming from operating and pension assets and to the leverage introduced by pension

[2] "Beta" measures the nondiversifiable or market-related risk of an asset, typically (as here) calibrated such that the beta of the S&P 500 is 1.00. Beta is explained in greater detail in the chapter on performance measurement, Chap. 7.

Table 5-3. Ralston Purina Company, Attribution of Market Risk (Beta), September 30, 1987*
Market Value Weighted

Market risk	Assets	Liabilities	Market risk
.00	Net working capital	Long-term debt	.30
.72	Operating assets	Pension "debt"	.30
.74	Pension assets	Common stock	.81
.67	Total Market Risk =	Total Market Risk	.67

*Sums may differ by 1 or 2 digits, due to rounding.

debt and other long-term debt. The details of the computations for this analysis are shown in Table 5A-4 in the appendix to this chapter.

Simply put, by issuing securities with less risk than the assets acquired by the firm, the stockholders shoulder the risk of the assets of the firm and then some. The role of leverage in adding to stockholder risk is spelled out by the following relationships:

$$\text{Stockholder Risk} = \text{Asset Risk} + \text{Leverage Risk}$$

$$\text{Leverage Risk} = \frac{\text{Debt}}{\text{Equity}} \times [\text{Asset Risk} - \text{Debt Risk}]$$

Ralston Purina's total leverage risk (Table 5-4) is relatively small,

Table 5-4. Ralston Purina Company, Sources of Risk, September 30, 1987*

Sources of Stockholder Risk		
	Beta risk	% of total assets
Net working capital	.00	6%
Operating assets	.72	84
Pension assets	.74	10
Total assets	.67	100%
Sources of Market Risk		
	Beta risk	% of total risk
Total assets	.67	83%
Leverage:		
Operating debt	.10	12
Pension liabilities	.04	5
Common stock	.81	100%

*Sums may differ by 1 or 2 digits, due to rounding.

though approximately one-third of that risk is attributable to pension liabilities. Total stockholder risk is made up of 83 percent asset risk and 17 percent leverage risk (5 percent from pension liabilities and 12 percent from long-term debt).

It is also important to note that the asset allocation decision as between stocks, bonds, and cash in the pension fund contributes to stockholder risk. In Ralston Purina's case, the risk of pension assets (0.74) is comparable to the risk of its operating assets (0.72).

Pension Asset/Liability Matching

The decision to immunize or dedicate a pension plan's liabilities is an alteration of capital structure that reduces aggregate corporate leverage by netting out bonds on the two sides of the augmented balance sheet. Immunization is frequently instituted in conjunction with a leveraged buy-out, which increases corporate debt. Pension asset restructuring partially offsets the leverage consequences of the additional new operating debt. On other occasions, the need for a close match is predicated by an imminent plan termination. This changes the pension funding and investment problem from that of an ongoing plan to an impending defeasance where the investment and liability accrual horizon becomes very short.

Pension Cost versus Pension Expense

FAS-87 pension expense numbers are overwhelmed by deferrals and amortizations. Pension cost versus pension expense is reconciled in Table 5-5. Ralston Purina reported pension expense was only $7 million versus a total increase in employee pension wealth for the year of $62 million. The difference is attributable to counting $172 million of stockholder investment income as negative pension expense, and some $116 million in amortizations and deferrals—which in itself is more than 15 times the reported expense number.

Augmented Earnings

Earnings for Ralston Purina were more than 20 percent higher than reported when adjustments for pension cost are made. The resulting

Table 5-5. Ralston Purina Company, Reconciliation of Pension Cost and Expense, September 30, 1987 (dollars in millions)*

Service cost	$ 24	
Interest cost	41	
Other gain (loss)	−4	
Pension cost (finance)	$ 62	Employee income
Investment returns	−174	Stockholder income
Amortizations & deferrals	116	Smoothing/goodwill
Other gain (loss)	4	
Pension expense (accounting)	$ 7	Disclosure

*Sums may differ by 1 or 2 digits, due to rounding.

revision in earnings for most companies is similarly very substantial. Without a myriad of other adjustments, however, our adjusted number cannot attempt to measure true earnings, as represented by the change in stockholder value over the period. The adjustments to reported earnings in Table 5-6 begins by backing out the reported accounting expense of $7 million and substituting our economic measure of pension cost of $62 million. The return on plan assets of $174 is added to stockholder income. The amortizations and deferrals are dropped. In the absence of a significant change in long interest rates, no capital gains or losses are reported, hence no partially offsetting adjustment for inflation was necessary.

In a recent study, one Wall Street research firm attributed some 44 percent of the gain in 1987 *reported* earnings for the S&P 500 companies to be attributable to the reduction in reported pension expense under

Table 5-6. Ralston Purina Company, Earnings Adjustments for Pensions, September 30, 1987 (dollars in millions)*

Reported earnings	$523
Reported pension expense	7
Total pension cost	−62
Return on pension assets	174
Pension adjusted earnings	$642
Change	22.8%

*Sums may differ by 1 or 2 digits, due to rounding.

FAS-87. The bulk of this "gain" is attributable to the fact that under FAS-87 the pension surpluses achieved by the majority of companies have gradually flowed through the income account. Hence, for the majority of companies that had pension surpluses, and earned investment returns in excess of assumed rates in those years, reported earnings were themselves significantly understated.

Conclusions

Our analysis supports the following conclusions.

- Current accounting falls well short of the objectives of the augmented financial statements we develop here. While FAS-87 is a major step forward, it is a very mixed bag.

    The good news is the development of most of the items needed for a complete financial analysis, which includes pension plans.

    The bad news is that not even the simplest cashflow data on benefit payments and contributions is presented and, more frequently than not, cannot be teased out of the disclosures, even though the FASB intended that they should be.

    Finally, the reported expense numbers are overwhelmed by the amortizations and deferrals that have been implanted both to smooth out the transition to the new standard and to absorb volatility.

- Pension debt adds to corporate leverage, and is a concomitant part of the capital structure of the firm, affecting stockholder risk and return.

- The pension fund asset allocation decision is ultimately a decision about capital structure.

- The capital budgeting decision is ultimately a competition (at the margin) between operating and pension assets. Many companies are investing about the same dollar amounts in each. The opportunity cost of the return on more operating assets is what they could have earned (essentially tax-free) in pension assets. Certainly, many of the larger sophisticated companies found the pension fund investment terms attractive.

The attention recently brought to pension finances in modern investment banking activities is simply a recognition that they are an integral part of corporation finance.

Appendix
Ralston Purina Example

More detailed background on the development of augmented balance sheet results is shown in this appendix using data taken from the financial statements of the Ralston Purina Company. Because of deficiencies in current accounting rules, several required data items are not available in published statements. In the following tables, items marked with a bracketed asterisk [*] were kindly provided by the company. Items marked E are estimated numbers not available as of publication of this book.

Market Valuation of Company Debt and Equity

Market closing prices are used to value total outstanding debt and equity as shown in Table 5A-1. Stock price multiplied times shares outstanding provides the market value for stockholder equity (Panel A). Changes in operating debt are disclosed in Panel B. Market prices for

Table 5A-1. Ralston Purina Company, Market Valuations: Equity and Debt, September 30, 1987 (dollars in millions)*

Panel A: Stock Valuation			
	Shares outstanding	Price per share, $	Value $
Open (9/30/86)	76,244	60.00	$4,575
Converted	54	68.00	4
Repurchased	−6,129	68.00	(417)
Close (9/30/87)	70,169	80.88	5,675

Panel B: Debt Valuation				
	Notes	Commercial paper	Bonds	Total
Open (9/30/86)	$189	$152	$1,772	$2,113
New			60	60
Redemptions	(106)	(152)	(223)	(481)
Close (9/30/87)	83	0	1,609	1,692
Market value	83	0	1,521	1,603

Table 5A-1. Ralston Purina Company, Market Valuations: Equity and Debt, September 30, 1987 (dollars in millions)* *(Continued)*

Panel C: Long-Term Debt			Book value	Market price	Yield	Market value
Sinking fund	7½	of '87				
bonds	7.70	of '96				
	12⅞	of '14	20.0	89.38	9.56	17.9
	9½	of '16	300.0	86.33	11.08	259.0
	9⅛	of '16	200.0	84.00E†		168.0
	conv. 5¾	of '00	1.7			1.7
Other debt						
Less than 1 year			293.4			293.4
	12¾	of '89	100.0	103.08	10.96	103.1
Singapore	4.38+	of '92	13.1			13.1
Swiss	4.3+	of '92	20.1			20.1
Swiss	12¾	of '94	50.1			50.1
	12	of '94	76.4			76.4
	11¾	of '95	132.3	104.01	10.91	137.6
	12	of '96	35.2	101.84	11.65	35.8
	9	of '96	200.0	91.60	10.49	183.2
	7¾	of '98	52.2	90.00E		47.0
Capital leases			16.9			16.9
Industrial revenue			61.5			61.5
Other			35.9			35.9
			$1,608.8	94.52		$1,520.7

*Sums may differ by 1 or 2 digits, due to rounding.
†E = estimated.

the bulk of outstanding debt were used, together with estimated prices when necessary to mark corporate debt to market (Panel C).

Pension Financial Data

The pension financial data are displayed in Table 5A-2 in four panels. Panel A shows opening and closing asset and liability and deferred account balances. Panel B reconciles these balances with the individual accounting flows. Panel C shows the sources and uses of cashflow for the pension fund. Panel D shows a breakdown of reported FAS-87 pension expense.

Table 5A-2. Ralston Purina Company, Financial Data, September 30, 1987 (dollars in millions)*

Panel A: Pension Fund Finances			
	9/30/87 Closing total	Change	9/30/86 Opening total
Liabilities			
Vested	$ 374		$346
Nonvested	25		25
Total ABO	400		371
Pay increases	142		132E†
Total Liabilities (PBO)	541	38	503
Assets	788	162	625
Surplus	246	124	123
FASB adjustments			
Amortization	−176		0
Adoption	−39		0
Prepaid expense	$ 32	−91	$123

Panel B: Changes			
Change in liabilities		Change in assets	
Interest	$ 41	Contributions	$ 16[*]‡
Service	24	Benefits	−23[*]
Amendments		Income	177
Gain (loss):		Expenses	−3 174
Actuarial			
Capital			
Other	−4		
Benefit payments	−23[*]	Other	−4
Net change	$ 38	Net change	$163

Panel C: Pension Fund Analysis of Cashflows		
Sources:		
Contributions	$16[*]	
Dividends + interest	38E	$53
Uses:		
Benefit payments	$23[*]	
Asset purchases	30E	$53

Panel D: Reported Expense	
Service	$ 24
Interest	41
Return	−174
Deferred & amortized	116
Expenses	$ 7

*Sums may differ by 1 or 2 digits, due to rounding.
†E = estimates of data not available.
‡[*] = supplied by company.

Pension Finance Tableaux

The several items of pension financial data in Table 5A-2 are pulled together and related to each other in the tableaux in Table 5A-3. Note that stockholder net pension wealth rises and falls with the market value of the plan's surplus (or deficit).

The accounts are set up such that:

1. Pension surplus increases by contributions and investment returns and decreases by cost of the plan.
2. Because benefit payments impact both assets and liabilities identically, they are a wash in affecting surplus. This is a feature common to both actuarial funding conventions and the surplus-driven FAS-87 architecture. This elimination of benefit payments by the netting of assets against liabilities contributes to their neglect in FAS-87.

Note the pension cost for Ralston Purina can be measured in any of at least three equivalent ways. First, it is the net change in pension liabilities or employee pension wealth ($541 − $503 = $38 million), plus benefit payments or cash received ($23 million), or $62 million (column 2). Second, it is the interest earned on past pension accruals ($41 million), plus pension rights earned this year or "service cost" ($24 million), plus gains or losses due to changes in interest rates and actuarial (demographic) assumptions (−$4 million), or $62 million. Finally, it is the increase (decrease) in pension surplus ($124 million) adjusted for contri-

Table 5A-3. Ralston Purina Company, Pension Finances and Disclosure, September 30, 1987 (dollars in millions)*

	Assets	Pension Liability (PBO)	Surplus
Opening balance (9/30/86)	$625	$503(@8%)	$123
Pension cost		62	−62
Benefit payments	−23	−23	
Contributions	16		16
Investment returns	174		174
Other	−4		−4
Closing balance (9/30/87)	$788	$541(@8⅛%)	$246
Change	$162	$ 38	$124

*Sums may differ by 1 or 2 digits, due to rounding.

butions ($16 million) and investment returns ($174 million and −$4 million of "other"), or $62 million (column 3).

The reconciliation of pension cost ($62 million) and accounting expense ($7 million) is essentially the difference between stockholder earnings on pension assets ($174 million) and net deferrals ($116 million).

Augmented Cashflows

The augmented statement of "sources and uses of funds" places the pension plan in the perspective of total company financial flows. A pension fund has its own sources of funds (contributions and dividend and interest income) and uses of funds (benefit payments and net asset purchases). In consolidating pension and corporate finance, this data becomes relevant to ascertaining the use of corporate cashflows for payments to investors, including employees, and reinvestment in the company, including investment in pension assets.

For Ralston Purina, these cashflows are relatively small (see Table 5A-4). The telling figure in many instances is the ratio of net investment in pension assets versus plant and equipment. For a large number of companies these two investment rates are about equal. Adjusting reported operating cashflows for contributions or gross asset purchases ($16 million) and interest and dividend income on plan assets ($38 million/ estimated) augments cashflows by $53 million. The augmenting balancing outflows are principal payments to investors or retirees ($23 million) and net purchase of plan assets ($30 million/estimated).

Pension Asset Allocation: Capital Structure and Stockholder Risk

The risk of the aggregate portfolio of Ralston Purina liabilities can be estimated from the risk measures for each component and the outstanding market values of each (see Table 5A-5). Using the BARRA (Barr Rosenberg Associates) published beta measure (0.81) for Ralston Purina, and some estimates for the fixed-income liabilities, the aggregate corporate risk (0.67) can be developed.

The aggregate risk of all of a firm's liabilities is the aggregate risk of the firm's assets. The risk of near-cash instruments is near zero, and the portfolio risk of pension assets is developed in part B of the table. It is

Table 5A-4. Ralston Purina Company, Analysis of Cashflows, September 30, 1987 (dollars in millions)*

Sources		
Net cashflows from operations:		
Reported	$ 439	
Interest payments	201	
Pension contributions	16[*]†	
Operating cashflow		$ 655
Pension fund interest & dividends		38E‡
Sale of operating assets		552
External financing:		
Interest rate swaps	104	
Stock issuance (net)	6	110
Total sources		$1,354

Uses		
Payments to investors:		
Interest payments	$ 201	
Principal payments	275	
Redemptions	149	
Bondholders		$ 625
Dividends	88	
Repurchases	493	
Stockholders		$ 581
Employee benefit payments		23[*]
Asset purchases:		
Plant & equipment	197	
Pension assets	30E	
Cash & securities	−101	$ 124
Total uses		$1,354

*Sums may differ by 1 or 2 digits, due to rounding.
†[*] = supplied by company.
‡E = estimates of data not available.

then possible to back into the risk of Ralston Purina's operating assets. It is noteworthy that the risk of Ralston Purina's operating assets and pension assets are almost identical (0.72 versus 0.74). The allocation of pension assets as between stocks, bonds, and cash clearly influences stockholder risk and return. Unlike Ralston Purina, for which pension assets are modest in comparison to operating assets, changes in pension asset allocation for many companies can have significant stockholder consequences.

Table 5A-5. Ralston Purina Company, Capital Structure Risk Analysis, September 30, 1987 (dollars in millions)*

Panel A			
	Market values	Capital structure	Capital risk (beta)
Bonds	$1,603	20%	0.30
Pensions	541	7	0.30
Stock	5,675	73	0.81
Liabilities	$7,820	100%	0.67
Working capital	$ 501	6%	0.00
Operating assets	6,588	84	0.72
Pension assets	729	9	0.74
Assets	$7,820	100%	0.67

Panel B			
	Market values	% Pension assets	Capital risk (beta)
Cash	$ 65	8%	0.00
Bonds	197	25	0.30
Stocks	525	67	1.00
= Pension assets	$ 788	100%	0.74

Panel C				
	Market values	Augmented debt/equity	Risk differential	Capital risk (beta)
Asset risk	$7,820			0.67
+ Leverage risk				
Pensions	$ 541	0.095	× (.67−.30) =	0.04
Bonds	$1,603	0.283	× (.67−.30) =	0.10
= Equity risk	$5,675	0.378		0.81

*Sums may differ by 1 or 2 digits, due to rounding.

6

How Securities Markets Work: Chess, Bingo, or Gin Rummy?

Investment Policy versus Investment Strategy

Augmented financial statements underscore the importance of pension asset management to company stockholders. As pension assets have grown relative to total corporate assets, their influence on stockholder value has also increased. Particularly where pension assets represent a substantial portion of the the market value of the company's shares outstanding, senior company management must assure itself that pension assets are effectively managed.

Hidden Assumptions: How the Investment World Works

How pension assets are managed reflects an understanding of how the securities markets work. Plan sponsors with fiduciary responsibility for pension assets are concerned with the development of long-range policy, the timely implementation of strategy, and the selection of investment managers for externally managed portfolios. Advice directed to each of these issues is plentiful, and it is almost always plausible based on the supporting assumptions. Since the advice can be no better than the assumptions on which it rests, the assumptions are critical. Yet, the most basic assumptions underlying the investment advice directed to the plan sponsor may not even be identified, much less, rigorously scrutinized.

Two polar assumptions underlying the management of pension funds are illustrated by a comparison between two familiar games—chess and bingo. If investing pension assets is a game of chess, the appropriate investment approach is not the same as if bingo were the most suitable analogy. The conclusion that investing is neither a game of chess nor a game of bingo but something in between, such as gin rummy, points to a still different response. These fundamental investment assumptions determine the kind of approach to investment management that makes sense.

Chess Analogy

The outcome of a chess game is determined almost wholly by skill. Each player begins the game with identical pieces arranged in exactly the same position relative to those of his opponent. Each player has complete information at all times about the decisions of his or her opponent. Since everything that happens in the game is determined by either of the two opposing players, the outcome clearly depends on their relative skill.

Application of the chess analogy to pension asset management is highly appealing to a free-enterprise society that stresses the rewards of individual skill and initiative competing in free markets. Athletic competition, which looms so large in American life, reinforces the message that victory is won by superior talent and trying harder. Similarly, business corporations stress the role of merit in determining promotions and in adjusting employee compensation. It is therefore not surprising that the chess-game concept is heavily weighted in the traditional view of investing: Superior investment skill produces superior investment returns. Conversely, poor investment results are readily attributable to one or more "mistakes" on the part of the investment strategist.

The chess-game concept of investment is consistent with vigorous, active management of pension assets. It explains many plan sponsor practices:

1. Stress on the selection of "smart" investment managers as the key to superior performance

2. Lack of interest in diversification, since skill should emphasize attrac-

tive investments and steer the portfolio away from investments with
no more than mediocre prospects

3. Low priority accorded to transaction costs and manager fees, since
they remain trivial compared to the potential advantages secured
from successful investment management

4. Measurement of investment managers against a standard that
equates the degree of skill with the level of investment returns. An
extreme standard—more common a few years ago than today—establishes a performance norm of 4 percentage points in excess of the
total rate of return for the S&P 500 in up markets and at least the
return from treasury bills in down markets. A more widely used current standard—which also incorporates the chess-game concept of
investing—measures each manager against the median return for an
available sample of managers without allowance for differences in either objectives or style.

Bingo: The Other Extreme

In terms of the skill required of the participants, bingo stands at the
other extreme from chess. The outcome of a bingo game is determined
entirely by chance. Each player receives a card with a random set of
numbers that form horizontal, diagonal, and vertical rows. An an-
nouncer calls another random series of numbers, which each player
matches against the numbers on his or her card. The player wins who is
first to match the numbers called against a complete row of numbers on
his or her card. No player has control of the outcome: Any kindergar-
ten child who has developed the ability to recognize numbers has the
same chance to win as the most talented adult.

The bingo-game concept of investing is supported by the extreme
form of the efficient market hypothesis. Proponents of this view point
to the large number of well-informed investors attempting to gain advantage over each other. As a result of their efforts, according to this
view, highly competitive, publicly traded securities markets so rapidly
discount available information that no investor will maintain a consistent advantage. While one investor may profit from a particular decision, it will just as likely be the turn of someone else next time.

The implications of the bingo-game concept of investing are the opposite of those supported by the chess-game concept:

1. Efforts to select superior active managers are futile. Apart from the
effects of consistent differences in transaction costs, an investment

manager who performed poorly in the past is just as likely as the manager with a superior record to achieve superior results in the period just ahead.

2. Efficient diversification of assets becomes the primary vehicle for improving expected return and controlling risk. Since assets can be combined so that risks are partially offsetting, efficient diversification permits a reduction in total risk relative to a given level of return. If efficient diversification can reduce risk relative to return, it can also provide incremental return for the level of risk the fund is willing to accept. In an efficient market, diversification is the only available free lunch.

3. Preference for passive management results in investment in highly diversified index funds. Such funds are designed to match closely the performance of issues in a designated index—the S&P 500, the Wilshire 5000, or, increasingly, a number of more specialized market segments. Although they forego opportunities for the incremental returns sought by active management, in return they avoid possible losses resulting from strategy failure and also the higher transaction costs and manager fees associated with active management.

4. Transaction costs and manager fees are minimized. Transaction costs are incurred only to maintain efficient diversification as income is received or as other contributions and withdrawals impact fund assets. Manager fees are negotiated to the lowest possible level and become an important element in the choice of managers. Because of the commodity-like nature of passive management, fees are subject to intense competitive pressures.

5. Measurement of the performance of investment managers focuses on their demonstrated ability to control risk (through limiting tracking errors in the matching of the targeted index) and to minimize expenses (both transaction costs and manager fees).

Gin Rummy, Contract Bridge, or Backgammon

The third possibility is that pension asset management is neither a chess game, decided on the basis of the skill of the players, nor bingo, where the outcome is purely a matter of chance. Most games—such as gin rummy, contract bridge, and backgammon—are somewhere in-between: Both luck and skill contribute to the final result. If the results from pension asset management similarly depend on both luck and skill, then neither the practices supported by the chess analogy nor those that follow from the bingo analogy are likely to be wholly appropriate.

It is just this third alternative—that pension asset management is somewhere in between chess and bingo—that best describes the investment world in which the plan sponsor actually operates. We offer the following comments to support this conclusion.

Evidence against the Chess Analogy. Even though investors, including plan sponsors, may act as if investing in publicly traded securities markets is a game of chess, the evidence is overwhelming that chance plays an extremely large role. The investor who is uncritically accepted as a genius based on a run of past success is often subsequently viewed as a bum when the results turn negative. At the same time, it is not unusual for yesterday's bum to become today's genius. Investors are much more likely than master chess players to generate erratic results. The academic community has heavily supported this conclusion with an accumulating library of statistical analysis, which shows that investing is clearly not a game of chess.

Limitations of the Bingo-Game Concept. Rejection of the chess analogy does not automatically mean acceptance of the bingo analogy, since there is plenty of room in between. Although academic research can provide overwhelming evidence to reject the chess analogy, it cannot prove the bingo analogy. Some investors, investment managers, and investment advisors have been able to demonstrate sufficient success with enough consistency to convince many observers that skill has played a significant role. Very few practical investors are willing to bet all their assets on the bingo concept of investing. To our knowledge, there is no major pension fund that has attempted totally to dispense with active management; in fact, we argue below that it is impossible to do so. Most pension fund assets include a substantial component of actively managed funds.

As a practical matter, the bingo-game concept of investing is impossible to implement in its pure form. In bingo, there are no choices left to the player, since the results are wholly determined by chance. For passive investment, in contrast, judgments must be made that often cross the line into the area of active management. As suggested by the three points made below, the plan sponsor who attempts to implement a passive program may actually shift assets as his or her hopes and fears about the investment outlook change.

1. Just the decision to begin a program of passive management involves a judgment on timing. For example, such programs usually begin af-

ter a period when experience with active management has been poor relative to index funds; the switch to index funds is made with the expectation of a performance advantage. If better performance does not follow, disappointment may lead to a rethinking of the index-fund approach.

2. Similarly, a passive approach still requires plan sponsors to select the combination of passive assets that best matches the trade-off of expected risk and return appropriate to their individual circumstances. It is not unusual for plan sponsors to view their risk tolerance differently as their assets rise or fall in value or as their judgments on the outlook for the various financial markets change.

3. The effort to avoid active management is further strained by the judgments required to allocate assets among disparate asset groups, including real estate and international investments. At least at present, such decisions cannot be made on a wholly objective basis.

Wrong Answer.   The plan sponsor, pulled one way by the hopes associated with the chess-game concept of investing and the other by proponents of the bingo-game concept, may attempt to resolve the dilemma by accepting some of both. Since the two games are so different, however, the key question is how the assumptions underlying each of them may be brought together into one useful operating framework. Just mixing passive and active management—in the absence of a logical plan to integrate the two approaches—does not resolve the issue.

Unambiguous Solution: Policy versus Strategy

The unambiguous solution is to establish a clear distinction between policy and strategy that permits the chess and bingo concepts of investing to complement each other.

   Policy should be based on the bingo analogy. It is a portfolio plan developed on the assumption that the investor has no advantage over the securities markets in forecasting returns for the various investment alternatives. The policy portfolio plan takes the form of a concrete statement of asset allocation, providing specific percentages for each of the major asset groups. *Policy serves to mandate the consequences of the plan sponsor's preferences for risk and return, imposes a long-term investment discipline, and establishes the framework for measurement of the success of strategy.*

   Once this view of policy is implemented, strategy, which reflects the spirit of the chess-game concept, governs the extent of departure from policy. Policy defines the portfolio plan that best meets the plan sponsor's objectives over the longer term and in the absence of superior forecasting ability. A *strategic departure from policy will occur only when a forecasting advantage over the securities markets is indicated.*

Plan sponsors too often lack the benefits of a carefully considered policy plan because they fail to recognize that investment policy is something quite different from investment strategy. Table 6-1 outlines the differences. As suggested by the various characteristics that distinguish policy from strategy, investment policy deserves at least as much attention on the part of the plan sponsor as investment strategy.

Completely Different Assumptions. *Policy* is a longer term concern, best based on the assumption that investing is a game of bingo. It therefore has no use for individual forecasts of future market prices or of any of the variables that could bear on future market prices. Most of the efforts of investment professionals, including the conclusions quoted in the financial press, are totally irrelevant to investment policy.

Strategy, on the other hand, assumes a temporary forecasting advantage over the market consensus, at least in areas selected for its application. The strategist who relies on various current factual information as measures of valuation may claim that he does not forecast. Such claims are misleading, since use of current information to determine undervalued securities implies a forecast of future changes in relative market prices. By way of illustration, a contrarian strategy will buy an issue because it is undervalued by historical standards for such measures as price-to-book value, price-to-earnings value, and yield. Such a decision is based on a forecast—presumably not shared by the market consensus—that the market price is likely to readjust within a given time horizon to a level more in line with historical norms.

Table 6-1. Investment Policy versus Investment Strategy

	Investment policy	Investment strategy
Assumption	Investing is a bingo game	Investing is a chess game
Purpose	To meet fund objectives	To achieve incremental returns
Critical input	Consensus views of securities markets	Forecasts differing from the consensus
Time horizon	Long term, often 10 years	Short term, usually 6–18 months
Accountability	For consistency with long-term goals	For return in excess of the policy plan

Contrast in Purpose. *Policy* aims to identify the combination of assets that provides the trade-off of risk and expected return most appropriate to fund objectives. The objectives of the fund depend on the characteristics of the sponsoring company, the condition of the pension plan, and the attitudes toward risk and return of the management of the plan sponsor. Because objectives can vary widely from one fund to another, pension fund policies are also likely to vary widely.

For *strategy*, the purpose is to achieve incremental returns relative to policy. Consequently, the point of departure is the policy plan as individually defined for each fund. At such time that strategy forecasts coincide with those already discounted by the publicly traded securities markets, the strategy portfolio will approximately match the policy plan. The strategy portfolio will differ from the policy plan only to the extent the strategy forecast differs from the market consensus.

Contrasting Definitions of Critical Input. *Policy*, accepting the views of the market consensus as the best estimate of future value, extracts forecasts of risk and return from prices in publicly traded securities markets. Policy uses these estimates to determine optimum diversification for the level of risk that the fund is willing to accept. How policy secures estimates of consensus forecasts of risk and return is covered in Chap. 7.

Strategy requires individual judgments of the future that differ from the market consensus. These judgments provide an advantage over the consensus, either because the information is more complete, or because it is better interpreted. In view of the wide availability of relevant investment information and the legal restrictions on the use of privileged information, it is virtually impossible for strategy to benefit consistently from better access to raw information. The advantage claimed by strategy is much more likely to be attributable to greater knowledge, understanding, and analytical ability. As computing power has become increasingly accessible, the growing number of quantitatively oriented analysts have increasingly attempted to secure advantage by incorporating a superior decision process in a valuation model. The decision process is covered in greater detail in Chap. 8.

Long Time Horizons versus 6 to 18 Months. The *policy* plan is concerned with a long time horizon. A widely used planning period is 10 years—long enough to allow for a wide variety of changes in investment conditions but not so long as to defer accountability far beyond the careers of those responsible for the planning. Despite the long time horizon, plan sponsors must also be concerned with shorter term possibilities. Choice of a policy plan is therefore a trade-off between the longer term and shorter term prospects for return and risk; the choice depends on the particular objectives of the plan sponsor.

Strategy, on the other hand, usually looks ahead 6 to 18 months. Prospects for periods less than 6 months ahead are often rather fully discounted by the securities markets, limiting opportunities to gain advantage. Prospects beyond 18 months are sufficiently far in the future to encounter rapidly diminishing visibility. Even if the superior forecaster could correctly anticipate a critical development (such as a world depression) several years in advance, the market consensus is unlikely to react until the events are closer in time. Studies of the relationship between stock prices and the business cycle, for example, suggest that the lead time for the stock market as an economic forecaster is on the order of 6 to 12 months.

Contrasts in Accountability. *Policy* is accountable for performance consistent with the objectives of the fund, as defined in terms of risk and expected return. A conservative fund, by way of illustration, should demonstrate less volatility in both up and down markets than a more aggressive fund would. An annual review of policy provides a basis for assessing its continued suitability to the purposes of the fund.

Strategy is accountable for return in excess of the policy plan. Since the results of policy are attainable without the incremental risk created by strategy, the only justification for strategy is a return better than that provided by policy.

Performance Contributions.   The distinction between policy and strategy, as outlined here, permits an unambiguous method of measuring the contribution of each to total fund performance. Because *policy* is precisely defined, its performance can be calculated on a pro forma basis. The return from the policy plan indicates the performance that could have been achieved on a purely passive basis, with no help from strategy. If the assets are managed actively, the actual fund portfolio will differ from the passive policy plan, and these differences will result in performance either better or worse than that of the policy plan. The contribution of *strategy* is the margin between the actual fund performance and that of the policy plan. With the aid of normal portfolios for each individual portfolio manager, the strategy contribution to total fund performance can be further separated into (1) the contribution from allocation of assets to the individual portfolio mangers and (2) the contribution of each individual portfolio manager. The analysis of the three sources of fund performance is the subject of Chap. 10.

7

Alternative Approaches to Investment Policy

Two Issues Determine Investment Policy

Development of investment policy involves two key issues. The first issue concerns the *investment objective* of the fund. Since expected return and risk are directly related, the fund objective is always a trade-off between two conflicting desires—for more expected return and for less risk. Our discussion in the pages that follow considers alternative ways to define the investment objective. The second issue requires identification of the series of asset-allocation plans that constitute an "efficient frontier." Each asset-allocation alternative included on an efficient frontier offers the highest expected return for a designated level of risk. Our comments on efficient asset allocation in the subsequent sections provide a summary of the steps necessary to determine an efficient frontier. The investment objective, as translated into a specific trade-off of expected return and risk, determines the selection of the most appropriate asset-allocation alternative from those on the efficient frontier.

Careful definition of the investment objective and the efficient frontier are each critically important, since together they determine the policy asset allocation that provides the framework for investment management. It follows that the plan sponsor may be poorly served by policy either because (1) the policy objective is inappropriate or (2) the asset allocation chosen to meet the objective fails to provide an efficient trade-off between risk and expected return.

Wrong Fund Investment Objectives Can Mean Trouble

Faithful adherence to the wrong objective exposes the fund to more risk—or to less expected return—than is necessary or appropriate given the financial circumstances and operating strategies of the firm. By way of example, suppose that fund A, because of its particular circumstances, requires a conservative policy and fund B, reflecting different circumstances, is well-suited to an aggressive policy. If fund A attempts to operate with an aggressive policy, it is subject to unacceptably large risks. At the extreme, the large losses for fund A may threaten the survival of the plan sponsor. There have been instances where an unprofitable company would have been an attractive merger candidate if its value for this purpose had not been more than offset by the unfunded liabilities in its pension plan. In contrast, fund B, if operating with an excessively conservative fund, is likely to miss out unnecessarily on opportunities for much larger returns.

Selection of the wrong policy objective increases the likelihood of ill-timed policy revisions. As changing conditions in the financial markets focus attention on the mismatch of fund policy with plan sponsor goals, pressures are likely to build for sudden lurches in investment position. Wide swings in asset mix significantly increase risk, but, in the absence of a forecasting advantage, they do not add to the probability of better returns. Fund A, if it attempts to operate with an aggressive policy objective, is likely to be particularly vulnerable to a conservative shift in policy under unfavorable investment conditions. As a result, fund A may "lock in" a significant portion of the large losses already incurred, limiting opportunities to recover when investment conditions again become more favorable. Conversely, fund B, if it misses out on highly favorable returns as a result of an unduly conservative policy, runs the risk of shifting to a more aggressive policy just in time for the next bear market.

Inefficient Asset Allocation Can Be Expensive

Even if a fund's objective is properly identified, the policy plan may be subject to the disadvantage of inefficient asset allocation. To illustrate our point, assume that both funds A and B have each chosen an efficient asset-allocation plan to meet their respective fund objectives. Because fund A requires limited risk, efficient asset allocation consistent with its objective would provide an expected return of 3 percent in excess of that for short-term treasury bills. Inefficient asset allocation, in contrast, may provide an excess return of only 2 percent relative to the same level of risk. Efficient asset allocation for fund B, meanwhile, may result in an expected excess return of 5 percent relative to the greater risk appropriate to this fund's circumstances. For the same level of risk, inefficient asset diversification would provide a lower return—perhaps 4 percent or even less. As pointed out in our introduction to this book, a small difference in pension fund returns, compounded over an extended period, can exert significant impact on the value of the plan sponsor's common shares.

Investment Objective: Risk-Return Trade-Off

Views of the Objectives

Getting the objectives right requires recognition of the role of the pension fund within the framework of the total corporation. There are three ways to view pension fund investment objectives: (1) as winning the performance race against other funds, (2) as matching the cashflows required to meet future pension liabilities, and (3) as supporting overall corporate goals. The following discussion of these alternatives stresses the need to view pension assets, together with pension liabilities, within the context of overall corporate goals. If policy planning does not explicitly address fund objectives in the framework of the total corporation, the officially designated objectives are likely to differ, perhaps even greatly, from the objectives that would best serve total corporate interests.

Performance Race. A view still too often evident among both plan sponsors and investment managers places pension fund returns in the perspective of a simple performance race against other pension funds. This view implies that all pension funds share the same objective and accept the same level of risk. Consequently, performance can be judged by the single number that ranks returns against those for other funds. No allowance is made for the likelihood that the policy that produces the highest returns under favorable investment conditions is also likely to be among the leaders on the downside under unfavorable conditions.

Differences in the characteristics of the pension plan itself, as well as differences in corporate goals, are ignored.

This view of the pension fund simply as an entrant in a single-category performance race is encouraged by a policy statement that includes palliatives which include conflicting objectives, such as "maximum return and preservation of capital." Since the official policy is universally appealing but impossible to achieve, it is a cop-out. Corporate directors or corporate executives with oversight responsibility for the pension fund are likely to interpret it as they see fit in the then-current investment environment. In the absence of quantitative articulation of asset-allocation objectives, the typical response is to focus on the returns of their fund relative to the median for other pension funds.

Despite the obvious shortcomings of the performance-race concept, it may dominate plan sponsor thinking simply by default. In the absence of clear reasons for a different formulation of fund objectives, "more" expected return always seems better than "less." While the goal of more rather than less is unassailable in general terms, the practical issue in the planning of investment policy is not so simple. In an investment world characterized by an uncertain future, each policy choice is expected to produce more under certain conditions and less under other conditions. Which policy choice for a particular fund will provide the most advantageous trade-off (assuming the fiduciary obligations imposed by ERISA are met) depends on the circumstances of the plan sponsor. To view the objectives of the pension fund within the framework of a performance race is to ignore the trade-off between expected return and risk in relation to overall corporate goals.

The problems that can arise from the performance-race concept are underscored by major changes in the investment environment. The investment policy designed to maintain leadership on the upside under favorable conditions is vulnerable to fourth-quartile performance under unfavorable conditions. Such wide variations in performance might be appropriate for a fund operating in a corporate context that can appropriately trade high volatility for the expectation of higher rewards over the long term. Where the fund objective is simply to win the performance race, however, fourth-quartile returns are likely to be regarded as a disaster. If the reaction is a shift toward a more conservative policy geared to unfavorable investment conditions, the stage has been set for another disaster when the investment environment again becomes favorable.

Unfortunately, a review of the performance records of individual pension funds suggests that this pattern of vacillation in an effort to win the performance race has too often prevailed. At a minimum, it is likely to result in a significant reduction in return relative to the risk the fund has accepted. At the extreme, the corporation and its shareholders may suffer from severe financial penalties as a result of an investment policy that is more conservative than necessary under favorable investment conditions or is subject to more risk than appropriate in an unfavorable investment environment.

Pension Assets in Relation to Pension Liabilities. A second approach to setting pension fund objectives views pension assets in reference to pension liabilities, as if the pension plan were an independent entity. This approach applies most appropriately to a terminated pension plan for a company that is no longer in business or imminently may not be. In this case, the assets must be invested to meet the cashflow required by the pension obligations with as little risk as possible. If the assets were sufficient, plan liabilities could be met through the purchase of an annuity contract to guarantee pension payments for all plan participants as long as required. Under these circumstances, the focus of attention shifts from the performance race with other pension funds; success is simply meeting the plan's legal obligations.

Need for Overall Corporate Perspective. While generating a return sufficient to meet pension liabilities is the appropriate investment objective in the above example, it does not apply so neatly to most pension funds. For an ongoing pension plan sponsored by a healthy corporation, this approach is too narrow for three reasons.

1. *Pension liabilities are driven by the plan sponsor's business.* Pension liabilities depend not only on the longevity of retirees but also on characteristics of active plan participants that are linked to the plan sponsor's business. Such employer-based characteristics include the changing size of the work force, the rate of employee turnover, changing levels of real wages, and changes in benefit provisions. Just this partial listing underscores the need for a view that integrates pension liabilities with the business of the plan sponsor.

2. *The pension fund holds the plan sponsor's IOU.* That is, the sponsor is obligated to the pension fund. As pointed out in Chap. 1, employees who participate in a pension plan effectively lend a portion of their wages to the plan sponsor. If the plan sponsor has not contributed sufficient assets to the pension fund to cover the present value of these liabilities (or loans), the pension fund will hold the equivalent of a promissory note issued by the sponsoring corporation. The plan sponsor is legally obligated to provide the present value of future plan liabilities, or, if payment is deferred, to provide more later to reflect accrual of interest. Consequently, it is clear that the financial strength of the spon-

soring corporation and the financial strength of the pension fund are interdependent.

3. *An integrated view addresses correlation of risks.* This view focuses on the relationship between the risks associated with the investment of pension assets and the operating risks of the plan sponsor's business. When there is a lack of correlation between returns on pension assets and returns on operating assets, risks will be partially offsetting. Consequently, the plan sponsor has an incentive to reduce risks that are highly correlated. Suppose, for example, a sharp drop in the market price of crude oil would result in both a 50 percent drop in earnings for the plan sponsor and a decline of 25 percent in the market price for oil shares held in the company's pension fund. Under these circumstances, the plan sponsor might consider lessening total company dependence on oil prices by reducing oil issues or by eliminating them from pension assets. As an alternative to constraints on the investments of individual portfolio managers, the pension fund could implement a policy of hedging oil investments by assuming a contrary position in oil futures.

Corporate View of Setting Objectives

Because the interests of plan participants and the interests of the sponsoring company are inextricably bound together, a broad corporate perspective is required to set objectives for pension investment policy. Within the constraints imposed by ERISA, management of the plan sponsor ordinarily retains considerable latitude to shape pension fund policy. The question is not whether pension fund investment policy should take into account corporate goals, but how the process is best accomplished.

Integration of pension fund assets and liabilities with the corporate balance sheet provides the framework required to identify pension fund objectives from the total corporate point of view. To construct an augmented balance sheet, as discussed in Chap. 5, pension assets and liabilities are added to the corporate balance sheet. All assets and liabilities are then restated, as closely as possible, to market values. Standard investment techniques permit the characteristics of the assets and liabilities listed on the augmented balance sheet to be reflected in the expected return and risk for the common stock of the corporation. Alternative asset-allocation policies may be tested by observing their effect, when inserted on the augmented balance sheet, on the characteristics of the company's common stock.

Pension Fund Support for Corporate Goals. The purpose of the integration of the pension plan with the plan sponsor's business is to select the trade-off of return and risk for the plan sponsor's common stock that is most consistent with overall corporate goals. The range of possibilities for pension fund policy is constrained by fiduciary obligations, as defined by ERISA, and management must be satisfied that these constraints have been met with a margin of safety. The policy choices are also limited to efficient portfolios,[1] as discussed in a subsequent section. Each of these portfolios is efficient because it maximizes expected return relative to a different level of risk. Consequently, corporate management does not attempt to identify the "best" investment policy, since each alternative is "best" for its level of risk. Rather, the challenge for corporate management is to identify the characteristics of the company's common stock, as modified by alternative investment policies for the company's pension fund, which best support overall corporate goals. Choice of the characteristics for the company's common stock, assuming fiduciary obligations under ERISA have been met, specifies the objectives of pension investment policy.

Case History: Augmented Balance Sheet in Practice. A brief example illustrates how top corporate management is able to identify the objectives of pension fund policy by focusing on the common stock of the corporation. Table 7-1 lists four alternative plans for policy asset allocation, designated A, B, C, and D, along with the implications of each for the risk-return characteristics of the company's common shares. (Chap. 5, specifically, Table 5-3, and the appendix to Chap. 5 explain the relationship between betas for the pension fund and for the common shares outstanding of the plan sponsor.) The information in Table 7-1, along with supporting data, was submitted to the management of a large industrial company by the officer responsible for pension investments. Management had previously defined the overall goal for the corporation: to achieve a total investment return for its common stock that would exceed that of the S&P 500. Success in achieving this goal in down markets received considerable emphasis, since the stock had long enjoyed a reputation as a relatively stable income stock. At the same time, management was strongly committed to building a record of superior performance for the company's stock over the longer term—3 to

---

[1]Use of options maintains portfolio efficiency as long as the option is purchased at a fair market price. The same conclusion holds for manufactured options created by portfolio insurance, assuming that the manufactured option performs as well as an equivalent listed option.

Table 7-1. Four Policy Alternatives for Asset Allocation

Policy alternative	Beta	
	Pension fund	Plan sponsor common stock
A	0.55	0.89
B	0.80	0.97
C	0.90	1.00
D	1.00	1.03

5 years—and the more extended time horizon increases the likelihood of a higher market.

One member of management supported a policy portfolio consisting entirely of fixed-income securities; it would be characterized by relatively low risk, much like that indicated for alternative A. The argument was made that this approach would facilitate accomplishment of the company's goals in the event another bear market in stocks should soon occur. Alternative A is a portfolio with the same expected return as the fixed-income portfolio, but, as a result of efficient diversification, it is subject to less risk. Analysis using the augmented balance sheet indicated that adoption of alternative A as investment policy for the pension fund (or the less efficient alternative of the all fixed-income portfolio) would reduce the beta for the common stock to less than 0.90 compared to 1.00 for the S&P 500. When other things are equal, the lower beta implies that the company's stock should be expected to perform better than the S&P 500 in an unfavorable investment environment.

Low-Fund Beta Conflicts with Long-Term Corporate Goals. Alternative A, along with the all fixed-income alternative, was rejected because of the unfavorable implications for success in meeting the corporate goal over the longer term. Given the likelihood of favorable returns for the S&P 500 over a 3- to 5-year time horizon and assuming other things are equal, the substantially lower beta for the company's stock would imply below-average performance. The goal of management of the sponsoring corporation was to add incrementally to returns through superior corporate strategy. Management recognized the danger that even a significant contribution to the performance of the company's stock from successful corporate strategy could be offset in a rising market by the negative effects associated with a low beta stock.

In the light of the problems associated with a common-stock beta substantially lower than 1.00, management looked with greater favor on alternatives B, C, and D. It was recognized that small differences in beta, ranging from 0.97 to 1.03, were not significant, but a shift to the highest risk portfolio could contribute in a small way to less-than-average performance in an unfavorable investment environment. The final choice was alternative C, with an indicated beta of 1.00. In effect, the pension fund policy was used to tune the characteristics of the common stock to avoid the likelihood that it would hinder the stock's performance relative to the S&P 500 in either an up or down market.

A company with different characteristics and goals might have chosen a very different policy plan for the pension fund. Suppose, for example, the beta for the company's stock would have amounted to 1.25 with alternative C as the pension fund policy. In this case, management might have determined that a conservative alternative, such as A, would be appropriate to lower the risk for the company's stock. On the other hand, management might have had reasons for preferring to continue a high beta for the company's stock, supported by an aggressive policy for the pension fund. Similarly, a company with a well-below-average beta for its common stock might consider a wide range of possibilities for its pension fund.

The policy choice from the alternatives available depends on the goals of management within the context of the particular corporate circumstances. To cite a specific example, government regulation of earnings, which limits the rate of return on capital, may be an important factor in shaping management decisions. For any company, a change in pension investment policy, through its impact on investment returns, will ultimately affect the level of corporate contributions to the pension fund. The question confronting management of a regulated company is how changes in contributions to the pension fund will be balanced by regulatory measures affecting the prices of company products or services.

like a defense contractor.

Appraising Risk and Return

If the investment objective is ultimately defined by a choice between alternative asset-allocation plans, how are the return-risk characteristics determined for the various alternatives? This is the second key issue involved in establishing investment policy for a pension fund.

Approaches to the Task

As summarized below, there are three broad possibilities. We stress the critical advantage of the second approach, which uses the consensus expectations of investors, but we also list the other two approaches to underscore their differences. Subsequent sections address the issues involved in implementing the consensus approach.

Judgmental Approach: Opens the Door to Uncontrolled Risks. The judgmental approach requires individual estimates of the outlook for the various financial markets. It misses the distinction between policy and strategy since it uses essentially the same approach—individual judgment. In its pure form, reliance on individual judgment (whether developed by an internal committee or by an outside "expert") may favor extreme positions—based on extreme views of the attractiveness of one asset class relative to another.

Consensus Approach: Permits Quantitative Assessment of Risk. The consensus approach is based on the assumption that the pension fund enjoys no forecasting advantage over other investors. The best estimate of future returns is therefore the consensus forecast already reflected in market prices. This approach infers expected return and risk for the various asset groups from prices recorded in highly competitive public markets. It makes possible a quantitative assessment of the trade-off of expected return and risk for each alternative policy.

Combination Approach: Creates Pitfalls.   The third category is a combination approach, which incorporates major elements of both the judgmental and consensus approaches. Our classification recognizes that the judgmental approach informally incorporates elements of the consensus approach to the extent it is influenced by what other pension funds are doing. Similarly, the consensus approach requires certain judgments, as we shall point out in our subsequent comments; it strives to avoid subjectivity but can never completely succeed.

The combination approach, in contrast, aims explicitly to mix the two approaches. It relies on a quantitative framework, using a standard statistical program, which appears to provide objective answers with precision. At the same time, the output of the model is driven by subjective inputs, usually a particular view of expected returns for one or more of the major asset groups. Often, little attention is directed to the inputs relating to risk measures for asset groups or correlations between asset groups. The unwary plan sponsor may conclude that the resulting asset allocation is a "scientific" answer to the formulation of policy, when, in reality, it is essentially the product of a particular subjective view of the future investment environment.

Consensus Approach Strives to Minimize Subjectivity

The consensus approach strives to minimize subjectivity in establishing the series of asset-allocation plans from which a policy plan is chosen. It uses probability analysis to focus policy asset allocation only on those portfolios included on the efficient frontier. As indicated previously, policy asset allocation is efficient when it offers maximum expected return for a given level of risk or minimum risk for a given level of expected return. Many other policy plans for asset allocation are possible, but they are ruled out because they are not efficient; they would require the plan sponsor to accept less expected return than could be achieved for the given level of risk.

Our purpose here is to address the principles underlying the construction of an efficiently diversified policy plan for asset allocation. Although the technical details are ordinarily provided by an outside consultant, plan sponsor executives with oversight responsibility for pension investments need to understand the process to appreciate the critical role of policy asset allocation—and also to recognize its limitations. An understanding of the conceptual framework is also necessary for the pension officer with direct responsibility for the assessment of the qualifications of candidates for the consultant's assignment.

Optimization of Return

Calculation of the set of portfolios that makes up an efficient frontier is a standard statistical exercise that optimizes expected return relative to risk. It requires three inputs for each asset category: (1) expected average rate of return, (2) variability of return, and (3) data relating to diversifiability (correlation between the returns of each pair of assets available for inclusion in the portfolio). The expected return is an estimate of total return, including both current income and capital appreciation. The other two inputs—the variability of return and correlations between returns—bear on the riskiness of the portfolio.

In sharp contrast to inputs to investment strategy, inputs to the policy optimization aim to represent the *consensus* views of investors as already reflected in current market prices. The goal of policy is to exclude individual judgments in order to control risk. The probable error in consensus expectations is quantifiable, using capital market theory supported by a widely accepted library of supporting research. By way of comparison, individual views of the investment outlook may defy conventional wisdom and still turn out to be very right, but there is no objective basis for advance assessment of their risks. Individual judgments are therefore the proper role of investment strategy rather than investment policy, since strategy risks can be controlled by limiting the role of strategy.

Two assumptions are critical to the establishment of investment policy. First, current market prices are the best estimate of value. Second, expected return is related to perceived risk.

Current Market Price Is the Best Estimate of Value. For the purpose of establishing investment policy, the consensus view is regarded as the best measure of current value in the light of currently available information. Although the consensus is made up of many disparate points of view, erroneous conclusions that are based on inadequate information or poor judgment tend to offset each other. Consequently, the current consensus view is reflected in current market prices, provided they are established in highly competitive public markets where material information is readily accessible to all participants. Consensus views may change substantially—and often do—as new information becomes available.

Expected Return Is Related to Perceived Risk. A second policy assumption is that investors are risk averse. They will hold an investment only when the expected return is sufficient to compensate for the associated risk. They will therefore price securities in the marketplace so that perceived higher risk is accompanied by higher expected return.

Expected Return Depends on Nondiversifiable Risk. The risk of significance to investors is the risk that cannot be diversified away (nondiversifiable risk). To the extent correlation of returns between asset groups is less than perfect, partially offsetting fluctuations for the individual asset groups eliminate some of the risk for the total portfolio. Therefore, in a competitive market, only nondiversifiable risk can expect to receive positive returns, on the average.

Nondiversifiable Risk Reflects the Market Portfolio. Nondiversifiable risk contributed by a particular asset in a portfolio depends not only on the correlation of returns with other portfolio assets but also on the proportion of the asset in the portfolio. For the consensus of investors, the relevant portfolio is their aggregate holdings, usually described as the *market portfolio*. As the proportion of an asset in the market portfolio increases, if other things are equal, it becomes more difficult to limit risk through diversification with other portfolio assets. As a result, the investor must be offered a higher expected return to induce holding the asset.

Measurement of Risk

Risk is measured by the variability of returns, usually from month to month over an extended period (such as 5 years). Common experience suggests that a record of wide variations in returns implies a high degree of risk in forecasting future returns, while relatively stable past returns indicate low risk. In highly efficient markets, such as U.S. markets for the most widely traded stocks and bonds, an analysis of historical variability of returns has been shown to provide useful forecasts of future variability. The widely used statistical measure of the variability of returns is the standard deviation, which quantifies the probability that future returns will deviate by a given amount from the expected average returns over the specified time horizon.

Benchmark Expected Returns

Expected return is derived in several different ways, depending on the asset group. The benchmark returns, used as reference points for estimating the returns of other assets, are those for treasury bills and the S&P 500.

Treasury Bills. The return on short-term treasury bills (usually 30 days or 3 months) is generally accepted as a proxy for the risk-free rate. No security can have a higher credit rating than a treasury obligation, and the very short maturity almost eliminates any risk due to changes in interest rates. As the minimum-risk investment, the return on treasury bills also serves as the benchmark for calibrating the "excess" returns for other asset groups. Since the reason for holding other more risky assets is to achieve returns in excess of the risk-free rate, policy planning focuses on expected returns in excess of those for treasury bills. (By definition, the excess return for treasury bills is zero.)

S&P 500. The excess return for the S&P 500, representing the predominant segment of the domestic equity market, is derived from long-term historical averages. Since investors attempt to avoid unnecessary risk, they will buy stocks only as long as the expected excess return is more attractive relative to the perceived risk. Similarly, they will sell stocks to the extent the expected return from stocks is inadequate relative to the risk. Thus, in highly competitive public markets, the continuing transactions of investors with conflicting views tend to price stocks so that the consensus view of expected excess return is equal to the return required to compensate investors for the level of risk represented by owning a share of the market. The actual excess return for any given year may turn out to be far different than expected by investors at the outset, since new information will continually result in reassessment of the investment outlook. Over a period of many years, nevertheless, the average of the excess returns actually achieved is likely to approach the average of the excess returns that had been expected. Based on this reasoning, the average of historical *excess* returns—subject to possible modification for demonstrated change in the level of risk—provides the best estimate of the consensus view of the expected excess return for the S&P 500. Policy studies generally use an expected excess return for the S&P 500 of about 5 to 7 percent.

Bond Market. The expected return for bonds is derived from comparison of nondiversifiable risk for the bond market with that for the S&P 500. Bonds are often represented by a comprehensive market index such as the Shearson Lehman Hutton Government-Corporate Bond Index. The risk demonstrated by bonds is usually greater than that for short treasury bills but less than that for the S&P 500. Because bond returns do not correlate perfectly with returns for stocks or other asset groups, part of the risk relating to bonds can be diversified away. Given an estimate of the proportion of bonds in the market portfolio and the correlation of bonds with other component asset groups, a standard statistical program permits calculation of the bond risk that cannot be eliminated through diversification. Bonds will be bought by investors, acting in their own self-interest, until prices have been bid to levels where the trade-off of expected excess return to nondiversifiable risk is the same as that for stocks. Consequently, it is the measurement of the nondiversifiable risk relating to bonds that is the clue to the consensus view of expected excess return. For policy planning, the excess return on long-term treasury bonds is usually estimated in the area of 1.5 to 3 percent.

Estimating Correlations of Returns

Although correlations may be deduced from market history, they may also require application of judgment. For example, the correlation between returns for stocks and bonds over the previous 5 years, in the absence of contrary information, constitutes a useful forecast of correlation for the years ahead. Yet history has also shown that correlations can change dramatically as the economic environment undergoes fundamental change. During the first two decades after World War II, returns for bonds and stocks were largely independent of each other. In the deflation of the 1930s, in contrast, returns for high-quality bonds were negatively correlated with those for stocks, and in the last two decades the returns demonstrated a large positive correlation. As changes in the environment become an issue, judgment necessarily enters into the process of estimating correlations of returns.

Major Components of Traditional Asset Groups

Diversification of the policy plan is facilitated by recognition that the traditional risky asset groups—stocks and bonds—are themselves composed of subgroups with less-than-perfect correlation of returns. The S&P 500, as a reflection of the stock market, is itself inadequate since it represents only about two-thirds of the market value of domestic common stocks traded in public markets. A separate equity group—described here as the non-S&P 500—therefore warrants a place in the policy plan. Similarly, in the area of fixed income, long bonds are frequently viewed as separate from intermediates. The fixed-income market may be represented by the Shearson Lehman Hutton Government-Corporate Bond Index, which aims to weight by market value the population of publicly traded taxable issues with maturities in excess of 1 year. For planning asset allocation, data is available separately for two major segments divided by maturity: (1) 1 to 10 years and (2) 10 years and over.

For these and other possible major segments of traditional asset groups—both common stock and fixed income—their characteristics can be estimated in much the same way as indicated for the total bond market. Measures of variability and correlation of returns, applied to estimates of the composition of the relevant market portfolio, determine the risk that cannot be diversified away. Comparison of their nondiversifiable risk with that for the S&P 500 provides the basis for estimating the expected return relative to the S&P 500.

Nontraditional Assets

Pension funds have increasingly invested in nontraditional assets in recent years. Traditional investments have focused mainly on large-company stocks, bonds, and cash equivalents, which are widely traded in highly competitive domestic markets. As suggested previously, the record of market prices for these traditional investments provides generally comparable evidence of nondiversifiable risk and correlations of returns necessary to estimate expected returns. The nontraditional assets of possible interest to pension funds constitute a long list, but the most important are real estate, international investments, and venture capital. For such asset groups, the market data necessary to derive consensus expectations is either absent or less than fully comparable with data for traditional asset categories.

For nontraditional assets—reflecting sparse historical data—inputs for expected returns, risks, and correlations require the use of analogy combined with a degree of judgment. Subjective judgment can be minimized, however, by a conscious effort to eliminate from consideration subjective opinions about the prospective investment environment. While estimates for nontraditional assets will still be influenced by greater subjectivity than those for traditional asset types, the effect on the policy asset plan is limited to the extent that these asset groups are candidates for a smaller part of the total plan. It is not unusual for the maximum policy percentage for real estate, for example, to be limited to 10 or 15 percent of the policy plan. In a similar way, policy constraints may be established for international investments and for venture capital. Because the estimates of consensus expectations for nontraditional assets are subject to greater uncertainties than those for traditional investments, such constraints are necessary. Even with such constraints, however, optimization still requires estimated characteristics for nontraditional asset groups. This information is necessary not only to establish the allocation of the asset within the range permitted by the constraints but also to allow for the interaction of these assets with other assets.

Real Estate.   Real estate provides the most prominent example of an asset group that requires extensive judgments about risk, correlations of return, and its proportion in the market portfolio. Data for the variability of returns for real estate funds notoriously understate risk, since reported variability is heavily distorted by use of appraisal data rather than actual transaction data. Real estate appraisals are based on a number of factors other than market prices because comparable market prices are frequently unavailable. Since each unit of real estate is unique, moreover, the appraiser must use discretion when applying prices established in another transaction to a particular property under review. The result is that appraisal values tend to be considerably more stable than stock or bond prices, which reflect actual transactions in highly liquid markets.

A review of the fluctuations in the value of real estate transactions over a wide variety of historical periods suggests that the risks in holding high-quality real estate may be similar to the risks associated with high-quality stocks as represented by the S&P 500. In a similar way, judgments may be made about correlations of returns with major asset groups. There have been periods like the 1930s when returns from real estate correlated positively with stocks, but in the 1970s the correlation turned negative for a substantial period. A judgment is required to determine the influences that are likely to bear on their correlation in the years ahead. An even more difficult judgment is to determine the proportion of real estate in the market portfolio that should be available to pension funds. As explained previously, the proportion of the asset in the market portfolio, the correlation of returns with other asset groups, and a measure of the variability of returns are all necessary to estimate the consensus view of expected returns.

International Investments. For international investments, market data for stocks and bonds may be similar to that for domestic markets, but the resulting consensus estimates are not wholly comparable even under the best of circumstances. Among the most important reasons are various barriers to the free flow of capital, including taxes levied on foreign investors, and the much higher transaction costs incurred in foreign markets. As stated above, an arbitrary limitation on the proportion of international investments in the policy plan is warranted.

Venture Capital. Data on venture capital returns are particularly unreliable, in part because there is no ongoing publicly traded market in these investments and also because the history of the industry is relatively short. Most of the data that we have seen is compiled with a heavy bias in favor of marketing venture capital partnerships; it is hardly useful as the basis for planning policy. One approach is to view venture capital as a segment of the market for very small capitalization stocks (for which data are available). Venture capital returns are highly dependent on the market for initial public offerings, since financial success for the venture capital partnership is ordinarily determined by the prices achieved as the individual ventures reach the stage where they can be offered to the public. When markets for the very small capitalization stocks are doing well, as they did from 1974 to 1983, the record of venture capital investments is also extraordinary. When very small capitalization stocks performed poorly in the 1969–1974 period, the venture capital business also encountered hard times.

Example of Assumptions Underlying Policy

An example of a set of policy assumptions is displayed in Table 7-2. The data were kindly provided by the Rockefeller Foundation, which manages a large endowment fund as well as a retirement fund for its own

Table 7-2. Capital Market Policy Assumptions

	Real return* %	Risk† %	Correlation coefficients					
			Equities	Bonds	Cash	Real estate	Foreign capital	Venture capital
Equities	6.7	20	1.00	0.50	-0.05	0.35	0.60	0.80
Bonds	3.0	11	0.50	1.00	-0.10	0.15	0.30	0.40
Cash	1.0	4	-0.05	-0.10	1.00	0.10	-0.05	-0.05
Real estate	6.0	16	0.35	0.15	0.10	1.00	0.25	0.20
Foreign capital	5.8	22	0.60	0.30	-0.05	0.25	1.00	0.60
Venture capital	9.0	35	0.80	0.40	-0.05	0.20	0.60	1.00

*Long-term inflation assumption = 5.5%.
†Annual standard deviation of returns.

SOURCE: Rockefeller Foundation (used by permission).

employees. These assumptions are based on analysis of the prices in the current financial markets within the framework of capital market theory and the historical record. Since financial markets change to reflect the changing investor consensus, policy assumptions are ordinarily reviewed at periodic intervals, such as once each year.

Limitations of Investment Policy

Although a clearly defined policy plan plays an essential role in investment management, it falls far short of meeting all plan sponsor concerns relating to asset allocation. Investment policy provides an objective framework for controlling risk—the risk of loss in unfavorable investment markets, as well as the risk of missing out under favorable conditions. A balanced view of investment policy, however, also acknowledges its limitations, which are as follows:

1. *Policy inputs cannot completely avoid subjective judgments.* While the role of policy in investment management depends on how well it reflects the consensus views of investors, the measurement of these consensus views is something less than a science. The subjectivity of judgments tends to increase as attention shifts from traditional to nontraditional assets.

2. *Consensus views change with new information.* Even if the consensus views could be inferred with complete accuracy, they may change substantially as new information emerges. Stock market risk, as measured by variability of returns, for example, was much lower over most of the postwar period than during the 1930s; by late 1987, there were indications, at least for a time, of a return to the variability demonstrated in the 1930s. Similarly, the very long-term data showing little correlation between returns of bonds and stocks have not served as a useful guide to the period of high correlations in more recent years.

3. *Actual return may differ greatly from expected return.* Given an accurate reading of consensus views and a high degree of stability in the measures bearing on risk and expected return for each asset group, actual performance may still differ significantly from the expected return over any time horizon. Pension officers sometimes seem to regard the policy estimate of expected return as the inevitable reward of long-term investing. This interpretation views shorter term volatility as only a temporary departure from the longer term trend. Such confidence overlooks the meaning of risk, because risk deals with the probability that the actual return will differ from the expected return over the full

range of possible time horizons. Risk of deviation from the annualized expected return diminishes as the time horizon increases but is never eliminated. When the policy performance substantially lags (or substantially exceeds) the expected return for an extended period, the plan sponsor patience with exclusive reliance on passive asset allocation—as it is incorporated in the policy plan—is almost certain to wear thin.

4. *Asset allocation: Long-term assumptions may change.* In recent years, long term planning for asset allocation has generally relied on the assumption that common stocks should be expected to return, on an average over the longer term, about 6 percent in excess of the return for short treasury bills. This projection of excess return is supported by the historical record from 1926 to 1988, as indicated by Fig. 7-1. Upon further analysis, however, this 63-year record also underscores the wide variations in return over extended periods.

The subperiods displayed in Fig. 7-1 divide the entire 63 years into three equal segments, each 21 years in length. The S&P 500 generated greater excess return in the 1947–1967 period—when the compound annual rate averaged 11.6 percent—than during the other two periods combined. For the initial 21 years (1926–1946), the annual compound rate of excess return averaged 5.3 percent, despite the collapse of stock prices that accompanied the Great Depression of the 1930s. Over the last 21 years, in contrast, the S&P 500 registered a compound rate of excess return of only 2.0 percent. Although this most recent period (1968–1988) included the extraordinary bull market of the 1980s, it also reflected the poor returns reported for the 1970s.

To a degree, investor assumptions about the long-term excess return for common stocks are shaped by a backward look at historical experience. The highly favorable market returns in the earlier postwar years—which largely coincided with the 1947–1967 period shown in

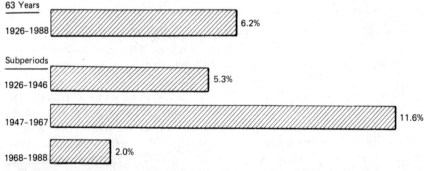

Figure 7-1. S&P 500: Compound annual rate of excess return.

Fig. 7-1—contributed importantly to the record necessary for development of current assumptions about the long-range target for excess return. Assumptions were much more conservative before the tremendous bull market that followed World War II. During the 1940s, most retirement funds held no common stocks at all, since contemporary expert opinion[2] had little confidence in the longer term superiority of common stock returns over those for fixed income.

Although current assumptions are supported by considerable data for other time periods in other countries,[3] investor confidence in an unknown long-range future requires continuing reinforcement. A significant bear market almost always raises questions about the validity of the long-range case for common stocks. If such a bear market were to occur during the next year or two—extending the relatively unfavorable record of equity returns since 1968—the currently accepted assumptions about the long-range future of equities would become increasingly open to challenge.

Avoiding Ill-Considered Lurches in Investment Policy

Mounting dissatisfaction with policy during extended periods when actual policy performance departs substantially from policy assumptions is likely to result in an ill-considered lurch in policy allocation. Revisions in policy will be appropriate from time to time, reflecting either a change in fund objectives or modifications in the alternatives available on the efficient frontier. Such revisions, however, should result from careful reassessment of the building blocks for policy rather than a hasty response to disappointing performance.

Since prevention is easier than cure, there are three avenues that the fund manager can pursue in an effort to maintain the overall effectiveness of a policy plan: (1) *maximum diversification,* which aims to strengthen the policy plan itself through minimizing dependence on any one asset type; (2) *hedging,* which, like policy, is a passive approach but changes the risk-return profile of the policy plan; and (3) establishment of *complementary roles for policy and strategy*—since combining ac-

---

[2]The most widely read textbook on investments in the 1940s was Benjamin Graham and David L. Dodd, *Security Analysis,* McGraw-Hill. The 1940 edition, p. 726, stated: "An institution that can manage to get along on the low income provided by high-grade, fixed value issues should, in our opinion, confine its holdings to this field."

[3]See Roger G. Ibbotson and Gary P. Brinson, *Investment Markets,* McGraw-Hill, 1987, Chap. 2.

tive management with passive management enhances opportunities for both policy and strategy to succeed in filling their respective roles.

Maximum Diversification

When in doubt about policy asset allocation, diversify. Under textbook conditions—where the inputs to policy optimization are assumed to be precisely correct and perfectly stable—policy diversification minimizes risk relative to expected return for assets with returns that are less than perfectly correlated. In a perfectly efficient market, diversification is the only free lunch. In actual practice, inputs to the optimization model, at best, are approximations and also may be subject to change in the light of fundamental change in the investment environment.

In the real world, diversification is even more important than under textbook conditions. Diversification over the maximum number of eligible assets, in addition to its textbook function, also tends to reduce vulnerability to errors in estimating the inputs to the optimization model or in recognizing fundamental change in the investment environment.

The generalization in favor of policy diversification applies only when prices are established in highly competitive public markets that incorporate generally available public information. By way of example, this principle favors holding the non-S&P 500 stocks as well as the S&P 500, since correlation of returns between these two major segments of the publicly traded equity market is less than perfect. The principle does not apply, on the other hand, when there are barriers to the efficient pricing of assets. The policy-diversification argument is therefore much weaker when applied to works of art or to rare coins. Market prices for these assets do not necessarily represent consensus views of investment value, in part because they are held for reasons other than investment and also because the transactions take place in less liquid, less efficient markets.

Hedging: Defensive Asset Allocation

Hedging is a method for changing the risk-expected return profile of a fund in response to the changing investment environment. It is often described as "portfolio insurance," since its aim is to limit risks of loss to a specified level. It is not insurance in the strict sense, since no underwriter provides a guarantee of a specified level of return. Rather, it is either (1) a purchase of puts on a listed index or (2) a dynamic strategy employing a rigorous mathematical rebalancing of holdings in a "risky asset" (usually equities) and a "reserve asset" (such as 1-year treasury bills) in a way to replicate the ongoing value of a put option.

In its original application, dynamic hedging was used in order to insure against a loss in an equities portfolio over a year. Recent applications are designed for various minimum floor returns (such as −5, +3, or +5 percent), for longer horizons of up to 3 years or more, and for other fixed-income assets as well as equities. Other versions of the method are based on the ability to deliver the better performing of the two assets (say stocks or bonds) or even multiple assets (for example, equity market performance across several countries).

Inherent Cost, or "Premium." To continue the insurance analogy, the inherent cost of either the listed index option or the program of dynamic hedging is described as the *premium*. In dynamic hedging, a cost is involved because the risky asset is sold progressively as the market declines (to control risk at a specified level) and is progressively repurchased as the market prices again rise (to avoid missing out in a bull market). The selling prices for these transactions will average less than the purchase prices, resulting in the premium paid each time the market fluctuates in the range where transactions take place. The cost of the premium in any year will depend on the number of whipsaws within the range where buying and selling take place. Costs other than the premium routinely include transaction costs as well as manager fees, but transaction costs are substantially reduced through the use of index futures contracts rather than cash purchases and sales.

Since there is no free lunch involved in dynamic hedging, the question is, why do it? The answer is that some investors may find the change in the risk-expected return profile more appropriate for their particular circumstances. For example, some pension funds were willing to hold more equities during the bull market of the mid-1980s than they would have in the absence of dynamic hedging. These funds were willing to trade the risks of increased costs of the dynamic hedging program—if the market fluctuations in a narrow range had created a series of whipsaws during these years—for the opportunity to participate more fully in a rising market.

Possible Problems in Highly Volatile Markets. The fund manager who contemplates the use of dynamic hedging must consider the possibility that transactions cannot be executed near anticipated levels in a highly volatile market that may become discontinuous (that is, suffer "gap" openings). Such was the case in the record market drop of October 19, 1987. Under the extreme conditions at that time, some dynamic hedging programs failed to work as planned and many dynamic hedging operations were suspended. Subsequently, dynamic hedging programs have been revised in an effort to lessen the problems encountered in such volatile markets, and they have been augmented by strategies employing listed index options.

Legitimate Method of Risk Control—at a Cost. Hedging, properly constructed and implemented, is a legitimate method of controlling risk. It may employ listed index options and/or dynamic rebalancing. Plan sponsors must assess, in the light of their respective fund objectives, whether these modifications in downside risk are warranted by the costs of hedging. The events of October 1987 have reminded investors, moreover, that the costs include penalties that can be incurred when markets are discontinuous. For this reason, newer technologies using portfolios of listed options with a range of strike prices have gained acceptance by avoiding reliance on the transactions required by dynamic approaches.

Complementary Roles of Policy and Strategy

An attempt to rely exclusively on passive asset allocation—the policy approach—is almost certain to open the way to back-door market timing and other poorly disciplined methods of injecting individual forecasts into investment decisions. When the performance of the securities markets seem inconsistent with policy assumptions for an extended period, the wisdom of rigid adherence to an earlier determined policy is almost certain to be subject to increasing question. Disavowal of active management does not eliminate strategy but, rather, encourages it to go underground, surreptitiously influencing revisions in policy. The likely result is that policy is handicapped in its role of controlling risk at the level most appropriate to fund circumstances. The strategy that is haphazardly reflected in policy, moreover, is at a competitive disadvantage relative to more carefully planned efforts to apply strategy on a continuing basis to a designated portfolio.

Integration of a separate strategy effort into the policy framework is advantageous to both major approaches to investment management. A role for strategy that is clearly delineated from policy lessens pressures to abandon policy during those periods when its performance proves disappointing. Strategy operating within the context of a carefully drawn policy plan, meanwhile, can be encouraged to pursue more aggressive active management. Since policy addresses the control of total fund risk, strategy can be accorded greater latitude to incur risk in its designated area of operations.

While the focus of this chapter is investment policy, the next two chapters concentrate on investment strategy. Chap. 8 presents an overview of the investment decision process, in order to provide a conceptual framework for evaluating the role of investment strategy in fund management. Chap. 9 specifically addresses the coordination of investment strategy with investment policy in the implementation of asset allocation.

8

Investment Management Process

Critical Role of the Decision Process

With investment policy firmly in place, the plan sponsor is in a position to consider investment strategy. Should a plan sponsor accept the incremental risks and costs associated with investment strategy in an effort to add value to policy? If so, how should these efforts be structured?

Since the success of investment strategy depends largely on how information is analyzed, our primary focus in this chapter is on the investment decision process. Information that may be legally employed for investment purposes is so widely available that no single investor is likely to benefit from a continuing information advantage. The value added by the individual investment manager therefore depends very heavily on the quality of the decision process that is applied to available information.

Elements that Determine Investment Value

Evaluation of an investment manager's decision process implies an understanding of the way the securities markets operate. The central question is: How well does a particular decision process address the elements that determine investment value? Figures 8-1 and 8-2, pages 107 and 108, provide a framework for reviewing these elements.

These two figures apply broadly to all asset groups and individual securities. For purposes of illustration, however, our comments focus on common stocks, specifically the S&P 500. To adapt Fig. 8-2 to fixed-income markets, for example, "interest coupon" would be substituted for "dividend." As a result, the rectangles referring to dividend change and dividend growth rate change would be eliminated, since their value would always be zero.

Investment Assumptions that Determine Managerial Decisions

Although investment managers may not define the investment issues exactly as outlined in Figures 8-1 and 8-2, their decisions reflect assumptions, either consciously determined or implied, that represent a resolution to each of these elements of value. The decision concerning the change in the risk premium—a term appearing in both figures—provides a familiar example. Few investment managers, when evaluating an investment, would claim that they specifically develop an estimate for the prospective change in the risk premium. Yet the investment manager who takes into account increasing investor confidence in reaching an investment decision is projecting a favorable change in the risk premium. At one extreme are the "contrarian" investment managers who buy low and sell high on the basis of widely used statistical measures. Their decisions largely depend on the assumption that the risk premium is temporarily exaggerated at depressed prices and unsustainably low when the market price is in the upper part of the historical range. At the other extreme are managers who stress long-term differentials in growth of earnings and dividends, systematically excluding factors that bear on fluctuations in investor confidence. Their decisions rest on the implied assumption that the risk premium does not change.

The advantages of careful definition of the framework for the investment process are several.

Persistent Bias in the Decision Process. One advantage is to increase the likelihood that appropriate consideration will be accorded each of the key factors affecting valuation. The investment manager introduces bias in a portfolio by regularly emphasizing certain issues in the decision process and according much less attention to others. Identification of an underlying bias can explain why a manager appears to be so much more effective in one kind of market environment than in another. A value manager, to cite an important example, thrives in an investment environment where the risk premiums are for the most part large and experience wide fluctuations. A growth-stock manager benefits from a general atmosphere of prosperity, with relatively low interest rates and only limited episodes of rising risk premium. Conventional versions of the dividend discount model, increasingly used during recent years, are likely to be particularly effective when interest rates are high and volatile. Each approach has its day because one part of the decision process is stressed while other areas receive much less attention.

Gaining Advantage from Bias.   Bias may be warranted where the manager can bring special skills to bear on the resolution of a particular issue, implying an advantage over other managers with the same orientation. Even though superior managers are usually expected to achieve favorable performance, they will seem to be doing poorly when their style is out of favor. Consequently, it is up to the plan sponsor to control total fund biases by selecting portfolio managers with special skills but with different decision biases. The plan sponsor's goal can be either to minimize total fund bias or, alternatively, to achieve a tilt consistent with his or her current assessment of the most advantageous strategy.

Interaction of Variables Affecting Value.   Another reason for examining the framework of the decision process is to trace the relationships of the various valuation elements to each other. The same estimate developed for one decision step can have different significance depending on the estimates for other steps. By way of illustration, the effects on market price of a given change in any one of the three investor assumptions that bear on market valuation—the risk premium, the risk-free rate, or the dividend growth rate—depends on the magnitude of the market's yield. If the yield is 5 percent, then a 0.1 percentage point change in consensus investor view of the risk-free rate would result in a change in market price of about 2 percent. If the yield were 3 percent, the same 0.1 percentage point change in the risk-free rate would change the market price by more than 3 percent. In contrast, a change in the current dividend payment, other things equal, would imply just as much change in market price when the market yield is low as when it is high.

Elements of Valuation

The point of departure in our analysis of the issues that determine investment value is the principle summarized in Fig. 8-1. As indicated by

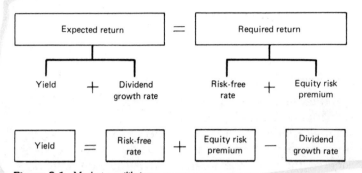

Figure 8-1. Market equilibrium.

the top line, market prices, in highly competitive, publicly traded markets, continually seek to adjust so that expected return equals required return. By way of example, suppose that investors expect a return higher than their required return from holding the S&P 500. Under these circumstances, they will bid up stock prices until equality is reached. Similarly, if investors conclude that the expected return is lower than their required return, they will sell stocks, until the discrepancy is eliminated.

The components of expected return and required return are displayed on the second line of Fig. 8-1. By definition, the required return is the risk-free rate, usually represented by short-term treasury bills (T-bills), plus a risk premium. The latter is the incremental return demanded by investors in order to compensate them for accepting the additional risk associated with holding stocks rather than treasury bills.

Expected return also consists of two parts. One part is the yield, based on the dividend payment indicated for the coming year. The other part is the changing value of the future stream of dividends as time passes and dividends grow. The pattern of prospective dividend changes, however viewed by investors, can be represented by an equivalent constant dividend growth rate.

Three Key Forces Define Yield

The bottom line of Fig. 8-1 defines dividend yield in terms of the three key forces shown on the right side of the equation. This expression results from subtracting the dividend growth rate from both sides of the equation in the upper part of the exhibit. Since market price is inversely related to yield, the change in yield is usually the most important single factor determining the level of stock prices over relatively short periods, such as a year.

Issues Deserving Special Attention

Figure 8-2 relates the valuation, shown at the top of the diagram, to the entire range of factors that influence it.

The large rectangles indicate the issues subject to particularly wide differences in the way they are resolved by investors. These are the issues that frequently dominate the ultimate conclusion on valuation. They deserve special attention from investment managers striving to improve their decision process and from plan sponsors who must evaluate investment managers.

Issues represented by the narrow rectangles, although subject to less controversy among investors than those enclosed by the large rectangles, must be addressed in the decision process to avoid substantial dis-

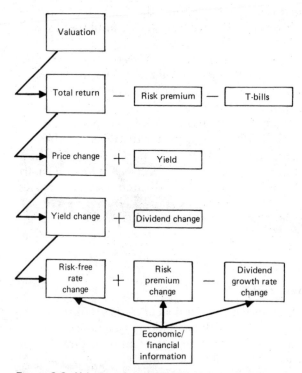

Figure 8-2. Valuation—overview.

tortion in the conclusion. A clear example is the current yield for a stock index, such as the S&P 500. The current price is a precise quantity, and variations in the estimates of the dividends to be paid over the coming year are unlikely to be sufficiently great to affect materially the calculation of the current yield. Omission of the yield from the estimate of total return, nevertheless, could significantly distort the conclusion on valuation.

Relative Valuation. The objective of an investment process is to determine relative valuation, and for this reason valuation is shown at the top of Fig. 8-2. The attractiveness of the S&P 500, which we are using as an example, depends both on the returns available on alternative investments and on the riskiness of the S&P 500 compared to other investments. Line 2 of the figure therefore shows total return less the sum of the estimates of the risk premium and the return for short-term treasury bills (which approximates the risk-free return). The return estimates ordinarily are calculated over a 1-year time horizon. Since each asset is valued relative to short-term treasury bills, the valuation of each of the risky assets may be readily compared with each other.

Valuation versus Relative Return. Table 8-1 provides an example of how focus on relative return rather than on valuation may lead to the wrong conclusion. Suppose the 1-year expected return on a venture capital fund is estimated at 17 percent compared with 13 percent for the S&P 500 and 12 percent for intermediate-term fixed-income securities. On the basis of expected return, venture capital appears relatively attractive. After subtractions for the risk-free rate and the risk premium, however, it is the intermediates that are undervalued—by five percentage points relative to venture capital. Based on these assumptions, venture capital should not be overweighted, despite the expected 17 percent return, and more likely should be underweighted, on the basis of the negative valuation.

Table 8-1. Valuation versus Relative Return (percent)

	Total return	−	T-bills	−	Risk premium	=	Valuation
Venture capital	+17		−7		−12		−2
S&P 500	+13		−7		−6		0
Intermediates	+12		−7		−2		+3

Total Return. Although it is necessary to allow for the risk-free rate and the differences in risk premium in calculating valuation, the most dynamic item listed on line 2 of Fig. 8-2 is the total return. The components of total return are shown on line 3. Over a 1-year time horizon, total return can be approximated by adding price change to the beginning yield. Since the beginning price is known and the dividend to be paid over the coming year can be projected with considerable accuracy, the yield estimate is shown in a narrow rectangle. The price change, in contrast, is subject to a wide range of possibilities. It is therefore enclosed in a large rectangle and analyzed separately on line 4.

Price Change. The price change over a 1-year time horizon can be analyzed in terms of two components—yield change and dividend change. In the absence of yield change, the market price of the S&P 500 would move exactly in proportion to the dividend change. Since the change in the dividend of the S&P 500 12 months ahead is largely known, this term can be estimated rather accurately. The critical variable is the yield change. Recognition that price change is an inverse function of yield change permits two useful conclusions. First, the same information affecting yield will have less effect on market price when yield is high than when it is low. Second, primary influences on market price can be identified most directly by determining the factors that influence yields required by investors.

Yield Change. Yield, as indicated in our earlier discussion of Fig. 8-1, is determined by three factors: (1) the risk-free rate, plus (2) the risk premium, less (3) the consensus assumption of investors about the long-term growth of dividends. Estimates of the change in each of these factors, as displayed in the three large rectangles, are derived from the information on economic and financial variables represented in the large rectangle at the bottom of Fig. 8-2.

Key Economic and Financial Variables

The range of economic and financial variables that can influence financial markets is so wide that is is virtually impossible to evaluate each of them individually. Apart from the sheer number, the impact of a change in one variable depends on its relationship to many other variables. Simple rules that attempt to establish direct cause-and-effect relationships between individual economic and financial variables and future returns for the financial markets are therefore doomed to failure; they are seeking to measure stable relationships when the relationships vary with changing circumstances.

Our graphic representation recognizes that a limited number of key variables summarize the net impact of a large number of supporting variables. For example, treasury bill yields depend on investor reaction to the growth of the money supply, the outlook for the federal deficit, prospects for business activity, and many other factors, particularly as they affect expected inflation. The investor-consensus expectation for treasury bill yields is the key variable; it contains the judgment of the investor consensus on all other factors that influence treasury bill yields. Even if the current consensus forecast ultimately turns out to be wide of the mark, it will be reflected in the financial markets (in this case, the S&P 500) until the consensus begins to change. In a similar way, the consensus view of prospective dividend increases will summarize the net effect of investor judgments about the course of business activity, the likely level of pretax margins, prospective changes in taxes, and the many financial factors that may influence the level of dividend payout. Other key variables required to analyze the S&P 500 include prospective corporate earnings and rates of inflation, since their relationships to other key variables, along with certain market price data, are indicators of the state of investor confidence in future dividends and interest rates.

Unanticipated Change Drives the Financial Markets

The major opportunity to gain advantage through application of the decision process is outlined in Fig. 8-2. New information about key economic variables is translated by the marketplace into changes in yield as investors adjust their assumptions about the risk-free rate, risk premia, and dividend growth rates. How changes in the key variables will affect these assumptions underlying the yield of the market depends on two factors. To what extent is the new information already anticipated by the financial markets? Of the new information not already discounted by market prices, how much will be regarded by the market consensus as a temporary fluctuation?

Example: Rising Interest Rates

By way of example, suppose the average yield on short-term treasury bills rises over the coming year by 100 basis points (one percentage point). If the financial markets had been discounting a 60-basis point rise, then only the last 40 basis points would represent a surprise. Not all of the 40 basis points, however, can be counted as an increase in the risk-free rate used to discount stock prices. Since treasury bill rates fluctuate, the market consensus may well conclude that a large part of the rise beyond the anticipated 60-point increase is subject to short-term reversal. The reaction of investors will depend on the volatility of interest rates, since a given change will seem less significant when volatility is high than when it is low. For the purposes of this example, suppose the unanticipated rise of 40 basis points results in an upward adjustment of only 5 basis points in the long-term assumption about the risk-free rate. With the yield of the S&P 500 at 4 percent, a 5-basis point rise in yield would warrant only slightly more than 1 percent decline in market price.

Changing Business Outlook

The market's response to the various business influences on expectations concerning the future dividend growth rate is tempered by the same two considerations—the proportion of change that has already been discounted, and, of the remainder, the proportion to be considered temporary by the market consensus. The residual is almost certain to amount to a small part of the total change, but it can still significantly affect market valuation through its impact on the current yield required by investors. Other things equal, current yield requirements are inversely proportional to the market consensus about future dividend growth.

Influences on Investor Confidence

Similar considerations apply to any appraisal of what impacts investor confidence. By way of example, evidence of a high rate of inflation will tend to increase the risk premium required by investors, with negative implications for stock prices. Even with no change in other factors that influence stock prices, the significance of the information on inflation will vary. It will depend on how much the inflation had already been anticipated in the marketplace and also on the investor consensus about how long it will last. Consequently, simple mechanical rules that attempt to relate the level of inflation to the level of the price-earnings ratio do not meet the test of past history.

Evaluating the Investment Manager

Although Fig. 8-2 aims to provide background for evaluating the investment process of individual managers, we do not expect each manager will formally address each issue represented in the diagram. For example, a manager could be highly successful in assessing the prospects for earnings and dividends for individual stocks but may largely ignore factors relating to changes in the risk-free rate and the risk premium. The manager's basic expertise in a particular area, nevertheless, may permit a performance advantage relative to a passive fund representing the same market segment (or the median of other managers who operate in the same universe of securities). Conversely, a manager may direct specific attention to each element listed in our diagram without providing evidence of value added.

Even though allowance must be made for wide differences among individual managers, comparison of manager decision processes with our diagram of the major investment elements is useful for two reasons. First, it provides assistance in identifying what the manager is attempting to do, what the manager does not attempt to do, and how the resulting bias favors or penalizes the manager depending on the market environment. Second, it can help determine the rigor a manager applies to his or her portfolio assignment. This part of the analysis discriminates between biases that reflect concentration on what the manager does well and those biases, unrelated to the manager's skill, that introduce continuing risk without offsetting advantages in terms of expected returns. The bias that emphasizes the manager's special skills is a positive factor, while the bias that adds unnecessarily to risk is a clear negative.

Review of the Manager's Decision Process

The underlying issue is whether an investment manager is able to present a carefully reasoned argument concerning how his or her decision process can expect to gain advantage over highly competitive securities markets. It is hardly adequate for the manager to state that he is a "Graham and Dodd" manager or a "growth" manager or uses "economic analysis" or "dividend discount models." A manager should be able to identify the information he or she uses and how it is processed to reach a conclusion. The following three broad questions provide a framework for discussion.

1. *Information Sources.* What are the manager's sources of information? Does he attempt to gain advantage through access to superior information, or does he use information widely available with the aim of applying superior analysis? Can she provide a persuasive argument either that her information is superior or, alternatively, that she has developed a superior method for closely tracking consensus information?

2. *Information Processing.*   How does the manager translate the economic forecasts that underlie his or her strategy into changes in the consensus assumptions that determine market valuations? Does the manager emphasize the differences in prospective gains in earnings and dividends? If so, the result is likely to be a persistent growth-stock bias, even as growth stocks go out of favor. In a similar way, focus on buying low and selling high (Graham and Dodd and other contrarian approaches) is oriented toward significant fluctuations in risk premia. It was particularly effective in the widely fluctuating markets of the 1930s and 1940s and came back in favor after the market collapse of 1973–1974. The recent popularity of dividend discount models, meanwhile, reflects the high degree of sensitivity in recent years of stock prices to fluctuations in interest rates.

3. *Rigor.*   How rigorously does the manager pay attention to the details? Even the steps represented by the narrow rectangles in Fig. 8-2 can make a substantial difference in the ultimate conclusion. The manager who does not allow for the difference between valuation and prospective total return will tend to bias decisions toward higher returns without adequate allowance for differences in risk. Similarly, total return must include current income as well as price change, and price change depends on change in dividend as well as on change in yield.

Portfolio Construction

The decision process can contribute to investment performance only if it is implemented in an actively managed portfolio. Implementation requires both selection and balancing.

Selection (which assets or securities to own) identifies the attractive securities (or asset groups), based on the perceived degree of undervaluation. Since it is the critical test of the skill of the active manager, it has been the principal subject of this chapter. It leaves unanswered, however, how the attractive alternatives are to be combined in an investment portfolio.

Balancing (how much to own) addresses relative portfolio weightings. Balancing may be accomplished in several ways. The most simple method uses standard rules that limit risk. For example, each security in an equity portfolio is accorded 3 percent of total assets (equal weighting) in order to maintain a high level of diversification. This approach provides for low exposure to the risks specific to each holding, but does not allow for factors that could result in wide variations in attractiveness of the different alternatives. A more refined solution would take into account estimates for expected return and for the effect of the addition of the security on total portfolio risk. On this basis, certain issues considered attractive on their own merits may play only a limited role in a particular portfolio because of their effect on total portfolio risk. Other securities may be assigned considerable variations in weights (risk-optimized weightings), depending on indicated differences in their effects on portfolio expected return and risk.

While the plan sponsor's primary concern should be the investment manager's skill in selecting attractive alternatives, it is also useful to review the manager's discipline for portfolio construction. Complex approaches are not necessarily better than relatively simple approaches, particularly if they require inputs that are themselves unreliable. In our view, the plan sponsor must be satisfied that the portfolio manager has a method for balancing the array of attractive alternatives that effectively controls risk. The absence of a clearly stated discipline would be cause for alarm.

Performance versus Decision Process

The only reason an investment decision process can be considered superior is because it increases the probability of favorable performance. Consequently, appraisal of an investment decision process should include analysis of past performance (which is the subject of Chap. 10). A period of mediocre or even unfavorable performance does not prove that the decision process is flawed, since risks taken with even highly favorable odds can turn out badly for a time. Because plan sponsors have no way of correcting for bad luck, however, they must remain highly skeptical of a decision process if it is not supported by a record of favorable results.

It does not follow that superior performance should be taken as evidence of a superior investment process. If all investment results were entirely due to chance, half of all investment managers would achieve performance above the median—over any time horizon. Statistical analyses have made clear, meanwhile, that past performance, in itself, is an inadequate predictor of future performance.

With passive alternatives to active management now readily available and widely used, the burden rests with active managers to show how they expect to gain advantage over highly competitive securities markets. They must make their case, first, in terms of a logical explanation of their decision process. A second criterion is the performance record Of the two criteria, the most difficult to demonstrate persuasively is the decision process—and it is by far the most important.

9
Role of Investment Strategy in Asset Allocation

Importance of Asset Allocation

For the pension fund manager, asset allocation presents both exceptional opportunity—and dangerous pitfalls. Various estimates have placed the proportion of investment performance attributable to asset allocation as high as 90 percent.[1] While the precise figure depends on the particular time period under consideration, the dominant contribution of asset allocation to performance is evident over any extended time horizon.

Two Fundamentally Different Approaches

Table 9-1 applies the fundamental distinction between investment strategy and investment policy, as discussed in Chap. 6, to asset allocation.

[1]See G. P. Brinson, L. R. Hood, and G. L. Beebower, "Determinants of Portfolio Performance," *Financial Analysts Journal*, July–August 1986.

Table 9-1. Policy and Strategy Asset Allocation

Stance	Purpose	Approach	Dynamics
Policy	To meet fund objectives	Passive	
	1. Long-term diversification	Static mix	Rebalancing
	2. Hedging ("insurance")	Reactive	Overbalancing
Strategy	To outperform policy	Proactive	Underbalancing

Hedging—commonly described as portfolio insurance and discussed in Chap. 7—is included in the policy classification. Distinctions between policy and strategy approaches to asset allocation are underscored in the three right-hand columns of the table.

Policy Asset Allocation. The basic framework for risk control is provided by investment policy, which constitutes the long-term framework for asset allocation. As explained in Chap. 6, investment policy requires a trade-off between expected return and risk according to the particular fund objectives. The major underlying assumption is the absence of any forecasting advantage. Policy attempts to be completely passive since it accepts consensus views of value already incorporated in current market prices. The result is a discipline that avoids, to the extent possible, the uncertainties associated with subjective judgments about the investment outlook.

Policy Diversification. The basic tool of policy is diversification of asset mix to establish the trade-off of expected return and risk consistent with the fund objectives. Since the aim of policy diversification is to provide a static mix for the longer term, it is subject to periodic rebalancing as market-price changes result in departures from the policy plan.

Portfolio Insurance. The policy plan may also incorporate a hedging program, or portfolio insurance. Portfolio insurance aims to limit downside risk while retaining upside potential. It is reactive. Using two assets (such as common stocks and cash equivalents), it "overbalances" by increasing exposure to the asset that has already increased as a proportion of the total portfolio because of relative price changes. Common stocks subject to portfolio insurance are purchased as their prices rise and are sold as their prices decline.

Tactical Asset Allocation and Other Asset Allocation Strategies.   In sharp contrast, investment strategy is proactive rather than reactive, since it strives to take action in anticipation of changes in the financial markets. It is concerned with establishment of the asset mix that is best positioned to exploit changes projected for the future. If it is successful, it will appear to underbalance the asset that has increased in proportion to the total portfolio as a result of relative price change. On average, successful investment strategy will have purchased common stocks after they have declined as a proportion of the total portfolio, and will have made sales (to purchase cash equivalents) after their market value has risen as a proportion of the total.

Need for an Asset-Allocation Strategy within a Policy Framework

Attempts to adhere totally to a passive policy framework are almost certain to falter as financial markets undergo major, unanticipated changes. The result, under such emotionally charged conditions, is likely to be strategic improvisation, much less carefully developed than if a specific role had been accorded strategy. We conclude that complete reliance on passive investing, in view of the several limitations discussed in Chap. 7, is virtually impossible. In practice, back-door market timing is the almost inevitable result: Active management creeps in the back door as dramatic changes take place in the investment environment.

How Market Timing Creeps in the Back Door.   In bull markets, for example, concern may develop that the long-term asset-allocation plan is actually too conservative. In bear markets, the pressures may be even more severe but in the opposite direction. Depending on the severity of bear-market fears, a plan sponsor's long-term objectives may be rather substantially reevaluated in the direction of preservation of capital and away from emphasis on superior returns.

By way of example, avenues of back-door market timing readily available to the plan sponsor in a bear market are listed below. The same methods can be adapted for back-door market timing under other market circumstances.

1. Review long-term policy assumptions, such as expected rate of return and variability for the various asset categories, in order to move them in the direction that will produce a more conservative result. Attribute change in asset allocation to reassessment of long-term objectives rather

than to recent changes in the investment environment.

2. Decide that immunization, which matches fixed-income securities against the expected cashflow required to meet pension liabilities, has long-term advantages (even though the advantages were not apparent at higher levels for the equity markets).

3. Terminate external investment managers who have registered less favorable performance because they follow higher risk policies (such as holding higher beta stocks or maintaining a fully invested position in equities). Replace them with more conservative managers.

4. Shift the internal staff assignments to provide a fresh perspective on the pension fund. After a top-to-bottom review of all pension plan operations—with special emphasis on the losses in the recent bear market—the new pension officer is likely to identify persuasive reasons for more conservative asset allocation.

The question is not whether active management is to be avoided but, rather, how it will be accomplished. As indicated by our examples, attempts to achieve a completely passive approach to asset allocation open the door to the hazards of back-door market timing. The alternative is to establish a separate role for investment strategy within the framework of a carefully planned investment policy.

Investment Strategy Seeks Advantage Relative to Investment Policy. Investment strategy complements investment policy since it seeks to gain performance advantage relative to investment policy. It is based on individual judgments that the investment manager considers superior to the consensus views already incorporated in stock prices. Implementation of an investment strategy implies departure from the investment policy, and the performance contribution of an investment strategy is the difference between the returns for the actively managed portfolio and its applicable policy portfolio.

The strategy risks of asset allocation are controlled by establishing maximum limits for departures from investment policy. In Table 9-2, column (1) represents a simple policy portfolio composed of stocks, bonds, and cash equivalents. In the absence of investment strategy, periodic rebalancing of fund assets would maintain asset allocation in line with these policy percentages. Columns (2) and (3) list ranges that define the extent of permissible departures from policy as the result of implementing the investment strategy. The narrow ranges in the second column severely limit the role of strategy, while the much wider

Table 9-2. Controlling the Role of Strategy in Asset
Allocation (percent)

	Policy	Permissible ranges of departure	
	(1)	(2)	(3)
Stocks	65	70–60	85–45
Bonds	30	35–25	55–0
Cash	5	10–0	55–0
Total	100	100	100

ranges in the third column accord investment strategy a very large role.
The appropriateness of one or the other approach—or something in
between—depends on the advantage anticipated as a result of the implementation of strategy. The advantage needs to be assessed in terms
of the expected incremental investment return relative to the incremental risk.

Active Asset Allocation

The application of investment strategy to asset allocation has been described by several different terms, including "market timing," "strategic
asset allocation," and "tactical asset allocation." These terms are sometimes associated with a particular approach to valuation and are not always used in the same way. We prefer an alternative definition less subject to a specific interpretation that covers all of these approaches: *active
asset allocation.*

Our consideration of various approaches to active asset allocation in
the remainder of this chapter focuses on common stocks. Common
stocks make up by far the most important asset group, usually accounting for half or more of fund assets. They also provide higher expected
returns than bonds or cash and are subject to wider variations in returns. Stock valuations, when compared with valuations for other asset
groups such as bonds and cash equivalents, ordinarily dominate the decision on active asset allocation.

Stock Market Valuation Simplifies a
Complex Investment Environment

Efforts to value the stock market require simplification of a very complex investment environment. Since the range of information that can

influence stock prices is almost unlimited, each valuation method stresses a limited number of factors that are considered particularly important. Ultimately, conclusions about valuation are in large measure shaped by a few key factors, organized judgmentally or within the framework of a quantitative model. The extent of the appraised under- or overvaluation provides the basis for over- or underweighting an asset relative to the policy standard.

Whatever the details of the decision process, all approaches to stock market valuation address one or more of the three key factors that drive stock prices. The left column of the table below defines these key factors using the terminology in Chap. 8. The right column lists the investment terminology that has been more commonly used to identify approximately the same influences on stock prices.

Key Factors that Drive Stock Prices	
Risk premium	Investor confidence
Dividend growth rate	Business outlook
Risk-free rate	Interest rate

Investor Confidence: "Contrarian Investing." A simple example of an approach to stock-market valuation that stresses change in investor confidence is the use of price-to-book ratios. For most of the past three decades, market prices for a broad stock index (S&P 400, in this case) have fluctuated from approximately 100 to 200 percent of book value. On average, low ratios of price to book are taken as an indication of low investor confidence. Under such circumstances, stocks are overweighted, based on the assumption that recovery of investor confidence will result sooner or later in a more normal ratio of price to book. Similarly, price-to-book ratios in the upper part of the range provide selling opportunities. They are considered evidence of excessive investor confidence, likely to be followed by a decline in market prices as investor confidence returns to average or even below-average levels.

In general, contrarian approaches to the valuation of stocks, even though they may consider a broader range of information than price-to-book ratios, depend on a repetitive pattern of fluctuations in investor confidence. Conclusions mainly attributable to the level of yields or price-earnings ratios clearly fall into this category. Perhaps the most familiar example is the discipline advocated by Graham and Dodd in *Security Analysis,* first published in 1934 and issued in a fifth edition in

1988.[2] This approach relates current market price to a calculation of "intrinsic value," with the objective of selling stocks as the market price rises above intrinsic value, and vice-versa. Calculation of intrinsic value does not depend on forecasts of future earnings, dividends, or interest rates, and wide fluctuations in market value either side of intrinsic value are attributed to excesses in investor pessimism and optimism.

Business Outlook: "Growth" Investing.   Active asset allocation based on business forecasting, in contrast to the contrarian approaches, emphasizes the outlook for earnings and dividends. In its extreme form, it remains invested in stocks as long as the outlook promises continued growth in earnings and dividends. The signal to sell stocks depends on identification of reasons to expect a significant downturn in business activity.

Emphasis on business forecasting, although it does not preclude concern with changing investor confidence and interest rates, tends to relegate such factors to a subordinate role in active asset allocation. Investor confidence, because it is difficult to measure and may seem to change unpredictably, is often differentiated from the fundamentals like sales and earnings that can be measured by hard statistics. Changes in interest rates, meanwhile, are likely to be viewed more in terms of their effect on the rate of future business activity than of their effect on the discount applied to the future stream of common stock dividends.

Interest Rates: "Discount Rate" (DDM) Investing.   During the past 15 years, increasing attention has been directed to interest rates as a powerful force driving stock prices. This period coincides with the increasing use of the dividend discount model (DDM). The DDM aims to value stocks based on a constant-growth model.[3] The basic equation, which also serves as a framework for more advanced models, is shown below:

$$\text{Price} = \frac{\text{Current dividend}}{\text{Risk-free rate} + \text{Risk premium} - \text{Dividend growth rate}}$$

The reliability of the DDM depends primarily on the estimates of the three factors that make up the denominator on the right-hand side of

---

[2]Sidney Cottle, Roger F. Murray, and Frank E. Block, *Graham and Dodd's Security Analysis,* McGraw-Hill, New York, 1988.

[3]Frank K. Reilly, *Investments,* Dryden Press, Hinsdale, Ill., 1982, pp. 208–209. This book provides a readily understandable derivation of the constant growth model. It was earlier developed by Myron J. Gordon and E. Shapiro, "Capital Equipment Analysis: The Required Rate of Profit," *Management Science,* 3:102–110 (October 1956).

the equation. The *current dividend,* shown as the numerator of the same term, is a largely known quantity. It represents dividend payments over the next four quarters, part of which have already been declared. Appraisal of the items in the denominator, in contrast, are subject to greater uncertainty. The *risk-free rate* is usually represented by the yield on a high-quality, long-term bond. While the bond yield is not the same as the risk-free rate, it provides a sensitive day-to-day measure of changes in interest rates for a competing long-term, fixed-income investment.

The *dividend growth rate* aims to reflect the average compound rate of increase for dividends over the very long term. Estimates usually take into account a projected rate of inflation and a real rate of earnings growth. Modifications may also include allowance for two or three stages of differing rates of dividend growth.

The magnitude of the *risk premium* is even more difficult to appraise than the dividend growth rate. Average levels of the risk premium can be inferred from long-term historical experience. For example, the difference between the average compound annual rate of return for the S&P 500 and the 20-year treasury bond is assumed to be the premium that investors require to accept the incremental risk associated with holding common stocks. The historical risk premium may be modified through the choice of historical base period or as a result of judgments on the change in the investment environment.

Because of the nature of the inputs, valuation of the stock market with the aid of the basic DDM is particularly sensitive to interest rates. The estimated dividend growth rate, which is oriented to the very long term, is likely to be little affected by change in the near- to intermediate-term business outlook. If the risk premium is based on an historical average, it will not change unless the base period is redefined. Bond yields, on the other hand, may swing widely in a matter of a few weeks. By way of example, suppose the stock market, currently yielding 4 percent, is judged fairly valued by a DDM. If the only change in the inputs to the model is a one-percentage point increase in the bond yield, the valuation would drop by 20 percent—resulting in a rather large overvaluation entirely as a result of a one-percentage point change in bond yields.

Changing Relative Importance of the Forces that Drive the Market

To the extent valuation does not appropriately address each of the three broad factors that drive stock prices, it is vulnerable to changes in their relative importance. Contrarian approaches, which depend on periodically wide swings in investor confidence, gained adherents in the highly volatile 1930s and 1940s. They seemed less relevant in the years after World War II, at least up to the 1973–1974 bear market. Forecasting the business outlook gained favor in the 1950s and early 1960s, when the growth trend for economic activity was strong, swings in investor confidence were muted, and volatility in interest rates was still mild. In more recent years, however, swings in investor confidence and interest rates have frequently overwhelmed the significance of changes in earnings and dividends. The basic DDM, which is highly sensitive to bond yields, has received increasing acceptance in the volatile interest-rate environment of the last 10 or 15 years. To the extent the DDM is driven by changing interest rates, its use may require patience when financial markets are primarily influenced for extended periods by other factors.

Broadening the Sensitivities of the Decision Process

For each of these basic approaches, refinements may be introduced to improve the sensitivity of the decision process to each of the three factors that drive stock prices. The basic DDM, by way of illustration, provides a number of opportunities for progress in this direction. The measure of the risk premium incorporated in the DDM may be based on option pricing or some other indication of changes in perceived market risk. Similarly, the estimate of the dividend growth rate may be adjusted for prospective business conditions over several stages of growth, including allowance for changes in payout ratio and return on equity.

An issue relating to such adjustments—apart from the accuracy of variables used as inputs—concerns the changing relative importance of the various factors as the investment environment changes. To address this issue, several innovative approaches to active asset allocation have been developed that aim to make valuation responsive to "what is important now." For example, does a one-percentage point change in interest rates have the same significance now as it did one year ago or 5 years ago? If the decision process incorporates a method for assessing "what's important now," it should be able to explain market returns over a wide variety of market conditions experienced over long time spans.

Implementation: Plan Sponsor Alternatives

Implementation of the insights gained through the valuation of the major asset groups may be accomplished in several ways.

Responsibility Rests with Individual Portfolio Managers

The plan sponsor may allocate responsibility for active asset management to each of the individual managers who handle stocks and bonds. We recommend against this approach for two reasons. First, few managers hired to handle equity or bond accounts are likely to be specialists in active asset allocation. Second, lack of coordination among the asset-allocation decisions of the individual managers may result in unanticipated risks as well as unnecessarily high transaction costs. Only the plan sponsor is in a position to control total fund risks associated with the changing asset mix of the total fund. Transaction costs will be unnecessarily high in proportion as individual portfolio managers implement changes in asset allocation to the extent that they are offsetting.

Plan Sponsor May Retain Responsibility

Alternatively, the plan sponsor may retain responsibility to move assets from one portfolio to another for the purpose of adjusting the fund asset mix. This option, if applied to actively managed portfolios, must be used sparingly to minimize interference with the investment activities of individual portfolio managers. Opportunities to implement plan sponsor decisions on asset allocation arise when the fund experiences cash inflow or outflow, new managers are hired, or existing managers are terminated. Plan sponsor flexibility is facilitated if a portion of the assets are held as index funds. Adjustment in the mix of assets committed to index funds incurs certain incremental costs but avoids conflict with the investment strategy of active portfolio managers and entails lower transaction costs than trading actively managed portfolios.

Delegation to Asset-Allocation Specialists

The plan sponsor may delegate responsibility to a specialist in active asset-allocation operations either as an overlay manager or as a swing-portfolio manager. Management may be internal, given the necessary resources, but will more likely be provided by outside specialists. The use of either approach permits pension fund management to concentrate asset-allocation strategy in the hands of those best qualified to demonstrate skill in this area. Consequently, it enhances the opportunity for active management to add value. The risks relating to strategy, meanwhile, are controlled in the swing portfolio by establishing guidelines to limit its role within the framework of policy.

Overlay Manager. The specialized role of the overlay manager is to command the asset allocation of the total fund, within the constraints established by the plan sponsor, through the purchase and sale of futures contracts. These contracts are bought and sold against assets held in other portfolios of the fund. Consequently, the plan sponsor instructs the master trustee to provide the overlay manager with continuing information on the composition of the fund.

Futures contracts, as used by the overlay manager, offer two advantages over cash transactions. First, they significantly reduce transaction costs; second, they operate without disruption of portfolio manager strategies relating to the selection of individual issues. Futures contracts, however, can present special risks as well as opportunities, since their pricing relative to the underlying securities can vary significantly from time to time. Maintaining a position in futures contracts over an extended period requires rolling them over periodically as they mature, each time requiring repurchase at the price spread then prevailing.

For example, contracts for future purchase of the S&P 500 at a specified price may be purchased against a holding of cash equivalents. Although the fund continues to hold the cash equivalents, its performance will be approximately the same as if it had shifted these assets into an S&P 500 index fund. In a similar way, S&P 500 futures may be sold against a current holding of common stocks. Although fund investments in the stock market are not disturbed, the exposure of the fund to a decline (or a rise) in stock prices has been reduced to the extent of the sale of futures contracts. Hence, this action is equivalent to selling stocks while still owning them. Professional institutional investors have rapidly increased their use of futures contracts during the 1980s. This trend seems certain to continue in view of their advantages in terms of transaction costs and liquidity.

Swing-Portfolio Manager. A more common practice in recent years has been for the plan sponsor to allocate a portion of the total fund to a swing-portfolio manager. In implementing an active asset-allocation discipline, the swing-portfolio manager may use either futures contracts or cash transactions, but, unlike the overlay manager, operates only with

Table 9-3. Swing Portfolio (percent)

Asset group	Asset allocation			Swing-portfolio effect on total fund		
	Policy	Other portfolio	Swing portfolio	10% stocks	10% bonds	10% cash
	(1)	(2)	(3)	(4)	(5)	(6)
Stocks	60	54	6	64	54	54
Bonds	30	27	3	27	37	27
Cash	10	9	1	9	9	19
Total	100	90	10	100	100	100

the assets dedicated to the portfolio. Management may be either internal or delegated to an external investment manager.

An example of a swing portfolio is provided in Table 9-3. Policy asset allocation for the total fund is shown in column 1, and the same policy percentages are applied to the 90 percent of assets in portfolios other than the swing portfolio (column 2). When the policy percentages are also reflected in the 10 percent of assets in the swing portfolio (column 3), asset allocation for the entire fund conforms to policy. The effects on fund asset mix of alternative changes in the swing portfolio are illustrated in the next three columns, where the 10 percent of total assets held in the swing portfolio are committed entirely to stocks (column 4), bonds (column 5), and cash (column 6).

The swing portfolio may move in intermediate steps between zero and fully invested positions, depending on relative valuations. By way of illustration, a decision to reduce by half the normal 6 percent of fund assets held as equities in the swing portfolio would bring total fund equities to 57 percent. Transaction costs can be controlled by the use of trading techniques developed for the construction of index funds and, as appropriate, derivative securities, such as S&P 500 futures contracts.

Adaptation of Swing Portfolio to Fund Circumstances. The proportion of fund assets committed to the swing portfolio may be larger or smaller than suggested by Table 9-3, and fund managers may specify other modifications to meet fund requirements. Alternatives include (1) different benchmark normals for the three asset groups, (2) limitations on the range of variation for one or more asset groups, and (3) flexibility to introduce "tilts" in the equity segment (such as value, growth, or small-capitalization stocks) and/or in the fixed-income segment (long-term bonds or intermediate-term securities).

10
Performance Measurement

Critical Role of Performance Measurement

Performance measurement is central to pension asset management. How performance is measured reflects a plan sponsor's understanding of the workings of the securities markets, as discussed in Chap. 6. It determines in large measure which managers will be chosen to manage fund assets, and obviously influences decisions relating to the termination of managers. Consideration of performance measurement therefore precedes our discussion of the selection of investment managers, the subject of Chap. 11.

Performance measurement, unambiguously defined and consistently applied, provides the plan sponsor with a powerful tool for controlling the way fund assets will be managed. Clearly, the actions of investment managers are shaped by their understanding of the way the plan sponsor will measure performance. Assumptions about performance measurement, even when they have not been explicitly stated, play an important role in virtually every investment decision.

To use an analogy from the playing field, performance measurement constitutes the rules of the game. Investment managers, like baseball or tennis players, are controlled by their understanding of the rules that will be used to evaluate their actions. In baseball, batters will attempt to hit the ball over the fence, because such action will be scored as a home run. Tennis players, in contrast, refrain from attempting to hit the ball over the fence, since they know that such action would produce a point for the opponent. In a similar way, investment managers aim to provide a result that will be scored favorably by the plan sponsor; but they cannot make the judgments necessary to guide their actions without an assumption about how the plan sponsor keeps score. A shift in a plan sponsor's benchmark for performance measurement is almost certain to receive the full attention of the investment manager, who is strongly motivated by economic considerations to retain the account. In effect, the plan sponsor reshapes portfolio strategy by sending to the investment manager changing signals about the way the game will be scored.

De Facto Performance Measurement

It is the de facto reaction of the plan sponsor to performance—which may not be the same as the conclusion reached by the formally stated method—that matters to the investment manager. The plan sponsor may establish a method of performance measurement for reasons other than complete dedication to it. For example, it may have been recommended by a consultant, included in a package of services provided by the master trustee, or adopted because of its widespread use by other pension funds. The formally designated method may produce a large amount of data along with various specialized statistical measures, but it does not necessarily determine the plan sponsor's evaluation of performance. Plan sponsor executives ultimately responsible for decisions relating to the pension fund may make judgments on another basis, perhaps even changing the method as circumstances change. To cite a common experience, comparisons with the returns on the S&P 500 may seem appropriate until the performance of the S&P 500 begins to lag well behind that of the median for the sample of equity managers compiled by an outside consultant or master trustee.

It is not unusual, moreover, for a plan sponsor to establish several simultaneous standards that individually call for different strategies. For example, the manager's returns may be measured against those for the S&P 500 *and* the median for equity portfolios *and* inflation plus 4 percent. The resulting confusion weakens the plan sponsor's role in managing the fund and means that the fund return, on the average, is likely to be lower than could have been attained for the assumed level of risk.

Four Competing Approaches to Performance Measurement

If the method of performance measurement is so important, how does the plan sponsor make the right choice? To respond to this question, a

Table 10-1. Performance Measurement Benchmarks

Benchmark	Underlying concept
Cash equivalents	Absolute return
S&P 500	Relative return
Risk-adjusted S&P 500	Single-index CAPM
Normal portfolio	Individual style

good starting point is a brief review of four approaches that compete for the plan sponsor's attention and are listed in Table 10-1. Our comments are directed to the application of these methods to equity portfolios but are readily adaptable to portfolios consisting solely of fixed income or various combinations of equities and fixed income.

While these benchmarks do not include all the standards used to evaluate investment performance, they are reviewed here because of their particular relevance to current performance measurement. The cash benchmark, although seemingly out of date under the conditions of recent years, remains intuitively appealing, particularly in bear markets. Measurement of return relative to the S&P 500 is probably still the most widely used standard for equity portfolios—at least on a de facto basis. The risk-adjusted approach became available to most funds—at least the large funds—in the 1970s; it continues in general use despite increasing recognition of its limitations. More recently, the normal portfolio—individually tailored for each situation—has been gaining favor among larger pension funds.

Cash Benchmark

The cash benchmark for performance measurement probably dates back to the earliest days of investment activity and cannot be attributed to any single source. It is the simplest and most obvious approach. In this case, the investment manager who achieves a return in excess of that attainable through investment in high-quality, short-term, fixed-income securities (cash equivalents) has succeeded. On the other hand, if the return is less than that of the cash equivalents—particularly if the return is negative—the manager has failed. As stated succinctly (but not precisely) by one portfolio manager: "The client knows what he wants—he wants to make money!"

The cash benchmark was largely unchallenged in the early years after World War II, reflecting conclusions drawn from the vantage point of the Depression years. Investors at that time were unaware of evidence that they should be paid for assuming risk. Since most investors in the stock market had experienced severe losses—if not financial ruin—in the bear markets of the 1930s, investment advisors who had demonstrated that they could do better than holding cash over a succession of bull and bear markets had clearly distinguished themselves. It was not until well into the postwar years that sustained inflation and an extraordinary bull market forced a rethinking of the cash benchmark for performance measurement.

Recognition of the change in the investment environment in the years after World War II does not mean that the cash benchmark has disappeared. Even among large plan sponsors—at least informally—it surfaces in bear markets. In the absence of a clear commitment to a carefully planned, unambiguous standard, it is easy for investors in periods of unfavorable investment conditions to drift in the direction of an absolute cash standard. Under such circumstances, investment managers who lose less money than others are likely to be evaluated favorably irrespective of their actual strategy contributions as measured by more meaningful standards. Where a de facto cash benchmark prevails on a continuing basis, equity will seldom, if ever, be fully invested.

S&P 500

In the years after World War II, the S&P 500 gained widespread appeal as a relative standard for measuring equity-management performance. The cash benchmark was rendered inadequate by postwar conditions as equity returns rather consistently exceeded returns from cash equivalents. The S&P 500, meanwhile, was available to fill the need for a comprehensive market value–weighted equity measure. Although in earlier years it included a smaller number of issues, it now represents about two-thirds of the total market value of publicly traded domestic equities. Other indexes include an even larger proportion of the equity market, but they lack the long market record, with accompanying earnings and dividend data, available for the S&P 500.

Even when more refined methods of performance measurement are available, the S&P 500 may serve as the de facto performance benchmark. It is not uncommon, for example, for corporate executives with oversight responsibility for a pension fund to be pleased with a portfolio manager's returns if they comfortably exceed those for the S&P 500 but register disapproval about portfolio results that lag behind those for the S&P 500.

The S&P 500 has shortcomings as the benchmark for equity portfolios in that it does not take into account significant differences in risk and style bias. A portfolio may achieve results superior to the S&P 500 in a bull market, simply because the investment manager is much more aggressive. If so, the portfolio is vulnerable to inferior results in a bear market. Even more common, portfolio results may be tied to a style bias. For example, a manager of small-capitalization stocks may achieve better returns than the S&P 500 for several years because the aggregate population of such issues is performing relatively well. The critical question about performance—which is left unanswered—is whether this manager was able to demonstrate skill in the attainment of better results than other managers using the same population of stocks as building blocks for the portfolio.

Risk-Adjusted Returns

The rapid acceptance during the 1970s of the concept of risk-adjusted returns was a major event in performance measurement. This approach attempts to separate the portfolio return attributable to the risk assumed by the manager from that due to superior skill. The concept was applied initially to the evaluation of equity portfolios, but, with appropriate adjustments, it is also applicable to fixed-income and other asset classes.

Several factors explain the widespread attraction of the new method. Comparisons with broad stock averages—such as the Dow Jones Industrial Average or the S&P 500—did not allow for differences in portfolio risk or style bias. The evolution of electronic data processing, together with the development of modern capital theory, opened the door to new possibilities. Explosive growth in pension funds in the first two decades after the war, meanwhile, created a large market for a more analytical way to evaluate pension fund performance.

The risk-adjusted method is based on the single-index capital asset pricing model (CAPM) developed in the 1960s. This approach requires an important simplifying assumption: Investment returns for individual equities can be explained by (1) the return for the equity market as a whole and (2) the uncorrelated returns specific to each individual equity. No allowance is made for correlations of returns among significant groups of equity issues not related to the returns for the total equity market. As we shall see, this underlying simplification opens the door to widespread misinterpretation of the significance of resulting performance statistics.

***Beta* as a Measure of Market Risk**.   The risk-adjusted method publicized the Greek letter *beta* as a measure of market risk. Beta, as previously mentioned, indicates the sensitivity of the returns for an individual equity, or portfolio of equities, to the returns for the S&P 500. (For this purpose, the S&P 500 is accepted as the proxy for the total equity market.) A beta of 1.0 for a randomly selected portfolio of stocks would mean that the portfolio returns, on the average, should approximate that of the S&P 500. Since betas for most equity portfolios differ from that of the S&P 500, individual portfolio returns must be adjusted to allow for such differences. A portfolio with a low beta—such as 0.8— would be expected to demonstrate lower returns than the S&P 500 in a bull market but higher returns in a bear market. Just the opposite expectations apply to a portfolio with an above-average beta, such as 1.2. How the adjustment is made will be discussed later in this chapter, since misunderstanding of the arithmetic involved is responsible for one of the frequent errors in the application of this method.

Alpha **as a Measure of Value Added**. The measure of the investment manager's skill provided by the risk-adjusted approach is represented by the Greek letter *alpha*. Given the underlying assumptions of the single-index capital asset pricing model, as indicated above, the performance of a randomly selected portfolio of stocks relative to the S&P 500 is predicted by beta. The fluctuations of the individual issues, to the extent they are uncorrelated with the S&P 500, are expected, on the average, to offset each other. For the actively managed portfolio, performance better than that predicted by its portfolio market risk, beta, is attributable to value added, alpha. For example, if performance attributable to the portfolio beta is 10 percent but the actual portfolio performance is 11 percent, the risk-adjusted method assumes that active management of the portfolio has achieved an alpha of 1 percent. Positive alpha—the difference between actual portfolio return and the return expected on the basis of portfolio beta—is regarded as evidence of the skill of the portfolio manager. Conversely, a negative alpha is generally taken as evidence of lack of skill.

Calculation of Risk-Adjusted Returns. A frequent misunderstanding in the calculation of risk-adjusted returns concerns the definition of beta. When the S&P 500 rises, it is sometimes erroneously assumed that, if other things are equal, the value of the portfolio should be expected to increase relatively in proportion to its beta. Under this assumption, a 25 percent increase for the S&P 500 would mean that a portfolio with a 1.5 beta should be expected to increase in value by 37.5 percent. Such calculation is at best imprecise and may lead to significant error in performance measurement. The beta applies not to the price of the S&P 500 but to the total return (change in capital value plus dividend income) less the risk-free rate, which is usually represented by the return

Table 10-2. Risk-Adjusted Returns (percent)

	S&P 500		Portfolio
Total return	+25%	Excess return (1.5 ×15)	+22.5%
Less risk-free rate	−10	Plus risk-free rate	+10
Excess return	+15%	Total return	+32.5%

on short-term treasury bills. Suppose in this example that the annual return on treasury bills amounted to 10 percent and the total return for the S&P 500 was 25 percent. Then the expected total return on the portfolio, as predicted by a beta of 1.5, would amount to 32.5 percent, as shown in Table 10-2.

Time Horizon Required for Significance. Almost as soon as the risk-adjusted method came into use, a widely publicized issue developed concerning the time period required for a measure of value added, or alpha, to be significant. While it is generally recognized that performance measurement requires a long time horizon, how long is necessary? Plan sponsors frequently identify the appropriate measurement period as 3 to 5 years—a time horizon that has historically been perceived to include a market cycle. Based on the assumptions underlying the method, statisticians relate the level of alpha to the volatility of the portfolio returns unexplained by beta in order to calculate the extent to which the results are due to chance.

Probability that Results Were Due to Chance. The probability that value added, or alpha, is due to chance, under the assumptions of the single-index CAPM, depends on the factors shown in Table 10-3. Two sets of calculations are shown for different levels of alpha and different time horizons. Returns for portfolio A fluctuate only moderately relative to the S&P 500, as measured by a residual standard deviation of 5 percent. (A residual standard deviation of zero would indicate portfolio returns identical to those for the S&P 500, and increasingly large per-

Table 10-3. Probability that Results Were Due to Chance (percent)

Alpha (annual rate)	Portfolio A			Portfolio B		
	1 yr.	3 yrs.	5 yrs.	1 yr.	3 yrs.	5 yrs.
1	42	36	33	46	43	41
3	27	15	9	38	30	25
5	16	4	1	31	19	13

centages indicate increasingly wide variations in returns.) Portfolio B is much more aggressive; its residual standard deviation is 10 percent.

For both portfolios A and B, the likelihood of manager skill increases with both the level of alpha and the time horizon, but it is inversely related to the residual standard deviation. An average alpha of 5 percent over 5 years is more persuasive than the same level of alpha for only 1 or 2 years. Equally important is the variability of the portfolio relative to the S&P 500 (residual standard deviation). An alpha of 5 percent is more significant if the portfolio performance ordinarily tracks returns for the S&P 500 rather closely, as indicated by the lower residual standard deviation for portfolio A, than if it usually is subject to wider fluctuations, as indicated for portfolio B.

Efficient Market versus Active Management. Calculations such as those shown in Table 10-3 are cited by proponents of the efficient market hypothesis in support of their position. They point out that an alpha of 1 or 2 percent, even when extended for 5 years, is subject to high probability (20–40 percent) that the results are simply due to random fluctuations rather than to skill. Statisticians generally consider that the probability of chance should be reduced to a much lower level before the results can be considered statistically significant.

Proponents of active management use the same figures to make two points in defense of their position. First, a 20–40 percent probability that favorable results are due to chance does not prove the absence of skill. On the contrary, these figures merely indicate that a much longer time is required to meet the rigorous standards of statistical significance. Second, they are able to show that occasionally portfolio returns are sufficiently favorable within a 3- to 5-year period to indicate statistically significant evidence of skill. Portfolio A, assuming the alpha averages 5 percent annually over 5 years, would qualify under certain widely used standards of statistical significance since there is a calculated probability of only 1 percent that the results were due to chance. The debate continues, nevertheless, since supporters of the efficient market hypothesis cite statistical arguments for remaining skeptical even of such favorable results.

Flawed Assumption Underlying Risk-Adjusted Returns. Our purpose is not to produce a scholarly resolution of conflicting interpretations of risk-adjusted performance figures, but rather to address a fundamental problem concerning the figures themselves. There is increasing recognition that a key assumption underlying the risk-adjusted approach does not adequately reflect reality. When the capital asset pricing model (CAPM) was introduced, the simplifying assumption was made that fluctuations in individual security returns not explained by beta were independent of each other. It is this assumption of zero correlation between residual returns of securities that is necessary to support the probabilities shown in the table. If the correlations of residual returns are substantially different than zero, the probability that value added, or alpha, reflects chance is higher than indicated.

Example. A brief example illustrates the relationship between correlation of residual returns and the probability that a favorable alpha results from chance. Suppose a portfolio of 30 individual issues equally weighted is restructured once each year. With a zero correlation of residual returns, the selection of each issue is an independent test of the manager's skill. If, on an average, 18 of the holdings achieve a positive alpha each year—bringing the average annual portfolio alpha to 3 percent over the 5 years—the investment manager has made a total of 90 correct decisions and only 60 incorrect decisions. The record, although perhaps not conclusive, is impressive.

In sharp contrast, the evidence of skill would be considerably less impressive in the absence of the zero correlation assumption. To provide an extreme example, suppose the manager makes only one decision at the beginning of the 5-year period—to commit the entire portfolio to an index fund of 30 issues selected to represent the population of small-capitalization growth issues. Further assume that the index fund performs much better than the S&P 500 3 years of the 5, resulting in an average alpha of 3 percent over the period. In this second example, the alpha is exactly the same as in the first example.

Yet the favorable results in the second example hardly represent useful evidence of skill in active management. The manager did not make individual decisions about each of the 30 issues in the portfolio but, rather, one decision about a style-based index fund at the beginning of the period. Clearly, one correct decision in only one attempt in the second example is much less impressive than 90 correct decisions in 150 attempts in the first example. Statistical inferences based on the assumptions of the first example may be highly misleading when they are applied to a situation where the assumptions do not hold.

Distortions Due to Persistent Style Bias. Suppose a manager, instead of holding a small-capitalization growth-stock index fund, concentrates on selecting the most attractive issues from that population. (For reasons addressed in the next section, each active equity manager tends to display a persistent set of portfolio biases relative to the S&P 500.) Although issues are selected for the portfolio because they are expected to perform better than the index, there is no assurance that this goal will be achieved. The issues may perform less favorably than the index. In the absence of special skill in selecting individual issues, the expected return for the manager's portfolio is the return of the index rather than the return of the S&P 500. For a portfolio drawn from a population of small-capitalization growth stocks, the benchmark should be adjusted accordingly.

Performance measurement based on risk adjustment relative to the S&P 500 is misleading when an investment manager operates in ways that maintain persistent biases. An example is provided by comparison of hypothetical performance for two managers in two subsequent 5-year periods. Suppose in the first 5-year period manager X simply held the small-capitalization, growth-stock index, with the result that a favorable annual alpha of 3 percent was achieved according to the standard risk-adjusted method. At this point manager X retired and was replaced by manager Y. In the second 5-year period, the performance of the index lagged behind the S&P 500; simply holding the index, as in the first period, would have resulted in an unfavorable average alpha of −5 percent. Active management of the portfolio by manager Y in this second 5-year period, however, permitted the manager to reduce the unfavorable alpha to −3 percent. Risk-adjusted performance measurement would then show an average annual alpha of −3 percent. In the first case, manager X would be credited with an alpha of 3 percent, clearly undeserved, and, in the second instance, manager Y's contribution would be judged as very negative despite a positive contribution of 2 percentage points.

Manager's Universe Reflects Self-Imposed Boundaries. The term "investment universe" is used here to describe the segment of the securities markets in which a manager persistently operates. Although the manager's universe may reflect limitations imposed by the client, it is defined for the most part by boundaries that managers impose on themselves. Only rarely does the manager's universe approximately coincide with the market value-weighted S&P 500, which is used as the benchmark for risk-adjusted performance measurement. Persistent differences in portfolio characteristics relative to the S&P 500 reflect the individual manager's "style" (such as bias toward growth, value, smallness, or other factors with important implications for the selection of individual issues).

Example of a Large-Pension-Fund. Figure 10-1 illustrates how portfolio managers restrict themselves to a universes of their own choosing. The data covers equity managers who handled pension accounts for a large pension fund over the period 1980–1984. An outside service (BARRA) analyzed each portfolio once every month to determine exposure to various common equity risk factors. One of the most impor-

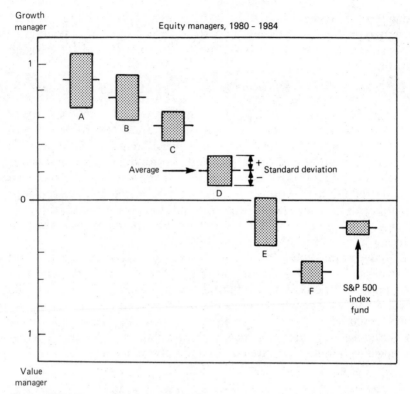

Figure 10-1. Persistence of manager bias.

tant of these factors is *growth orientation,* which indicates the extent to which the manager selects issues with growth characteristics. Positive numbers for this growth-orientation index (vertical scale) indicate growth-stock managers while negative numbers are characteristics of value managers. Data for six active managers (labeled A through F) and an S&P 500 index fund are displayed in the figure. For each manager, the horizontal line indicates the average of the growth-orientation index over 60 months. The vertical bar is a statistical measure (one standard deviation) of the dispersion of individual monthly readings, demonstrating that monthly fluctuations did not diverge very much from the 5-year average in each case.

Figure 10-1 underscores the persistence of style bias for each manager. Growth managers remained growth managers throughout the 5-year period. Similarly, value managers were consistent in maintaining their respective characteristics. There has been little evidence that either group of managers attempted to tilt their portfolios away from their respective growth or value orientation as the investment environment changed. This conclusion does not reflect in any way on the skill of these managers in selecting individual issues or in strategically favoring one industry over another; it merely points out that there are certain persistent characteristics that frequently define a manager's universe and are most unlikely to change.

Reasons for Persistent Style Bias. Why does the investment manager limit operations to an investment universe that accounts for only a part of the available opportunities? There are three good reasons. The primary reason is the manager's *investment philosophy*, which shapes the firm's decision process to focus on the selection of issues consistent with it. Since investment philosophy is based on a view of how the investment world works and supporting fundamental principles, it does not readily change.

A second reason is the *orientation of the firm's investment staff*, which has learned to work within the framework of the firm's decision process. Since no investment organization can process all the information relating to the entire spectrum of investments, it must necessarily concentrate on developing the specialized knowledge necessary to implement the firm's investment philosophy. It is extremely difficult to change significantly the persistent biases that define the manager's universe without changing the staff.

Finally, the firm's *identification in the marketplace* plays an important role. Clients, prospective clients, and consultants who assist plan sponsors in selecting investment managers respond warily to the introduction of an approach that represents a break with the manager's past history. They have been conditioned by the manager and supporting salespeople to associate the manager's past success with faithful adherence to the principles that underlie the existing investment universe. A firm with a revised investment philosophy, new staff members in key positions, and a greatly changed sales presentation, at best, faces the prospect of starting over in the marketplace.

Normal Portfolio as Performance Benchmark

Development of a style-based normal portfolio as the benchmark for performance measurement follows logically from recognition of the role of the manager's investment universe in active portfolio management. The *normal portfolio* for a particular manager is an index of securities designed to replicate the investment universe in which the manager routinely operates. It represents the neutral position for the manager in the absence of strategic insights. Consequently, implementation of investment strategy takes the form of a departure from the appropriately identified normal portfolio.

Total investment returns for a normal portfolio are measured by imputing to each asset group the total return for the index representing that asset group. No allowance is usually made for transactions costs, since turnover in the normal portfolio is ordinarily very low from one measuring period to the next. Certain normal portfolios, however, may be subject to higher turnover—because they require periodic rebalancing of equally weighted indexes or for other reasons. Under these circumstances, it is useful to estimate transaction costs in order to allow for this factor in determining the performance of the normal portfolio.

Use of a normal portfolio as a benchmark for performance measurement avoids penalizing or crediting a manager for the performance attributable to the manager's universe. Manager performance is measured by the value added relative to the applicable normal portfolio. Since fluctuations in the performance contribution of the normal portfolio may be very large, performance measurement using a normal portfolio will at times differ dramatically from returns measured against the S&P 500 or under the risk-adjusted method. The ascendance of normal portfolios for the purpose of controlling risk and measuring performance reflects the shortcomings of the risk-adjusted approach using beta relative to the S&P 500. The normal portfolio, as discussed earlier, recognizes the effect on performance of the correlation of returns between individual securities.

Performance of Plan Sponsor Strategy. If portfolio managers are responsible only for value added relative to their applicable normal portfolio, who deserves credit or should receive blame for the performance of the normal portfolio itself? Since the normal portfolio is a "permanent" characteristic of the manager, the plan sponsor has the responsibility for its identification. When the portfolio manager is hired, the plan sponsor implements two decisions: (1) to commit funds to the manager's universe and (2) to accept the results of the manager's skill (or lack thereof) in making strategy commitments that depart temporarily from the applicable normal portfolio. If a manager's normal portfolio does not meet the policy or strategy requirements of the plan sponsor, the latter has the opportunity—and the responsibility—to select a qualified manager from a list of those who also provide the appropriate normal portfolio. Since the plan sponsor determines the combination of normal portfolios that represent the different investment styles in the pension fund, the plan sponsor cannot escape direct responsibility—and accountability—for their aggregate performance.

The plan sponsor's contribution to strategy is measured relative to the performance of the plan sponsor's policy portfolio. As indicated in Chap. 6, investment policy is defined by the portfolio that a fund would hold in the absence of any forecasting advantage over the publicly held securities markets. It is that *passive* asset-allocation plan that best meets the objectives of the fund. The plan sponsor will therefore match the aggregate universes of the individual portfolio managers with the investment policy portfolio unless a temporary advantage is expected to result from a departure from policy. Since such departures are determined by the plan sponsor, it is the plan sponsor who is accountable for their impact on total fund performance. The plan sponsor's performance is simply a matter of subtraction, as suggested by the example in Table 10-4.

Construction of the Normal Portfolio. Consultants frequently assist plan sponsors in establishing normal portfolios since the plan sponsor is unlikely to have the staff, the experience, or the access to the technical services required for this specialized effort. It is important, nevertheless, for the plan sponsor to take an active role in developing normal portfolios for three reasons: (1) plan sponsor strategy is accountable for the performance of the normal portfolios that make up the fund; (2) selection of the appropriate consultant requires perspective on what the normal portfolio is to accomplish; (3) a detailed understanding of the normal portfolio is necessary to use it effectively in working with the portfolio manager whose performance will be measured against it.

As a starting point, we recommend that the plan sponsor review presentations of several of the consultants who offer help in developing normal portfolios. The time spent on this effort will not only help identify the qualifications of the consultants but will also provide background needed to work with the managers in the application of normal portfolios. As a framework for such review, we offer a checklist of eight key points taken from our experience in pioneering their installation.

1. *Investment philosophy*: Active managers should be able to state their investment philosophy by summarizing how they expect to achieve

Table 10-4. Sources of Fund Performance

	Total return, %
Aggregate manager normal portfolios	9.8
Less policy portfolio	−8.2
Plan sponsor strategy	1.6

superior results. For example, one manager may stress a high rate of return on capital as an essential criterion for stock selection. If so, the manager automatically excludes—or at least limits—use in the normal portfolio of issues with average-to-low return on capital.

2. *Decision process*:   The decision process shows how the investment philosophy is implemented. Review of the manager's decision process provides more precise detail about what is included and what is excluded from his or her portfolio. It also helps identify the weighting of the individual portfolio components. By way of illustration, the equity manager who stresses a high rate of return on capital should be able to identify the pool of securities considered eligible for screening, the relevant information sources, and the steps necessary to process the information to achieve the targeted results.

3. *Characteristics of the firm*:   Useful information includes the amount of money under management, the size of the staff, the distribution of staff members in various investment activities, the background of the key people, and the history and reputation of the firm. To cite the simplest of examples, a very large firm, out of concern for market liquidity, is more likely to emphasize larger capitalization issues than is a small firm.

4. *Cash reserve policy*:   The proportion of cash in the normal portfolio is related to the range of cash reserves that the manager will hold as the investment environment changes. For example, the normal portfolio for a manager who moves between 5 and 50 percent cash reserves would warrant a higher cash position than that for a manager who limits cash reserves to a range of 5 to 10 percent. It is important, however, to reflect what the manager actually does rather than what the manager claims to do.

5. *History of the portfolio*:   While discussion with the manager may uncover much of the information required to construct an initial version of the normal portfolio, a review of persistent portfolio characteristics over past years provides additional information. It is useful to use a service, like that provided by BARRA or Wilshire Associates, to identify persistent common risk factors.

6. *Trial run*:   Once a tentative normal portfolio has been identified, it is essential to compare its performance in recent years with actual portfolio results. Returns for the actual portfolio should differ from those of the normal portfolio as the manager implements strategy to gain advantage, but significant departures should be explainable in terms of the explicit strategy in use at the time.

7. *Discussion of unexplained differences*:   Where differences between performance of the actual and the normal portfolio cannot be

readily explained in terms of then-current strategies, additional discussion may well uncover persistent portfolio characteristics that have been overlooked. To cite an example from our experience as a plan sponsor, a manager had decided—as a long-term policy—to commit 15 percent of the portfolio to small-capitalization, high-growth stocks. Although this policy was not mentioned in the discussions with the manager, it was identified by comparing the performance of a test normal portfolio with actual results.

8. *Mutual agreement*:   It is essential to secure mutual agreement between the plan sponsor and a portfolio manager about the manager's normal portfolio. The agreement should include such details as the weighting of the issues or indices to be included in the normal portfolio, the frequency with which it is rebalanced, and measures of risk, diversification, and manager style bias. Unless the agreement is incorporated into written guidelines in advance, the portfolio manager will be in a position to argue strenuously, when results turn out badly, that the plan sponsor is using an unfair benchmark.

Normal Portfolio in Operation.   The normal portfolio in itself is not a new concept. What is new in recent years is the construction of individually designed normal portfolios to address individual manager biases. The cash benchmark, when used to evaluate performance, serves as the normal portfolio. It can be appropriate in certain special circumstances. In a similar way, the use of the S&P 500 implies that it is the normal portfolio. The underlying assumption is that the active manager, in the temporary absence of special insights, would hold a portfolio that mirrors the characteristics of the benchmark—home base, as it were.

Since all performance measurement implies the continuing operation of a normal portfolio, the question is not whether to use a normal portfolio but, rather, which normal portfolio is most appropriate. The cash benchmark and the S&P 500 can be viewed as alternative versions of the normal portfolio to be used to the extent portfolio objectives are consistent with the underlying assumptions. Where such is not the case, the resulting performance measurement would be misleading. Performance measurement based on an inappropriate normal portfolio is unfair not only to the manager, who may be erroneously accorded credit or blame, but also to the plan sponsor, whose judgment about managers and their portfolios is obscured by misleading information.

Limitations of the Normal Portfolio.   Does the use of carefully selected normal portfolios for performance measurement provide the precise information about investment-manager skill that is otherwise lacking? Our answer is loud and clear: Normal portfolios, no matter how carefully they are developed, cannot make performance measurement an exact science. Even the most carefully selected normal portfolios may be far from perfect, but they are simply much better than the alternative— a standard benchmark applied indiscriminately to the performance measurement of a wide range of portfolios with very different characteristics.

It should also be recognized that normal portfolios will not work without the full commitment of the plan sponsor to making them work. Construction of normal portfolios requires special effort and background. They will not automatically be accepted by investment managers, moreover, unless the plan sponsor can show that they have been fairly selected and will serve as the de facto method of performance measurement.

Properly constructed normal portfolios can significantly reduce error in the evaluation of the manager's skill, and they permit the plan sponsor better control of the risks in the pension fund. The improvement is a matter of degree, since the role of chance can be reduced but never eliminated. Performance measurement alone—even with optimal normal portfolios in place—is not an adequate basis to judge a manager. As discussed in Chap. 11, manager selection also depends importantly on other factors, to be considered together with the performance record.

Need for Written Guidelines.   Written guidelines are essential to control risk and to communicate unambiguously the benchmark for performance measurement to an investment manager. An example of guidelines prepared by the sponsor of a large pension fund is provided in the appendix to Chap. 11. The guidelines provide a clear measure of the sponsor's attitude toward risk and return, all other comments, spoken or written, notwithstanding. Development of such guidelines requires that plan sponsors understand what they want, since what they get will be heavily influenced by how performance is measured. Inconsistency between what the plan sponsor wants and how performance is measured will mean that the investment manager will likely ignore the former and concentrate on the latter.

11
Managing People
Who Manage Money

Manager Selection Requires
Answers to Key Issues

The selection and management of investment managers is the final topic in our discussion of pension fund management—and for good reason. Effective management of people who manage money requires answers about questions raised in earlier chapters. So far, our discussion has dealt with three broad issues: (1) the goals of pension fund management (in relation to pension liabilities and the goals of the plan sponsor), (2) the complementary roles of investment policy and investment strategy (in securities markets that are neither a game of bingo nor a game of chess), and (3) clear accountability for the application of investment strategy (through unambiguous performance measurement).

It is only after addressing these issues that the plan sponsor is ready to allocate assets of the pension fund to the portfolios of individual investment managers. How these issues are resolved determines the criteria for selection of investment managers. For example, it makes a difference whether the pension fund is viewed primarily as the plan sponsor's entry in a performance race with other pension funds—or as an integral part of a larger unit that includes pension liabilities together with other corporate assets and liabilities. Similarly, manager skill is evaluated differently, depending on the role accorded chance in the outcome of investment decisions. A reordering of priorities in the way managers are chosen is also likely to result from the establishment of clear accountability for the sources of performance, especially the identification of the separate performance contributions of the plan sponsor and the investment manager.

Our analysis, as presented in the earlier chapters of this book, identifies four characteristics of investment managers critical to the selection process. These key characteristics are listed below in order of importance:

1. Normal portfolio (investment style)
2. Investment decision process
3. Organization and key people
4. Performance record

Our focus in this chapter places the performance record immediately after discussion of the normal portfolio and before the other two topics. We address these topics in this order—with this one change from the order listed above—because the comments concerning performance provide background for consideration of the investment decision process and organization and key people. Subsequent sections discuss the balance between active and passive management as well as the control of investment managers after they are hired.

Normal Portfolio (Investment Style)

A manager's normal portfolio, as the essential building block for plan-sponsor strategy, heads the list of criteria for manager selection. Chapter 10 considered the use of the normal portfolio in performance measurement and focused on methods to identify it. An equally significant application of the normal portfolio in overall fund management is its role as a building block for plan sponsor strategy. Identification of a manager's normal portfolio is necessary not only to assess the manager's contribution to strategy but also to implement plan sponsor strategy.

The importance of the normal portfolio to plan sponsor strategy is underscored by a brief review of the role of plan sponsor strategy within the framework of total fund management. *Investment policy*, as defined in Chap. 6 and analyzed in Chap. 7, is a specific plan for asset allocation designed to meet the fund objectives. Its appropriateness for the total pension fund depends on the particular objectives of the fund—represented by the trade-off of expected return and risk—and the identification of the most efficient passive mix of major asset groups that best meets these objectives. Once the policy portfolio mix has been determined, it provides the benchmark for managing strategy.

Investment strategy is a temporary departure from the policy mix that aims to gain performance advantage over policy; it may be implemented by either the plan sponsor or individual investment managers.

Plan Sponsor Strategy Focuses on Allocations Across Normal Portfolios

Plan sponsors implement strategy by shifting assets between managers with different normal portfolios. Plan sponsor strategy therefore reflects the relationship of the current aggregate normal portfolio of the fund to the fund's predetermined policy portfolio. The *aggregate normal portfolio* is the weighted sum of the normal portfolios of the individual investment managers. An *individual normal portfolio* may include only one asset class, such as stocks, bonds or real estate, or a combination of two or more asset classes, such as stocks and cash equivalents.

Plan sponsor strategy contrasts with investment manager strategy. Investment managers implement strategy through transactions in the securities markets, which cause the actual portfolio to differ from the normal portfolio. Consequently, an individual manager is responsible only for that portion of the performance of the actual portfolio that differs from that of the applicable normal portfolio.

Neutral versus Active Plan Sponsor Strategy

Plan sponsor strategy may be classified as neutral or active, depending on its purpose relative to the policy portfolio. A *neutral strategy* aims to eliminate risk of poor performance relative to the policy portfolio but also foregoes opportunity to achieve performance superior to policy. An *active strategy*, in contrast, willingly accepts risk of less than policy performance in the expectation of achieving a performance advantage.

Implementation of Neutral Strategy. Plan sponsors implement a neutral strategy when they select investment managers with normal portfolios in amounts that, in the aggregate, match the policy portfolio. There is no requirement that the normal portfolio of any individual manager match the plan sponsor's policy portfolio, since the plan sponsor may select investment managers with complementary normal portfolios. For example, funds could be allocated to a growth manager, a value manager, and a manager of small-capitalization stocks to achieve an aggregate normal equity portfolio that approximates the characteristics of the Wilshire 5000 Stock Index (assuming this index represents the equity portion of the policy portfolio).

Active Strategy Departs from Investment Policy. Alternatively, the plan sponsor may aim at an active strategy. To this end, the plan sponsor allocates assets among investment managers to provide a mix of normal portfolios that, in the aggregate, differ from the policy portfolio. To continue the example described in the previous paragraph, the plan sponsor could withdraw assets from the growth manager and place them with a value manager; the result would be a plan sponsor strategy in the equity portion of the fund that tilts away from growth in favor of value. The plan sponsor is accountable for the difference in return between the aggregate normal portfolio and the policy portfolio. Consequently, an active strategy will be limited to those occasions when the plan sponsor expects to benefit from an insight that has not yet been discounted by the securities markets.

Plan Sponsor Strategy Precedes Manager Selection

Recognition of the clear distinction between plan sponsor strategy and manager strategy places responsibility on the plan sponsor to define plan sponsor strategy before addressing the allocation of funds to individual portfolio managers. Plan sponsor strategy either aims to match the policy portfolio, providing a neutral strategy, or it attempts to benefit from insights not yet discounted by the securities markets, resulting in an active strategy. The only way the plan sponsor can implement either strategy is through the allocation of funds to investment managers, which, in combination, provide the appropriate aggregate normal portfolio. If a portion of the pension fund is internally managed, the normal portfolio for these assets, as for the assets supervised by external managers, is necessarily included in the aggregate normal portfolio of the total fund.

Poor Excuses

A plan sponsor can readily identify reasons for avoiding accountability for plan sponsor strategy. They are, in each instance, poor excuses. We list below six possible excuses along with our response in each case.

1. No Means for Identifying Normal Portfolios

Excuse. "We do not implement plan sponsor strategy because we do not have the means for identifying normal portfolios."

Response. All plan sponsors implement plan sponsor strategy—if only implicitly—because they allocate fund assets to normal portfolios. Each manager operates within the framework of a normal portfolio, whether or not its characteristics are identified. When you hire managers, you assemble an aggregate normal portfolio that either approximates your policy portfolio or differs from it. You cannot avoid the performance implications of its composition because you do not address the issue.

2. Lack of In-House Expertise

Excuse. "Our financial people, although very good at what they do, do not have the specific background necessary to identify normal portfolios."

Response. When your company operates a division with assets as large as your pension fund, it assembles the necessary resource internally or secures the appropriate outside help to run it successfully. If the risks and returns associated with the company's pension fund are important to your earnings statement, it is equally important to secure the resources—internal or external—required to achieve your goals.

3. Manager Candidates Lack Normal Portfolios

Excuse. "It is impossible to use normal portfolios in manager selection since the normal portfolio of a manager candidate will not be developed until the manager is hired. Consequently, screening the population of managers on the basis of performance—and the identification of superior managers—must continue to be based on the standard industry benchmarks, such as the S&P 500 or a widely recognized bond index."

Response. This excuse overlooks two important points. First, preliminary screening is better accomplished on the basis of investment philosophy than on the basis of performance record. For example, if the plan sponsor seeks a large-capitalization value manager to meet current plan sponsor strategy, it is counterproductive to compare the record of managers in this category with managers who focus on small-capitalization growth stocks. Once a list of candidates with investment philosophy that is generally similar and broadly consistent with plan sponsor requirements has been assembled, the preliminary screening can continue, as suggested in this chapter, on the basis of the decision process, the key people, and the quality of organization. At this stage, relative performance is not a reason for selecting a manager, but it can be a reason for dropping managers from further consideration. Managers may be screened out if their performance has clearly been unfavorable relative to the broad category of normal portfolios under consideration.

Our second point takes issue with the assumption that the normal portfolio cannot take shape until the manager has been hired. On the contrary, our position is that the manager candidate's normal portfolio should be well defined before the final decision on hiring is made. Any interview with a manager candidate that covers investment philosophy, decision process, the amount of money under management, the policy on raising cash reserves, and an explanation of the record provides an approximate identification of the appropriate normal portfolio. Before the final choice is made, the plan sponsor (or the consultant assisting the plan sponsor) should be able to complete the work necessary to pin down the normal portfolio more precisely.

4. Lack of Opportunities to Implement Plan Sponsor Strategy

Excuse. "Even when normal portfolios are in place, it is just not practical to reallocate funds among manager portfolios to implement plan sponsor strategy. It would interfere with the operations of our active managers and increase transaction costs."

Response. While it is important to avoid interference with manager operations, the point of view presented above overlooks a range of opportunities for implementing plan sponsor strategy without affecting the strategy or the transaction costs of the active managers.

Index funds. Since many funds now hold a portion of assets in passive form, necessary adjustments to the aggregate normal portfolio can often be made in passive portfolios. Such adjustments do not affect the strategy of the active managers and are subject to much lower transaction costs than are adjustments in actively managed portfolios.

Swing portfolio. A continuing opportunity to adjust the aggregate normal portfolio for the total fund is provided by the use of a swing portfolio, which includes stocks, bonds, and cash. For example, the plan sponsor may alter on a quarterly (or monthly) basis the normal asset allocation for the swing portfolio as a means of adjusting the normal asset allocation for the total fund. The active manager of the swing portfolio can adapt readily to such changes in the applicable performance benchmark; it is the role of the swing portfolio to achieve a high degree of flexibility with low transaction costs (by using "informationless" trades or derivative securities). Chapter 9 provides an example of a swing portfolio.

Completeness fund. Passive managers now prepare "completeness" portfolios in order to provide a passive fund tilted to bring the aggregate normal portfolio in line with the plan sponsor objective. The completeness portfolio can be routinely rebalanced to change the bias in the aggregate normal portfolio to conform to the plan sponsor strategy.

Financial futures. Futures contracts provide opportunities for adjustment of the fund asset mix without disruption of existing portfolios. They provide for purchase or sale at a specified price on a specified future date for various equity and fixed-income indices. The most widely traded contracts cover the S&P 500, long treasury bonds, and treasury bills. These markets are very liquid and subject to very low transaction costs.

Net cashflows. Reallocation occurs rather frequently in pension funds because cashflow to the fund is either positive or negative and managers are terminated for reasons other than rebalancing of normal portfolios. Each of these events is an occasion to implement changes in the aggregate normal portfolio.

5. Conflict between Normal Portfolio and Manager's Skill

Excuse. "We prefer to choose the best managers, in terms of their ability to add value, rather than to choose managers on the basis of their normal portfolios. We don't want normal portfolios to get in the way of picking the most able managers."

Response. Since plan sponsor strategy is determined by the aggregate normal portfolio for all of the individual portfolios that make up the fund, it can allow for considerable flexibility in the selection of individual normal portfolios. For each manager, the normal portfolio may differ substantially from plan sponsor strategy. The goal of the plan sponsor is to construct the combination of normal portfolios that both includes the managers who qualify in terms of their own skill and also meets the requirements of plan sponsor strategy.

A conflict between plan sponsor strategy and the normal portfolio of a specific manager does not necessarily preclude hiring that manager. As discussed earlier, the plan sponsor can correct for an unwanted combination of manager normal portfolios in several ways in order to make room for the manager who shows high promise of superior skill. On occasion, the obvious solution may be the termination of an existing manager with a similar normal portfolio but with little evidence of superior skill. Since replacement of one manager with another generates substantial transaction costs as one portfolio is liquidated and another is purchased, this approach depends primarily on the strength of the case for termination. Other opportunities arise as routine cash inflows or outflows may be used to modify the weighted combination of normal portfolios that make up the fund.

Where a portion of the funds are held passively, they may be tilted by the passive manager to compensate for the addition of the manager with an unwanted normal portfolio. For example, the passive fund may reduce holdings of smaller capitalization growth issues to offset the emphasis on such issues in an actively managed portfolio. In this way, the bias of the total fund to small-capitalization growth issues is unchanged, but the fund can expect to benefit from the skill of the active manager in the selection of such issues. The passive portfolio may be shaped—and reshaped as necessary—to compensate for the discrepancy between plan sponsor strategy and the aggregate normal portfolios of the active managers. As a result, the combination of normal portfolios (which now includes the passive portfolio) can always be approximately in accord with plan sponsor strategy. A number of passive managers welcome the opportunity to provide such service.

6. Need for Top-Level Support

Excuse. "The approach presented here, as desirable as it may be, requires radical changes, which are just not likely to come about without initiative from the chief executive officer or the chief financial officer—and they are busy with other matters. For example, the top people involved in making decisions concerning the pension fund may continue to focus on comparisons of equity performance with the S&P 500 rather than with the applicable normal portfolios. In this event, the S&P 500 rather than the normal portfolios remains the de facto basis of equity performance measurement."

Response. Show the top decision makers what the addition of one percentage point to the the total return of your fund would add to earnings per share. Translate into dollars the effect of reducing the loss in the market value of the assets in your pension fund—in a severely unfavorable investment environment—by five percentage points. And present them with a copy of our book.

Manager Skill Does Not Replace Plan Sponsor Strategy

Plan sponsor focus on manager skill without attention to the manager's normal portfolio generates unnecessary risks, as illustrated by the following example. Suppose plan sponsor strategy calls for a manager with a normal portfolio represented by the S&P 500, but the plan sponsor chooses a manager on the basis of superior skill in selecting small-capitalization, high-growth stocks. Over the 5 years previous to this new assignment, the manager's record showed an average annual return six percentage points greater than that for the S&P 500. This favorable performance is attributable both to the normal portfolio of small-capitalization, high-growth stocks (five percentage points) and to manager strategy (one point). In the year after selection of the manager, the manager's normal portfolio performs very poorly relative to the S&P 500—by ten percentage points. Even though the manager's skill this time contributes a positive three percentage points, total performance of the manager's portfolio amounts to a shortfall of seven percentage points relative to the S&P 500.

In this hypothetical example, poor portfolio performance relative to the S&P 500 during the first year of the new assignment is due to plan sponsor strategy rather than investment manager strategy. The manager deserves commendation for continued positive contribution to performance relative to the properly identified normal portfolio. It is the plan sponsor who assumed an unnecessary risk by the choice of a manager with a normal portfolio that did not conform to plan sponsor strategy.

Performance Record

Since the goal of active management is superior performance, any list of criteria for manager selection must include an evaluation of past performance. Yet performance records—no matter how favorable—can be highly misleading in the absence of attention to important qualitative factors. For this reason, as indicated earlier in this chapter, we rank both investment decision process and organization and key people ahead of the performance record in our criteria for manager selection. Nevertheless, we address the performance record before discussion of these other issues, since the limitations of performance measurement underscore the need to emphasize qualitative factors.

Performance Measurement and Its Limitations

Perhaps the most common error in performance measurement is to attribute the entire difference between the total portfolio return and that of a standard benchmark index (such as the S&P 500) to the skill of the manager. As discussed in Chap. 10, the margin of superior return may simply result from failure to measure performance against an appropriate style-adjusted normal portfolio. Adjusted for a realistic definition of the normal portfolio, an initially favorable record may become an unfavorable record or, conversely, a record previously viewed as unfavorable may be shown to be favorable.

Even when performance is measured against a carefully chosen normal portfolio, a favorable record is far from conclusive. A carefully chosen normal portfolio provides a better benchmark than readily available standard indexes such as the S&P 500, but it is still subject to a significant margin of error. No one can claim that the normal portfolio is defined with absolute accuracy. Even if the normal portfolio were perfect, performance measurement would still reflect the substantial role of chance, especially over relatively short periods of only 2 or 3 years.

Since an active manager necessarily makes decisions based on probabilities, the role of chance looms large in performance measurement. If a manager actually possesses superior skill, the odds on any one decision may be upgraded from the 50–50 attributable to chance to perhaps 60–40 in favor of a correct decision. These odds, applied to even a large number of independent decisions, are unlikely to provide statistically significant results over commonly used measurement periods, often as short as 3 to 5 years. Many investment decisions, moreover, are not independent of each other. A manager who switches 15 issues in a 50-stock portfolio may have actually made only two or three key decisions; other decisions depend on the correctness of the few key decisions. With so few key decisions, favorable results for even an extended period do not necessarily assure the presence of skill, just as unfavorable results do not necessarily prove its absence. There are numerous examples of plan sponsors who have placed great stress on hiring only those managers with extremely impressive performance over the previous 3 to 5 years only to find, once the managers were hired, that the past results offered little basis for a projection of future results.

Favorable Record—Necessary, but Not Sufficient

These comments are made, not to argue against the use of performance records in manager selection, but, rather, to stress great care in their use. Since a performance record should never be the primary criterion for the assessment of manager skill, our ranking accords priority to qualitative factors, as listed above and discussed in the next sections. If analysis of qualitative factors provides reason to evaluate favorably the skill of an investment manager, the positive conclusion is reinforced by a positive performance record—or is subject to reservations as a result of the lack of a record.

In general, a favorable performance record is necessary, but not sufficient, for selection of an investment manager. In certain cases, a manager may qualify for an assignment even without a meaningful performance record if special advantages relating to the decision process and other qualitative factors are sufficiently impressive. The converse is never true: No manager should ever be hired primarily on the basis of the past record.

Investment Decision Process

In highly efficient securities markets, superior strategy results from a decision process that is in some way itself superior. At one time it was possible to secure an advantage through the use of material information not generally available to other investors. In these earlier days, an important investment-manager resource was access to corporate directors, corporate officers, and other sources of what would now be labeled "inside information." Since the transmittal and use of such information became illegal some years ago, investment managers have had to look for advantage in the processing of information that is rapidly available to all investors.

Although there is no sure way of identifying a decision process that will gain advantage over the securities markets, discussion with the manager of the questions listed below is likely to improve the chances of success. At the very least, managers can be eliminated from further consideration because of lack of satisfactory answers.

1. *What's different?* Since the same information is generally available to all investors, it is unlikely that any one investor can gain consistent advantage by utilizing decision rules widely used by other investors. Persistent emphasis on low price-earnings ratios or, alternatively, on high growth is an example of a widely used decision rule that defines, in the first case, a value manager and, in the other case, a growth manager. This rule does not explain why a particular decision process is likely to benefit from something other investors miss. Probably no decision process, without continuing evolution, can expect to maintain an advantage indefinitely. Opportunities for innovative decision processes that can provide an advantage arise from new technology (such as the increasingly sophisticated use of electronic data processing), new forms of investment (such as derivative securities), and continuing research on finance and capital market theory.

2. *Is the decision process consistent with the investment philosophy?* What is the manager's investment philosophy, and does it make sense in securities markets that can be compared neither to a game of chess nor to a bingo game? Does the decision process follow logically from the investment philosophy, or is the investment philosophy a conglomeration

of platitudes that have little relevance to decisions that are actually made?

3. *How thorough is the decision process?* Figure 8-2 in Chap. 8 outlines the elements involved in the valuation of any asset. Does the decision process address only one or two of these elements? If so, there is likely to be a persistent bias that can influence future returns. Is there some way in which the risks relating to such bias can be controlled?

4. *What are the implications for transaction costs?* Transaction costs depend heavily on turnover, which is driven by the decision process. (Other factors affecting transaction costs include such characteristics of a security as volatility and liquidity, which relate more to the characteristics of the securities represented in the normal portfolio than to the decision process.) If other things are equal, low transaction costs are better than high transaction costs, since transaction costs represent a direct subtraction from performance. High transaction costs could be warranted if they can be expected to more than pay for themselves through better performance. The burden of proof, however, is on the manager. The higher the transaction costs, the more advantage the manager must be able to secure in competition with other investors. There is no rule about the maximum turnover or transaction costs that seem reasonable, but we would become increasingly demanding concerning the evidence of the superiority of the decision process as the magnitude of transaction costs rises.

5. *Does the record indicate that the decision process operates in practice as the manager claims?* When, for example, the decision process in the past has provided a negative valuation, does the manager sell? Or is there a de facto decision process, different from that presented by the investment manager, which actually determines what happens in the portfolio?

Organization and Key People

If the plan sponsor is attracted by the decision process of a manager operating with a normal portfolio consistent with plan sponsor strategy, the next step is to review the organization and key people.

1. *Are the current key people those who have been responsible for what is attractive in the firm—the investment philosophy, the decision process, and the performance record?* For this purpose, the key people may be defined as anyone who has a significant role in shaping the investment

management that will be delivered to the client. The key people would ordinarily include portfolio managers, research specialists, and traders.

2. *Is the organization strong and stable?* Does the firm have enough resources to do what it claims to do? Does it offer sufficient incentives to hold on to the necessary staff? Is there sufficient depth so that the results would not be greatly affected by the loss of any individual, should it occur?

3. *What is the condition of the firm's book of business?* Is it growing, or have a number of terminations recently occurred? What effect are these changes having on the distribution of accounts by size and the number of accounts per portfolio manager? Growth in the business, even the addition of prestigious clients, is not necessarily evidence of favorable future results. On the other hand, loss of business may reflect client factors unrelated to the quality of investment management, including company takeovers, plan terminations, and restructuring. In either case, such information should be available to the plan sponsor.

Passive Managers versus Active Managers

Since the 1970s, passive management has become an increasingly available alternative to active management. Most large pension funds now use passive management to maintain a "core" portion of their assets in conformity with a specified benchmark. The benchmark may be (1) a widely recognized index, such as the S&P 500 for equities or the Shearson Lehman Hutton Government-Corporate Bond Index; (2) a specialized index covering a particular market segment, such as small-capitalization stocks or long-term bonds; or (3) a customized index designed for a specific purpose. By way of example, the customized index may replicate the population of growth stocks or value stocks, or, given certain persistent biases in the remainder of the fund, may provide a mix of issues to offset these biases.

The rapid growth of passive investing raises an issue concerning the proportion of pension assets that might advantageously be held in passive form. Allocation of assets to passive managers affects neither investment policy nor plan sponsor strategy. The plan sponsor may allocate assets to passive managers to match the policy plan or may depart from policy to implement a particular strategy. Only the opportunities and risks associated with investment manager strategy are eliminated.

How much of a particular pension fund should be shifted from active to passive management depends on the plan sponsor's appraisal of the value added by active management. The critical comparison is the incremental return anticipated from active management in relation to its incremental cost and its contribution to increased volatility. Active management costs more than passive management because the fees are significantly higher. In addition, active management must benefit sufficiently from successful strategy to offset the higher turnover and higher costs per transaction associated with active management. Combined management fees and transaction costs for active management are likely to exceed those for passive management by at least 1 percent of assets annually. For some active managers, the cost burden is significantly higher. If the plan sponsor were certain that he or she could hire superior active managers who, through superior investment strategy, could more than offset these incremental costs, passive management could not be justified. Absolute certainty that superior active managers are impossible to identify in advance would warrant the opposite conclusion—to the extent possible, the entire fund should be managed passively.

Balance between Active and Passive

Our view supports an intermediate conclusion concerning passive management, a position consistent with that of the majority of sponsors of large pension funds. Plan sponsors, recognizing the difficulty of identifying in advance the limited number of superior managers, have in many cases shifted one-fourth to one-half of equity assets to passive managers. The proportion of fixed-income assets under passive management, although not yet so large, is also becoming significant. To our knowledge, no major pension fund has shifted its entire assets to passive management.

Controlling Investment Managers: Investment Guidelines

The critical element in controlling investment managers is unambiguous guidelines for specific responsibilities, constraints, and methods of performance measurement. The appendix to this chapter provides a sample set of guidelines that illustrate those prepared by the sponsor of a large pension fund for the fund's equity managers. Once the guidelines are in place, monthly monitoring of the manager's portfolio provides a continuing flow of information about the manager's observance of the guideline constraints as well as data on performance.

Communications with Investment Managers

Provided the guidelines are carefully drawn and receive the full agreement of the manager, it is unlikely that the plan sponsor will find information in the monthly portfolio reports that indicates need for remedial action. An example of the use of monthly reports in controlling manager adherence to guideline constraints is provided by the changing exposure to stock market risk. Suppose cash reserves in the manager's portfolio rise to 12 percent, perhaps because of market action affecting equity holdings, when the guidelines specify a maximum of 10 percent. In such an event, the plan sponsor may phone to make certain the manager is aware that cash limits have been exceeded and to explore the manager's future plans for the portfolio. The combination of monthly portfolio reports and clearly written guidelines permits the plan sponsor to react quickly to actions on the part of an investment manager that conflict with mutually agreed limitations.

With the continuing monthly analysis of portfolio data, formal meetings with the manager may be required only semiannually. The meeting provides the manager with an opportunity to explain the recent operation of the firm's decision process, to raise evolving issues about the normal portfolio or method of performance measurement, and to report on changes in organization or key people that might affect the management of the account. The purpose of the meeting is *not* to provide the manager with supplementary instructions that do not appear in the guidelines. If the guidelines should be changed, a specific proposal should be presented to the manager for agreement, and the revised guidelines, redefining the responsibilities of the manager, should then become effective on an agreed date. Without formal change in the guidelines—including any change in the performance benchmark—transmittal of the plan sponsor's opinions on the outlook for the securities markets or on management of the portfolio can only serve to create confusion.

Manager Terminations

Standards for manager termination are much the same as those for manager selection. For example, a normal portfolio that no longer meets the requirements of plan sponsor strategy provides a compelling reason for termination of the portfolio manager. In this case, the manager is terminated, not because of reappraisal of the manager's competence, but simply because the services are no longer needed.

A change in the normal portfolio by the manager is also reason to review the manager's role. Manager changes in normal portfolio are rare in the absence of significant replacement of key people. Even then, substantial modification of the normal portfolio may not occur unless there is reaction to an extended period of poor performance. If a manager were to shift to a new normal portfolio, the plan sponsor would have to determine whether the revision is appropriate in the perspective of plan sponsor strategy. The process is essentially the same as the selection of a new manager.

Reevaluation of a manager's decision process or increasing reservations about organization and key people are also reasons for termination. By emphasizing qualitative factors over the performance record, termination for cause may be accomplished before the full effect of deteriorating skill is evident in the performance record. A clear record of poor performance is the least advantageous reason for termination of the manager, since the plan sponsor has already paid a heavy price. While poor performance in itself may warrant termination in certain circumstances, earlier detection of developing problems through monitoring qualitative factors, where possible, is the better alternative.

Appendix
Investment Guidelines for ABC Associates

[The following guidelines, which apply to a portfolio manager designated here as "ABC Associates," illustrate those prepared by the sponsor of a large pension fund for the fund's equity managers. Similar guidelines were issued to each of the managers of the fund, with variations due principally to differences in normal portfolios.]

Guidelines for the ABC portfolio are an integral part of our plan for the total pension fund. Because of this interrelationship between the role of individual managers and our overall requirements, the first section of these guidelines summarizes the policy framework for our total fund. A second section lists the specific standards that will apply to the portfolio actively managed by ABC Associates. A final section defines the method that will be used to evaluate performance of the portfolio.

Policy Framework for the Total Fund

The investment objective of our total fund is differentiated from the individual objectives of any one of our active managers. The fund objective, which we have established after careful planning, reflects the trade-off between the risk and expected return considered most appropriate for our total pension fund. The individual objectives of active managers, in contrast, relate to the special role that each has chosen as the best opportunity to add investment value.

Basic Portfolio Plan

Our Basic Portfolio Plan provides the broad policy framework required to respond to the investment objective of the total fund. To this end, it assigns each asset category (i.e., stocks, bonds, real estate, and cash equivalents) a "normal" position in the total fund. The Basic Portfolio Plan contributes directly to the performance of the fund in two ways:

1. *Reduction of risk through diversification.* The Basic Portfolio Plan affords downside protection in periods of adversity in financial markets, since it controls risk at a level consistent with the requirements for our fund. Risks for the individual asset categories partially offset each other to the extent their returns are out of phase. Combined risks for the diversified mix of assets specified by the Basic Portfolio Plan are therefore considerably less than the weighted average of the risks for the component asset categories.

2. *Contribution to expected return.* Equally important, the discipline incorporated in the Basic Portfolio Plan enables the total fund to aim at incremental rate of investment return over the longer term. Since overall risk is reduced by asset diversification, the fund is able to include a greater proportion of aggressive investment vehicles than would otherwise be the case. The Basic Portfolio Plan, by our calculations, provides a probability of more than 50 percent that *real* returns will average in excess of 4 percent annually over a 10-year period. Less carefully diversified portfolios, *subject to the same risk limitations,* would have to aim at an average annual return that would be lower by as much as a full percentage point.

Active Manager's Investment Universe

Within the broad framework of the Basic Portfolio Plan, each active manager is expected to operate in his or her own "investment universe." Subject to individually prepared guidelines, each manager will pursue his or her own strategies within the population of securities that he or she prefers. Our coordination of guidelines for the individual managers assures that the combined efforts of our managers will be consistent with the overall objectives of the fund. The benefits for the active manager of our approach are twofold:

1. *Concentration in areas of special skill.* Through appropriate definition of his or her preferred investment universe, the individual manager will be able to concentrate in those areas of special skill. The designated investment universe will exclude segments of the financial markets in which research coverage is absent. It will concentrate investment efforts in activities that are most likely to be advantageous on the basis of the manager's investment philosophy and decision process.

2. *Intensification of risk-taking.* Once the preferred investment universe is defined, the active manager can enhance opportunities to add value by aggressively exploiting his or her convictions. The preferred investment universe of each manager will be carefully coordinated with the investment universes that make up the remainder of the fund. As a result, the sum of our managers' efforts can be controlled to avoid unacceptable deviations from the normal positions specified for the Basic Portfolio Plan. Given careful planning and control for the total fund, the potential negative implications of intensified risk-taking by individual managers will be limited.

Portfolio Standards

Standards for the ABC portfolio follow from identification of the investment universe in which the firm prefers to operate. The investment universe, in turn, is defined by an index and a range of deviation from this index.

The index for the ABC portfolio is designated the "ABC" Index. It will be calculated by determining each month the change in value of a portfolio made up of 90 percent equities and 10 percent treasury bills.

Equities included in the index will consist of stocks selected from the S&P 500:

- All issues with market values of $5 billion or more will be included. These issues will be equally weighted, since ABC's decision process ignores market values of large-capitalization issues.

- Issues with market values of less than $5 billion are included only if they meet a minimum standard of +0.1 on the BARRA index of growth orientation. The growth tilt reflects a continuing policy of ABC, which dedicates about 15 percent of its managed portfolios to high-growth, smaller capitalization stocks. These issues with market values of less than $5 billion are market value–weighted, reflecting liquidity considerations made necessary by the volume of funds under management.

Latitude for implementation of investment strategy within the preferred investment universe is indicated by the range of deviation of the ABC portfolio from the ABC Index. Portfolio standards are provided for both market risk and equity diversification. Subject to these broad standards, equities may be purchased from time to time which are not included in the ABC Index, and fixed-income securities with maturities over 1 year may be purchased opportunistically up to a limit of 25 percent of the portfolio. There is an understanding between ABC Associates and the sponsor, nevertheless, that the ABC Index will generally represent the median characteristics of the ABC portfolio over an extended period of changes in strategy.

Market Risk

Market risk (systematic risk) will be defined in terms of the portfolio beta. As is the standard practice, portfolio beta will be measured against the S&P 500. ABC may alter the portfolio beta within the bounds indicated by the range shown below as changes in the financial markets are anticipated. Adjustment in portfolio beta can most quickly be achieved through adjustment of cash reserves but may also be attained through modification of the mix of securities held in the portfolio.

	ABC Index	Portfolio range
Beta	0.98	0.85–1.30

The beta coefficient for each individual equity will be calculated on the basis of the investment fundamentals as provided by BARRA. Cash equivalents will be assumed to provide a zero beta. Betas for long- and intermediate-term bonds will be determined, as necessary, on the basis of an in-house risk model.

Diversification

Diversification for the ABC portfolio relative to its benchmark will be defined by the residual standard deviation (RSD) relative to that benchmark, as shown below:

	Portfolio range
RSD relative to ABC Index	2.5–10.0%

Within the limits specified for diversification, ABC is expected to concentrate the portfolio in order to exploit as fully as possible the firm's strategic insights. Where such insights warrant high confidence, the residual standard deviation is likely to approach the high end of the range. During periods when strategic insights are accompanied by low confidence, portfolio diversification will tend to move toward the low end of the range.

Other Standards

Other standards guiding ABC investment management are summarized below:

1. Private placements or other investments without active trading markets will not be made without our prior approval.

2. There are no restrictions relating to dividends or earnings of the stock held in the portfolios.

3. Securities turnover is warranted by the need to alter strategy as prospects for the financial markets change. Commission costs are included in the management fee, but hidden costs relating to the market impact of transactions are a charge against our pension assets as well as the performance of ABC Associates. It is therefore mutually agreed that turnover will be maintained at the lowest level consistent with implementation of strategy.

4. There are no requirements for, nor restrictions against, realization of net investment gains or losses during the calendar year.

5. No securities of the plan sponsor are to be purchased.

6. There are to be no short sales, trading on margin, purchase or sales of options, nor lending of securities.

Portfolio Evaluation

ABC Associates will be evaluated in terms of its demonstrated ability to add value relative to the ABC Index. The ABC Index, which has been described previously in these guidelines, will be calculated on a monthly basis.

A shortfall from the index under favorable market conditions will be regarded negatively, as would failure to attain relative gains under unfavorable market conditions. Over a period of changing market conditions, active management is expected to demonstrate a cumulative net gain over the applicable standard of measurement.

Standards established for the ABC portfolio reflect our mutual agreement as of the date of the guidelines. Guidelines will be reviewed at least annually, and more frequently as required.

ABC Associates will promptly advise us at any time these guidelines no longer seem appropriate. A compelling reason would be significant change in the evaluation by ABC Associates of the expected real return or risk over the longer term for the assets that comprise the firm's preferred investment universe. Upon mutual agreement, the standards for the portfolio will be changed to assure the latitude necessary for exercise of the special skills of ABC Associates in active management.

12
Summing Up—
Three Critical
Issues

How the corporate pension fund is managed ultimately depends on the resolution of three critical issues. Although they may be stated in somewhat different ways, we have summarized them in three short questions: (1) What is the goal of pension asset management? (2) How much risk should the fund accept? and (3) What is the appropriate mix of active management and passive management? This latter issue involves the role of investment strategy relative to investment policy.

Much of traditional thinking about pension fund management bypasses these critical issues to concentrate on forecasting the course of the financial markets. For example, the senior executives who gather to participate in meetings with the pension investment committee are likely to concern themselves primarily with the condition of the economy and the probable implications for stock and bond markets. At the same time, they may view the principal challenge for pension officers as the selection of the investment managers who are able to achieve advantage over the financial markets. While such questions relating to investment strategy merit attention, their role in pension fund management is subordinate to the three policy issues listed above.

Those responsible for management of pension assets, both internally and externally, operate within a philosophical framework—explicit or implied—represented by the resolution of these critical issues. If these issues are not addressed, they are still resolved by default—and not necessarily in a way that is advantageous either to the plan sponsor and its stockholders or to the plan participants. The purpose of our book is to address these critical issues. This final chapter serves as an overview, summarizing our conclusions. It is offered as a checklist for the chief executive officer who must be concerned with the "big picture" decisions affecting the company's total business as well as a review for everyone involved in management of the pension fund.

What Is the Goal of Pension Asset Management?

We conclude that the goal of pension asset management, within the rather broad framework permitted by ERISA, is to support the corporate goals for the company's common stock. Our book, as stated at the beginning of Chap. 1, aims "to legitimize pension finance in general, and management of pension assets in particular, as an important ongoing corporate-finance function." This legitimization requires stripping away important misconceptions fostered by elements drawn from actuarial and accounting conventions as well as from federal statutes (ERISA). These widely held misconceptions are inconsistent with the economic content of pension plans in practice (Chaps. 2, 3, and 4). The foundation laid in Chaps. 1 through 5, by focusing on the pension plan as an integral component of corporate finance, presents the case for a broad corporate perspective on the management of pension assets (as well as pension liabilities).

Our position, as discussed in Chap. 7, contrasts with two alternative views that seem to receive considerable support. One view looks at pension fund management as a performance race, with the objective of securing higher returns than other fund managers do. The other view looks at the pension fund as part of a pension plan separate from the business of the sponsoring corporation, with little regard for differences from one plan sponsor to another in relation to business prospects, company resources, or management goals.

Modification of Investment Policy to Support Corporate Goals

Focus on plan sponsor goals may seem to the casual observer to conflict with the fiduciary obligations required by ERISA, but, for a healthy, ongoing corporation, such is not the case. Within the framework of strict compliance with ERISA, there is wide latitude to modify investment policy to support corporate goals. The pension fund may be invested wholly in fixed-income securities, widely diversified among the various asset groups, or heavily skewed toward common stocks. For an ongoing corporation, moreover, the strength of its pension fund ultimately depends on the strength of its operations. An extreme emphasis on avoiding risk in the pension fund, for example, could prove counterproductive for the plan participants if it contributed to a weakening of the sponsoring corporation over the longer term.

Pension Costs Are Independent of Pension Fund Returns

The point of departure of our analysis is to recognize the role of the pension plan in corporate finance. As explained in Chap. 4, the cost of the pension plan is independent of the investment return attained on pension assets. No matter how the assets are invested, the cost of the pension plan is the present value of the fixed-income securities that would have to be purchased to provide the future cashflows required to pay for future benefits. Establishment of a pension plan is therefore equivalent to the issuance of the debt necessary to pay future benefits. As described in Chap. 3, the present value of this debt is subject to revision as a result of both changes in the prevailing level of interest rates and changes in factors affecting the level of future benefits, including the effects of inflation on wage rates.

How the plan is funded and the assets are invested are decisions separate from the cost of the plan. A return on assets in excess of the cost of the plan is a gain for the shareholders, since it reduces the company contribution to the pension fund. Similarly, an investment program that returns less than the cost of the plan represents a loss for the shareholders. Clearly, the shareholders of the corporation sponsoring the pension plan have a direct stake in management of pension assets as well as management of the company's operating divisions. All of these assets have to outperform the cost of money in the debt market if shareholders are to benefit. It is the role of the chief executive officer, once the requirements of ERISA have been met, to assure that pension fund management supports corporate goals.

Growing Role of Pension Plans in Corporate Finance

A generation ago, pension assets and liabilities were often too small to merit much attention from those in charge of the overall financial structure of the corporation. Now, as pointed out in the introduction to this book, fund assets (for defined benefit plans alone) may average close to 30 percent of the market value of the plan sponsor common stock and are much larger in certain instances. As a result, how the pension fund is managed can significantly affect corporate results and the value placed on the company's common shares. The growing role of the pension plan in corporate finance has been underscored by the influence of pension assets and liabilities in takeover calculations. For some companies, surplus pension assets have contributed to a materially larger valuation, while in other cases, large unfunded pension liabilities have severely reduced valuations. At the extreme, the large unfunded pension liabilities have effectively precluded sale of a corporate entity.

Cash does not have to be withdrawn from a pension fund for pension surplus to contribute to the price realized in a takeover. Although the calculations supporting a takeover price are not generally made public, the underwriters hired by the buyer to value the acquisition are certain to scrutinize the pension plan for "hidden values." In one case, where recognition of the values in the pension plan added about 10 percent to the winning bid, these values were realized through elimination of cash contributions to the pension plan for several years into the future. The new owners were able to divert cashflow, previously directed to the pension fund, to the servicing of the heavy debt created by the leveraged buyout.

How Much Risk Should the Fund Accept?

How much investment risk is appropriate for a pension fund in light of the corporate goals of the plan sponsor? The answer requires a realistic view of the way financial markets work. Chapter 6 examines two very different views of investment management, depending on the underlying assumptions about financial markets. It compares investment management to a game of chess (where superior skill almost always assures success) and to a game of bingo (where skill does not matter), but concludes that the best analogy is something in between, such as contract bridge or gin rummy.

The Chess Analogy Implies Full Reliance on Active Management

If the chess analogy were valid, risk and expected return would be inversely related. An investment manager with superior skill, like the master chess player matched against an opponent of lesser capability, would be expected to win more times than not and the risk of losing would be correspondingly reduced. Since high expected return would be accompanied by low risk, there would be little reason for one fund to accept more risk than another fund. All funds would attempt to achieve low risk and high returns by securing the services of the most skillful investment managers. Since the quality of investment management could be rather easily deduced by the ranking of returns, pension management would constitute a simple performance race with other pension funds.

The Bingo Analogy Calls for Passive Management

The bingo analogy, in contrast, implies that risk is directly related to expected return. Given the same expected return, investors prefer less risk rather than more risk. If no investor has advantage over another, the only reason for an investor to accept higher risk would be to seek higher return. Consequently, securities would be priced in the marketplace so that expected return and risk are directly related. The composition of one pension fund would differ from that of another to reflect differences in fund objectives, as defined by the trade-off between expected return and risk.

Hazards of Mixing Chess and Bingo

In the absence of a clear distinction between the two points of view, the plan sponsor's decision process is likely to be muddled and inconsistent. At times the plan sponsor may commit to active management as if the chess analogy were essentially valid. At other times, the problem may be an overly simple view of passive management, as if the rules that govern the outcome for passive investments are as reliable as those that relate to a contest between bingo players. Risks of a negative outcome over time may be compounded if plan sponsor decisions vacillate between the two approaches, particularly if the shift takes place without recognition of the underlying conflict. It is tempting, for example, to agree at the top of the stock market to continue to hold a full commitment of stocks because "no one can time the market" (bingo analogy); but later on, at the bottom of the market, the same decision maker may sell equities because it is clear that market prices have not yet discounted the extremely negative outlook (chess analogy).

Clearly Defined Separation of Roles
for Policy and Strategy

The first step toward a solution, as proposed in this book, is to define separate roles for policy and strategy.

Investment Policy. Policy assumes that no investor has advantage over another (bingo analogy) and that risk and expected return are directly related. Policy risk and policy expected return, moreover, are subject to quantification (based on the objective evidence provided by analysis of historical data). Since policy does not depend on superior forecasting and looks to the longer term, it serves as a useful framework for planning the appropriate level of risk for the pension fund.

A very simple example of policy asset allocation is sometimes described as a "standard" or "policy" mix. It consists of 60 percent S&P 500 and 40 percent fixed-income securities, the latter often represented by one of the widely used bond indexes. It meets the definition of policy to the extent it represents a long-term plan that assumes no forecasting advantage over publicly traded securities markets. For most funds, however, this simple asset mix cannot qualify as a good policy choice for two reasons. Unless there are unusual constraints limiting the range of assets held in the fund, the trade-off between expected return and risk can be substantially improved through increased diversification (into such areas as smaller capitalization domestic stocks, foreign stocks and bonds, and real estate). Even more important, there is no standard policy mix appropriate for all pension funds. Because fund objectives vary widely, fund investment policies must be tailored to reflect the differing requirements of each fund.

The steps necessary to select the appropriate policy plan to meet corporate goals for the company's common shares are outlined in Chap. 7. Construction of an augmented balance sheet (Chap. 5) requires (1) addition to the balance sheet of both pension assets and liabilities and (2) marking to market of all balance sheet items. The augmented balance sheet permits formulation of a series of alternative pension fund policies to be reflected in the risk and expected-return characteristics of the plan sponsor's common shares. By viewing the implications of these alternatives for the company's stock, the appropriate level of risk for the pension fund can be identified.

Investment Strategy. With policy in place, investment strategy is defined as a departure from policy that aims to secure incremental return. By way of illustration, suppose the policy percentage for common stocks is 60 percent, as suggested in the above example. When the plan sponsor (or strategy advisors) considers common stocks to be overvalued, the actual percentage might be temporarily reduced to 45 percent, with the proceeds held as cash equivalents. Investment strategy is responsible for the contribution to fund performance—positive or negative—resulting from the difference between the policy percentage of 60 percent and the strategy percentage of 45 percent. At the same time, another plan sponsor, working with a policy allocation to stocks of 40 percent, might increase the stock percentage to 45 percent to reflect a bullish view of the stock market. Both plan sponsors, in this example, hold the same percentage of common stocks, but the first is accountable for a strategy underweighting of 15 percent while the second is accountable for a strategy overweighting of 5 percent.

We have used the chess analogy to describe the rationale of investment strategy, since, in a chess game, superior skill enjoys a clear advantage. Similarly, investment strategy—to the extent it is superior—limits investment risk and increases expected return. Assessment of strategy risk and strategy return, however, is highly subjective, depending on individual appraisal of the skill of the strategist. Since strategy is competitive, the net strategy losses for all investors must balance their net gains. Hence, expected returns from the implementation of strategy cannot be matched by actual results across all investors in the market. This disparity between the goals of strategy and the actual outcome for investors taken as a whole generates the background for the third critical issue involved in management of pension assets: the appropriate mix between active and passive management.

What Is the Appropriate Mix between Active and Passive Management?

The mix between passive and active management is an issue that has come to the fore in the 1980s. Passive management did not become formally available as a product until the 1970s, and it did not compete in a major way for pension fund business until the 1980s. As this book is written, it is possible to meet all the requirements of the policy plan, at least for common stocks and fixed-income securities, through the purchase of passively managed index funds. Active management, which strives to apply superior strategy to secure performance superior to that attainable by policy, had once accounted for almost all of fund management, but during recent years has ceded a rapidly increasing portion of its market share to passive management.

Where should the plan sponsor draw the line? Some large pension funds have strenuously resisted the shift to passive management, and their funds, in total, continue to be actively managed. Other large funds have shifted as much as 50 percent of assets to passive portfolios, and most large funds have at least a portion of their assets in passively managed portfolios. Recent trends, indicating continuing rapid growth in passive management, suggest that the active/passive question is a major issue confronting plan sponsors.

As a broad generalization, the mix between passive and active management depends on the plan sponsor's assessment of the likelihood that active management will add value relative to passive management. If the plan sponsor can identify active managers who benefit from superior investment skill, there is no reason to permit fund assets to be passively managed. On the other hand, lack of ability to identify superior active managers would suggest reliance on passive management.

Identification of Superior Active Managers

How can plan sponsors be reasonably certain that they have identified superior active managers? While there are no easy answers, steps can be taken to avoid important pitfalls. Our recommendation for selecting active managers recognizes that a favorable record is a necessary but not sufficient basis for a decision. As explained in Chap. 11, we stress four criteria, ranked below in order of importance.

Normal Portfolio. The manager's normal portfolio, even though it does not reflect manager skill in applying investment strategy, heads the list of criteria for manager selection. The plan sponsor must be satisfied that the combined normal portfolios that constitute the fund meet the requirements of plan sponsor strategy. If a manager of value stocks is required, addition of a growth manager with the same degree of skill in stock selection would unnecessarily increase overall risk. In this example, it is necessary either to seek a qualified value manager or, alternatively, to rearrange the fund's normal portfolios to accommodate the addition of a growth manager.

Investment Decision Process. The superior active manager—who claims to add value beyond that which might result from chance—must be able to explain the advantage afforded by a superior decision process. Privileged information is not an alternative, as indicated by our review of the decision process in Chap. 8. Consequently, it is a fair question to ask the prospective manager what he or she does differently that provides a margin of superiority over the financial markets.

Key People and Organization. Do the people involved have the background and experience necessary to implement the decision process, and does the organization provide the structure and depth required to deliver the product with a high degree of consistency?

Performance Record. In judging managers, we rank the performance record after the other criteria for two reasons. First, the record is often misleading because an inappropriate benchmark is used for performance measurement. For instance, a common error is to measure the performance of equity managers who concentrate on smaller capitalization issues against the S&P 500, which is dominated by large-capitalization issues with a significantly different industry pattern. How to minimize this problem is the subject of Chap. 10, which addresses the construction of normal portfolios. A second reason for reservations about the performance record relates to the role of chance in influencing the outcome of strategy decisions. Even if performance measurement over several years is based on the optimal normal portfolio, the favorable record may still result from chance rather than from skill.

Passive Management

In the absence of superior active management, passive management offers two clear advantages: (1) lower transaction costs because of both lower turnover and "informationless" trading and (2) lower management fees. In addition, passive management seeks reduced risk through maximum diversification.

Even a complete shift to passive management, however, cannot avoid the need for investment judgments, particularly those for asset allocation. The subjective aspects of the assumptions underlying the passive approach are outlined in Chap. 7. Another issue is timing. When should passive management be initiated—after a period when it seems to have performed better than active management? For passive equity or bond portfolios, moreover, judgments are required to determine which index funds in what proportion should be included in the fund.

Active/Passive Mix

As a broad generalization, we favor a diversified approach to the active/passive issue. The two approaches complement each other. To the extent a portion of the fund is passively managed—effectively implementing investment policy—active management can be encouraged to be more aggressive within the limits established for its operations. For example, the plan sponsor may limit the number of issues held in an equity portfolio to perhaps ten or fifteen names—in order to encourage more concentrated risks in the issues considered to be most attractive. Similarly, investment policy can benefit from a component of the fund committed to carefully selected active management. Pressures on investment policy to adjust to a particular current view of the investment environment may become especially intense during periods of extreme gloom or extreme optimism in financial markets. Such pressures on policy—which may lead to back-door market timing as described in Chap. 9—are moderated when the responsibility for interim strategy is specifically assigned to a portion of the fund that is actively managed.

The case for a balance between passive and active management does not preclude continuing changes in their manner of application. Long before the availability of index funds, a plan sponsor could have emphasized passive management in the area of asset allocation while stressing active management in the selection of individual issues. Under such circumstances, for example, the equity portfolio may have been concentrated in a relatively few issues subject to rapid turnover, but the percentage allocation to equities remained relatively static. With the advance of investment technology as well as capital market theory, the areas of application for passive and active management have expanded. Now, active management in the selection of individual issues competes with a passively managed index fund. At the same time, active management may be implemented through flexible adjustment in holdings of various index funds—with major implications for the performance of the total fund.

Employer's Accounting for Pensions: Financial Accounting Standards Board—Standard No. 87

[We have excerpted from the extensive material that the FASB published as FAS-87 in order to highlight the depth of the Board's thinking and insights that went into this accounting standard. The text also illuminates the severe compromises forced on the Board by accounting precedent and the strong aversion to volatility voiced by "many respondents." Numbered paragraphs are as in the standard itself.[1]]

Why FAS-87?

The Need for a New Standard

This Statement supersedes previous standards for employers' accounting for pensions. The most significant changes to past practice affect an employer's accounting for a single-employer defined benefit pension plan, although some provisions also apply to an employer that participates in a multiemployer plan or sponsors a defined contribution plan.

Measuring cost and reporting liabilities resulting from defined benefit pension plans have been sources of accounting controversy for many years. Both the Committee on Accounting Procedure, in 1956, and the Accounting Principles Board (APB), in 1966, concluded that improvements in pension accounting were necessary beyond what was considered practical at those times.

After 1966, the importance of information about pensions grew with increases in the number of plans and amounts of pension assets and obligations. There were significant changes in both the legal environment (for example, the enactment of ERISA) and the economic environment (for example, higher inflation and interest rates).

---

[1]SOURCE: Financial Accounting Standards Board. Used with permission. This reprint does not include the appendices to FASB—Standard no. 87. These appendices are an integral part of the document.

Problems with the Prior Standard

Critics of prior accounting requirements, including users of financial statements, became aware that reported pension cost was not comparable from one company to another and often was not consistent from period to period for the same company. They also became aware that significant pension-related obligations and assets were not recognized in financial statements.

The Nature of the Exchange: Future Promises for Current Consideration

Findings

79. The Board's conclusions in this Statement derive from the basic idea that a defined benefit pension is an exchange between the employer and the employee. In exchange for services provided by the employee, the employer promises to provide, in addition to current wages and other benefits, an amount of retirement income. It follows from that basic view that pension benefits are not gratuities but instead are part of an employee's compensation, and since payment is deferred, the pension is a type of deferred compensation. It also follows that the employer's obligation for that compensation is incurred when the services are rendered.

Comments

109. Some respondents disagreed with the Board's basic view of the nature of the employer's obligation under a defined benefit pension plan. They argued that the employer's only obligation is to make periodic contributions sufficient to support the plan. In this view, it is the plan—as a distinct legal entity—that has an obligation for benefits promised to employees. They concluded that the schedule or budget for making contributions determines the amount of the present obligation and current period cost and that contributions scheduled for future periods, although based upon past events, are future obligations.

110. The Board concluded that viewing the obligation and the cost only in terms of scheduled contributions does not reflect the fundamental difference between the inherent promise and the resulting obligation under a defined benefit plan and the promise and obligation under a defined contribution plan. An employer that has undertaken an obligation to provide defined pension benefits based on service already rendered may view it as an obligation directly to the employees (looking through the fund-

ing arrangement) or as an obligation to make future contributions to the plan, but the employer has a present obligation based on the defined benefits either way.

111. The Board believes that creating a separate legal entity to receive and invest contributions and pay benefits does not change the nature of the employer's obligation to pay promised benefits to retirees. Viewing the plan as a truly separate economic entity raises the question of what consideration the plan received for making benefit promises to employees. Although legal requirements are only one factor to be considered in determining accounting standards, the Board also notes that Congress, in enacting ERISA, chose to base the definition of an employee's rights under a defined benefit pension plan on the benefits promised rather than on the amount the employer has contributed or is scheduled to contribute.

112. Those who subscribe to the separate legal entity idea also argued that plan assets are not the assets of the employer. The Board noted that the employer's future contributions to the plan will be increased or decreased by the performance of the plan assets so that the employer bears the risks and reaps the rewards associated with those assets. The Board also observed that numerous recent situations in which significant amounts of assets have been withdrawn by employers provide compelling evidence that rebuts that argument.

Why a Balance Sheet Pension Liability Is Recognized

Comments

144. *Preliminary Views* proposed requiring recognition of a net pension liability or asset based on the difference between the projected benefit obligation and the fair value of plan assets. However, the net gain or loss not yet included in net periodic pension cost was also unrecognized for purposes of measuring the net pension liability or asset, thereby reducing the volatility of that balance. An intangible asset would have been recognized when a plan was amended, increasing the projected benefit obligation. Respondents objected to the proposal for a number of reasons, both conceptual and pragmatic. Some of those objections, based on doubts about the nature of the employer's obligation, were discussed previously.

145. A number of respondents argued that increased pension benefits granted in a plan amendment are exchanged for employees' *future* services, even when the amount of the benefit is computed based on prior service. In this view, the employer's li-

ability for such benefits arises only as the future services are rendered. Some also argued that a plan amendment is a wholly executory contract and for that reason should not be recognized. The Board agrees that the obligation is undertaken by the employer with the expectation of future economic benefits but believes that does not provide a basis for not recognizing the obligation that arises from the event or for arguing that no obligation exists. The Board does not agree that a plan amendment is a wholly executory contract. To the extent that an amendment increases benefits that will be attributable to future services, neither party has performed. The Board has never proposed to recognize any liability for those benefits. However, to the extent the increased benefits are attributed by the benefit formula to services already rendered, the Board concluded that one party to the contract has performed and the agreement is at most only partially executory.

146. Some respondents argued that the obligation could not be measured with sufficient reliability (or precision) to justify recognition. The Board notes that the measurements of net periodic pension cost and unfunded accrued pension cost, which are based on the same assumptions, are no more or less precise than measurements of the accumulated and projected benefit obligations. In addition, insurance companies often undertake obligations that will be determined in amount by future events (although not by future compensation levels), and those obligations are recognized. When an insurance contract involves obligations similar to pension obligations (for example, an annuity contract), measurement of those obligations involves some of the same assumptions used in pension accounting. The Board concluded that information about pension cost and obligations based on best estimates of the relevant future events is sufficiently reliable to be useful. The Board recognizes that pension (and other postemployment benefit) liabilities are, as some respondents argued, different from the other recognized liabilities of most employers, but that is because most enterprises other than insurance companies do not ordinarily take on obligations of comparable significance that depend on unknown and uncontrollable future events to define the amount of future sacrifice.

147. Those respondents who challenged the reliability of liability measures based on actuarial calculations generally supported recognition of part of that same liability based on unfunded accrued pension costs. FASB Concepts Statement No. 2, *Qualitative Characteristics of Accounting Information,* defines reliability as a combination of representational faithfulness and verifiability. In the Board's view, the obligation based on the terms of the plan and the unfunded accrued cost are equally difficult to verify, but the former is a more faithful representation of a liability because it is an estimate of a present obligation to make future cash out-

lays as a result of past transactions and events. The unfunded accrued cost does not purport to be a measure of an obligation; it is a residual resulting from an allocation process and, therefore, it cannot be a faithful representation of a liability.

148. A number of respondents argued that a pension liability must be limited either to the amount that would have to be paid on plan termination or to the amount of vested benefits. Those arguments were based on the view that the employer has discretion to avoid any obligation in excess of those limits. Some who preferred no recognition nevertheless agreed that it is difficult to argue that at least unfunded vested benefits are not a liability.

149. The Board concluded that, in the absence of evidence to the contrary, accounting should be based on a going-concern assumption that, as applied to pensions, assumes that the plan will continue in operation and the benefits defined in the plan will be provided. Under that assumption, the employer's probable future sacrifice is not limited to either the termination liability or amounts already vested. The Board believes that the actuarial measurement of the obligation encompasses the probability that some employees will terminate and forfeit nonvested benefits. Benefits that are expected to vest are probable future sacrifices, and the liability in an ongoing plan situation is not limited to vested benefits. However, the Board was influenced by respondents' views of the nature of vested and accumulated benefit obligations in its decision that a reported liability should not be less than the unfunded accumulated benefit obligation. Some Board members were also influenced by arguments that the accumulated benefit obligation, which requires no estimate of future salary levels, is more reliably measurable than is the projected benefit obligation.

The Separation of Funding and Expensing

This Statement reaffirms the usefulness of information based on accrual accounting. Accrual accounting goes beyond cash transactions to provide information about assets, liabilities, and earnings. The Board has concluded, as did the APB in 1966, that net pension cost for a period is not necessarily determined by the amount the employer decides to contribute to the plan for that period. Many factors (including tax considerations and availability of both cash and alternative investment opportunities) that affect funding decisions should not be allowed to dictate accounting results if the accounting is to provide the most useful information.

The conclusion that accounting information on an accrual basis is needed does not mean that accounting information and funding decisions are unrelated. In pensions, as in other areas, managers may use accounting information along with other factors in making financial decisions. Some employers may decide to change their pension funding policies based in part on the new accounting information. Financial statements should provide information that is useful to those who make economic decisions, and the decision to fund a pension plan to a greater or lesser extent is an economic decision. The Board, however, does not have as an objective either an increase or a decrease in the funding level of any particular plan or plans. Neither does the Board believe that the information required by this Statement is the only information needed to make a funding decision or that net periodic pension cost, as defined, is necessarily the appropriate amount for any particular employer's periodic contribution.

81. Opinion 8 stated, ". . . it is important to keep in mind that the annual pension cost to be charged to expense...is not necessarily the same as the amount to be funded for the year" (paragraph 9). However, Opinion 8 allowed any of a range of funding methods to serve as the basis for determining net periodic pension cost, with the result that annual net pension cost and the amount to be funded for the year were commonly the same. This Statement reaffirms the APB's conclusion that funding decisions should not necessarily be used as the basis for accounting recognition of cost. The amount funded (however determined) is, of course, given accounting recognition as a use of cash, but the Board believes this is one of many areas in which information about cash flows alone is not sufficient, and information on an accrual basis is also needed. The question of when to fund the obligation is not an accounting issue. It is a financing question that is properly influenced by many factors (such as tax considerations and the availability of attractive alternative investments) that are unrelated to how the pension obligation is incurred.

What's Old?

In applying accrual accounting to pensions, this Statement retains three fundamental aspects of past pension accounting: *delaying recognition* of certain events, reporting *net cost,* and *offsetting* liabilities and assets. Those three features of practice have shaped financial reporting for pensions for many years, although they have been neither explicitly addressed nor widely understood, and they conflict in some respects with accounting principles applied elsewhere.

1. Delayed Recognition

The *delayed recognition* feature means that changes in the pension obligation (including those resulting from plan amendments) and changes in the value of assets set aside to meet those obligations are not recognized as they occur but are recognized systematically and gradually over subsequent periods. All changes are ultimately recognized except to the extent they may be offset by subsequent changes, but at any point changes that have been identified and quantified await subsequent accounting recognition as net cost components and as liabilities or assets.

Comments

104. The Board acknowledges that the delayed recognition included in this Statement results in excluding the most current and most relevant information from the employer's statement of financial position. That information is, however, included in the disclosures required, and . . . certain liabilities previously omitted will be recognized.

150. Some respondents objected to the accounting proposed in *Preliminary Views* on the grounds that delaying the recognition of gains and losses as part of the measurement of the net pension liability or asset could cause an employer to report a net liability when the fair value of plan assets exceeded the projected benefit obligation, or to report a net asset when the projected benefit obligation exceeded the fair value of plan assets. The Board noted that delayed recognition of the effects of price changes is an inherent part of historical cost accounting and that the problem results from the Board's retention of the delayed recognition and offsetting features of past pension accounting.

2. Net Cost

The *net cost* feature means that the recognized consequences of events and transactions affecting a pension plan are reported as a single net amount in the employer's financial statements. That approach aggregates at least three items that might be reported separately for any other part of an employer's operations: the compensation cost of benefits promised, interest cost resulting from deferred payment of those benefits, and the results of investing what are often significant amounts of assets.

3. Offsetting

The *offsetting* feature means that recognized values of assets contributed to a plan and liabilities for pensions recognized as net pension cost of past periods are shown net in the employer's statement of financial position, even though the liability has not been settled, the assets may be still largely controlled, and substantial risks and rewards associated with both of those amounts are clearly borne by the employer.

What's New?

[Within those three features of practice that are retained by this Statement, the Board has sought to achieve more useful financial reporting through three changes.]

1. Single Method for Cost Recognition and Measurement

This Statement requires a standardized method for measuring net periodic pension cost that is intended to improve comparability and understandability by recognizing the compensation cost of an employee's pension over that employee's approximate service period and by relating that cost more directly to the terms of the plan.

The Board believes that the understandability, comparability, and usefulness of pension information will be improved by narrowing the past range of methods for allocating or attributing the cost of an employee's pension to individual periods of service. The Board was unable to identify differences in circumstances that would make it appropriate for different employers to use fundamentally different accounting methods or for a single employer to use different methods for different plans.

The Board believes that the terms of the plan that define the benefits an employee will receive (the plan's benefit formula) provide the most relevant and reliable indication of how pension cost and pension obligations are incurred. In the absence of convincing evidence that the substance of an exchange is different from that indicated by the agreement between the parties, accounting has traditionally looked to the terms of the agreement as a basis for recording the exchange. Unlike some other methods previously used for pension accounting, the method required by this Statement focuses more directly on the plan's benefit formula as the basis for determining the benefit earned, and therefore the cost incurred, in each individual period.

2. Immediate Recognition of Minimum Liability

This Statement requires immediate recognition of a liability (the minimum liability) when the accumulated benefit obligation exceeds the fair value of plan assets, although it continues to delay recognition of the offsetting amount as an increase in net periodic pension cost.

The Board believes that this Statement represents an improvement in past practices for the reporting of financial position in two ways. First, recognition of the cost of pensions over employees' service periods will result in earlier (but still gradual) recognition of significant liabilities that were reflected more slowly in the past financial statements of some employers. Second, the requirement to recognize a minimum liability limits the extent to which the delayed recognition of plan amendments and losses in net periodic cost can result in omission of certain liabilities from statements of financial position.

Recognition of a measure of at least the minimum pension obligation as a liability is not a new idea. Accounting Research Bulletin No. 47, *Accounting for Costs of Pension Plans*, published in 1956, stated that "as a minimum, the accounts and financial statements should reflect accruals which equal the present worth, actuarially calculated, of pension commitments to employees to the extent that pension rights have vested in the employees, reduced, in the case of the balance sheet, by any accumulated trusteed funds or annuity contracts purchased." Opinion 8 required that "if the company has a legal obligation for pension cost in excess of amounts paid or accrued, the excess should be shown in the balance sheet as both a liability and a deferred charge."

The Board believes that an employer with an unfunded pension obligation has a liability and an employer with an overfunded pension obligation has an asset. The most relevant and reliable information available about that liability or asset is based on the fair value of plan assets and a measure of the present value of the obligation using current, explicit assumptions. The Board concluded, however, that recognition in financial statements of those amounts in their entirety would be too great a change from past practice. Some Board members were also influenced by concerns about the reliability of measures of the obligation.

3. Expanded Disclosures

This Statement requires expanded disclosures intended to provide more complete and more current information than can be practically incorporated in financial statements at the present time.

The Board believes that users of financial reports need information beyond that previously disclosed to be able to assess the status of an employer's pension arrangements and their effects on the employer's financial position and results of operations. Most respondents agreed, and this Statement requires certain disclosures not previously required.

This Statement requires disclosure of the components of net pension cost and of the projected benefit obligation. One of the factors that has made pension information difficult to understand is that past practice and terminology combined elements that are different in substance and effect into net amounts. Although the Board agreed to retain from past pension accounting practice the basic features of reporting net cost and offsetting liabilities and assets, the Board believes that disclosure of the components will significantly assist users in understanding the economic events that have occurred. Those disclosures also make it easier to understand why reported amounts change from period to period, especially when a large cost or asset is offset by a large revenue or liability to produce a relatively small net reported amount.

106. The components of net periodic pension cost and the net funded status of the obligation are among the more significant disclosure requirements of this Statement. One of the factors that made pension information difficult to understand was that past practice and terminology combined elements that are different in substance into net amounts (assets with liabilities and revenues and gains with expenses and losses). Although the Board agreed to retain from past practice the basic features of reporting net cost and offsetting liabilities and assets, the Board believes that disclosure of the components will significantly assist users in understanding the economic events that have occurred. Those disclosures also make it easier to understand why reported amounts change from period to period, especially when a large cost or asset is offset by a large revenue or liability to produce a relatively small net reported amount.

Costs Components: Cost as Separate from Financing

16. Net periodic pension cost has often been viewed as a single homogeneous amount, but in fact it is made up of several *components* that reflect different aspects of the employer's financial arrangements as well as the cost of benefits earned by employees. The cost of a benefit can be determined without regard to how the employer decides to finance the plan. The **service cost component** of net periodic pension cost is the **actuarial present value** of benefits attributed by the plan's benefit formula to services rendered by employees during the period. The service cost component is conceptually the same for an unfunded plan, a plan with minimal funding, and a well-funded plan. The other components of net periodic pension cost are **interest cost** (interest on the **projected benefit obligation,** which is a discounted amount), **actual return on plan assets, amortization** of **unrecognized prior service cost**, and **gain or loss**. Both the return on plan assets and interest cost components are in substance financial items rather than employee compensation costs.

Prior Service Cost: Plan Initiation and Amendments Require Future Recognition

24. **Plan amendments** (including initiation of a plan) often include provisions that grant increased benefits based on services rendered in prior periods. Because plan amendments are granted with the expectation that the employer will realize economic benefits in future periods, this Statement does not require the cost of providing such **retroactive benefits** (that is, **prior service cost**) to be included in net periodic pension cost entirely in the year of the amendment but provides for recognition during the future service periods of those employees active at the date of the amendment who are expected to receive benefits under the plan.

Gains and Losses: The First Accounting Standard to Recognize Unrealized Values?

29. **Gains and losses** are changes in the amount of either the projected benefit obligation or plan assets resulting from experience different from that assumed and from changes in assumptions. This Statement does not distinguish between those sources of gains and losses. Gains and losses include amounts that have been realized, for example by sale of a security, as well as amounts that are unrealized. Because gains and losses may reflect refinements in estimates as well as real changes in economic values and because some gains in one period may be offset by losses in another or vice versa, this Statement does not require recognition of gains and losses as components of net pension cost of the period in which they arise.

Explicit Assumptions: Unbundling of Assumptions Required for Accurate Financial Analysis

Findings

43. Each significant assumption used shall reflect the best estimate solely with respect to that individual assumption. All assumptions shall presume that the plan will continue in effect in the absence of evidence that it will not continue.

Comments

191. This Statement requires that each significant assumption used in determining the pension information reflect the best estimate of the plan's future experience solely with respect to that assumption. That method of selecting assumptions is referred to as an *explicit approach.* An *implicit approach,* on the other hand, means that two or more assumptions do not individually represent the best estimate of the plan's future experience with respect to those assumptions, but the aggregate effect of their combined use is presumed to be approximately the same as that of an explicit approach. The Board believes that an explicit approach results in more useful information regarding (a) components of the pension benefit obligation and net periodic pension cost, (b) changes in the pension benefit obligation, and (c) the choice of significant assumptions used to determine the pension measurements. The Board also believes that the explicit approach is more understandable. Most respondents who addressed the question agreed.

Interest Rates and Projected Wages

195. Most respondents focused their comments on assumed discount rates and compensation levels. Those are generally cited as the assumptions that have the greatest effect on measures of pension cost and benefit obligations, and they are related because both are affected by some of the same economic factors (such as the expected future rates of inflation). Some respondents also believe those assumptions (particularly the discount rates) are less likely than others to reflect real differences among plans.

Assumed Discount ("Settlement") Rate: Pension "Bonds" Require Market Rates

Findings

44. Assumed discount rates shall reflect the rates at which the pension benefits could be effectively settled. It is appropriate in estimating those rates to look to available information about rates implicit in current prices of annuity contracts that could be used to effect settlement of the obligation (including information about available annuity rates currently published by the Pension Benefit Guaranty Corporation). In making those estimates, employers may also look to rates of return on high-quality fixed-income investments currently available and expected to be available during the period to maturity of the pension benefits.

Assumed discount rates are used in measurements of the projected, accumulated, and vested benefit obligations and the service and interest cost components of net periodic pension cost.

Comments

196. The Board considered a requirement that all employers use common benchmark discount rates, such as those published by the Pension Benefit Guaranty Corporation (PBGC). One reason for that consideration was its concern that rates previously used for disclosure purposes varied among employers over an unreasonable range. In spite of that concern, however, the Board concluded that requiring use of benchmark rates would be inappropriate, in part because no readily available rates seemed fully suitable. Instead, the Board decided that this Statement should describe more clearly the objective of selecting the discount rates with the expectation that a narrower range of rates used would result. Although the Board concluded that it should not require use of PBGC rates, it noted that certain of those rates, as currently determined, are one source of readily available information that might be considered in estimating the discount rates required by this Statement.

197. The Board notes that discount rates are used to measure the current period's service cost component and to determine the interest cost component of net periodic pension cost. Both of those uses relate to the liability side of pension accounting. From an accounting (as opposed to funding) perspective, they have nothing to do with plan assets. The same assumptions are needed for an unfunded plan.

199. Interest rates vary depending on the duration of investments; for example, U.S. treasury bills, 7-year bonds, and 30-year bonds have different interest rates. Thus, the weighted-average discount rate (interest rate) inherent in the prices of annuities (or a dedicated bond portfolio) will vary depending on the length of time remaining until individual benefit payment dates. A plan covering only retired employees would be expected to have significantly different discount rates from one covering a work force of 30-year-olds. The disclosures required by this Statement regarding components of the pension benefit obligation will be more representationally faithful if individual discount rates applicable to various benefit deferral periods are selected. A properly weighted average rate can be used for aggregate computations such as the interest cost component of net pension cost for the period.

200. An insurance company deciding on the price of an annuity contract will consider the rates of return available to it for investing the premium received and the rates of return expected to be available to it for reinvestment of future cash flows from the ini-

tial investment during the period until benefits are payable. That consideration is indicative of a relationship between rates inherent in the prices of annuity contracts and rates available in investment markets. The Board concluded that it would be appropriate for employers to consider that relationship and information about investment rates in estimating the discount rates required for application of this Statement.

201. Some believe that year-to-year changes in pension information as a result of changes in assumed discount rates should be avoided to the maximum extent possible. In their view, some averaging technique should be used to smooth potential year-to-year changes so that assumed rates are changed only when it is apparent that the long-term trend has changed. The Board recognizes that long-term interest rates must be considered in determining appropriate assumed discount rates. However, it rejects the view that material changes in long-term rates should be ignored solely to avoid adjusting assumed discount rates.

Projected Wages and Salaries (to Include Projected Inflation)

Findings

46. The service cost component of net periodic pension cost and the projected benefit obligation shall reflect future compensation levels to the extent that the pension benefit formula defines pension benefits wholly or partially as a function of future compensation levels (that is, for a final-pay plan or a career-average-pay plan). Future increases for which a present commitment exists as described in paragraph 41 shall be similarly considered. Assumed compensation levels shall reflect an estimate of the actual future compensation levels of the individual employees involved, including future changes attributed to general price levels, productivity, seniority, promotion, and other factors. All assumptions shall be consistent to the extent that each reflects expectations of the same future economic conditions, such as future rates of inflation. Measuring service cost and the projected benefit obligation based on estimated future compensation levels entails considering indirect effect, such as changes under existing law in social security benefits or benefit limitations that would affect benefits provided by the plan.

Comments

202. The Board also addressed assumed compensation levels and concluded that they should (a) reflect the best estimate of actual future compensation levels for the individuals involved and (b) be consistent with assumed discount rates to the extent that both

incorporate expectations of the same future economic conditions.

222. Some respondents opposed disclosure of assumed future compensation levels because providing that information to employees could affect labor negotiations. The Board concluded that the information is likely to be available to labor negotiators from other sources and that the usefulness of the information to financial statement users justifies its disclosure.

Future Compensation Levels, Wages, and Inflation

138. In response to the Exposure Draft and earlier documents issued as part of this project, some respondents argued that, based on the definition of a liability, pension benefits dependent on future increases in compensation cannot be a present obligation and, therefore, the liability measurement should be based only on actual compensation experience to date. They also noted that if the plan were terminated or if an employee with vested benefits did not render future services, the employer's obligation would be limited to amounts based on compensation to date.

139. Among those respondents who argued that obligations dependent on future compensation increases are excluded by the definition of a liability, very few were prepared to accept a measure of net periodic pension cost that was based only on compensation to date. The Board notes that under the double entry accounting system, recognition of an accrued cost as a charge against operations requires recognition of a liability for that accrued cost. Thus, excluding future compensation from the liability and including it in periodic pension cost are conflicting positions.

140. The Board also considered the arguments of respondents who noted that it would be inconsistent (a) to measure pension cost or the obligation ignoring future compensation increases that reflect inflation and (b) to use discount rates that reflect expected inflation rates in making those measurements. In this view, discounting a benefit that does not include the effects of inflation amounts to removing the effect of inflation twice. Those respondents suggested that the effects of inflation should either be considered for both purposes or be eliminated from both. The latter approach would involve use of inflation-free (or "real") discount rates. The Board considered that possibility but concluded that the use of explicit rates observable in actual transactions ("nominal rates") would be more understandable and would present fewer implementation problems, as noted below.

141. The Board notes that at present few private pension plans in the U.S. provide benefits that are increased automatically after an employee retires based on either compensation levels or inflation. If

future compensation increases were incorporated *implicitly* by reducing the discount rates used to compute the present value of the benefit obligation, projected benefit increases during the postretirement period would be incorporated automatically at the same time unless different (explicit) discount rates were used for those periods. Using inflation-adjusted (implicit) discount rates would, in effect, anticipate postretirement benefit increases, which would be inconsistent with the Board's decision that future plan amendments should not be anticipated unless there is a present substantive commitment to make such amendments.

142. Other respondents disagreed with the argument that a measurement approach based only on current compensation would be inconsistent with use of nominal interest rates (paragraph 140). They argued that the assumed discount rates should reflect the rates at which the obligation could be settled—for example, by purchasing annuities or perhaps by dedicating a portfolio of securities. They argued that future interest rates (and therefore forecasts of future inflation) are irrelevant.

143. The Board concluded that the pension obligation created when employees render services is a liability under the definition in Concepts Statement 3. That definition, however, does not resolve the issue of whether the measurement of that liability should consider future compensation levels. After considering respondents' views, both practical and conceptual, the Board concluded that estimated future compensation levels should be considered in measuring the service cost component and the projected benefit obligation if the plan's benefit formula incorporates them. The Board perceives a difference between an employer's promise to pay a benefit of 1 percent of an employee's *final* pay and a promise to pay an employee a fixed amount that happens to equal 1 percent of the employee's *current pay*. Ignoring the future variable (final pay) on which the obligation in the first case is based would result in not recognizing that difference. The Board also concluded that the accumulated benefit obligation, which is measured *without* considering future compensation levels, should continue to be part of the required disclosure and should be the basis on which to decide whether a minimum liability needs to be recognized.

Suggested Disclosure: What Was Left Out That Shouldn't Have Been

Findings

223. The Exposure Draft would have required the following disclosures in addition to those noted in the preceding paragraphs.

a. The ratio of net periodic pension cost to covered payroll.
c. Information about the cashflows of the plan separately showing employer contributions, other contributions, and benefits paid during the period.
d. The amount of plan assets classified by major asset category.
f, g. The change in the projected benefit obligation, [and service cost and interest rate component of net periodic pension cost cost, (*sic*)] that would result from a one-percentage point change in (1) the assumed discount rate, and (2) the assumed rate of compensation increase.

Comments

224. Those disclosures had been suggested by respondents to previous documents issued as part of this project and the Board had concluded in the Exposure Draft that they would provide useful information and would not be unduly costly to provide. However, many respondents to the Exposure Draft commented that the volume of the proposed disclosures was too great. The Board agreed and concluded that the disclosures described in the preceding paragraph should not be required. The Board believes those disclosures are relatively less useful or (in the case of the last two items listed) relatively more costly than the disclosures required by this Statement. The Board also believes it would be appropriate for employers to consider disclosing those items if they decide to disclose more information about pension plans than the minimum required by this Statement, for example, because their plans are large relative to their overall operations.

Fair Value of Plan Assets: All Assets Carried at Market

Comments

117. The Board concluded that plan investments should be measured at fair value for purposes of this Statement (except as provided in paragraph 30 for purposes of determining the extent of delayed recognition of asset gains and losses). Fair value provides the most relevant information that can be provided for assessing both the plan's ability to pay benefits as they come due without further contributions from the employer and the future contributions necessary to provide for benefits already promised to employees. The same reasons led to a similar decision in Statement 35.

118. The Board recognizes that there may be practical problems in determining the fair value of certain types of assets. Notwith-

standing those difficulties, the Board believes that the relevance of fair value of pension assets is so great as to override objections to its use based on difficulty of measurement. In addition, most pension assets are invested in marketable securities and are priced regularly for investment management purposes.

119. The Board considered the use of an actuarial value of assets instead of fair value. A number of different methods of determining actuarial asset values are available, generally based on some kind of average of past market values or on long-range projections of market values intended to eliminate short-term market fluctuations. The Board concluded that those methods produce information about the assets that is less relevant and more difficult to understand than fair value. Specifically, if an actuarial asset value were used to measure the minimum net liability defined in paragraph 36, it would sometimes result in recognition of a liability when the fair value of the assets exceeds the obligation, and at other times it would result in no recognition when a net unfunded obligation exists based on the fair value.

120. The Board understands that measuring investments at fair value could introduce volatility into the financial statements as a result of short-term changes in fair values. Some respondents described that volatility as meaningless or even misleading, particularly in view of the long-run nature of the pension commitment and the fact that pension investments are often held for long periods, thus providing the opportunity for some gains or losses to reverse. The Board also recognizes that some changes in the fair value of investments are related to some changes in the measurement of the pension liability because they are affected by the same economic factors.

For example, a change in the level of interest rates would be expected to affect the liability by changing the discount rates and would also affect the fair value of at least some types of investments (such as bonds). In many cases such fluctuations in the pension benefit obligation and in the fair value of plan investments would tend to offset each other.

121. The Board concluded that the difference between the actual return on assets and the expected return on assets could be recognized in net periodic pension cost on a delayed basis. Those effects include the gains and losses themselves. That conclusion was based on (a) the probability that at least some gains would be offset by subsequent losses and vice versa and (b) respondents' arguments that immediate recognition would produce unacceptable volatility and would be inconsistent with the present accounting model.

123. The Board discussed whether securities of the employer held by the plan should be eliminated from plan assets and from the employer's financial statements as, in effect, treasury securi-

ties. The Board concluded that elimination would be impractical and might be inappropriate absent a decision that the financial statements of the plan should be consolidated with those of the employer, but that disclosure of the amount of such securities held would be appropriate and should be required.

Accommodating Financial Statement Impact and Subsequent Volatility

Transition Asset (or Liability) to Be Amortized: A 16-Year Boost in Reported Earnings!

Findings

77. For a defined benefit plan, an employer shall determine as of the measurement date (paragraph 52) for the beginning of the fiscal year in which this Statement is first applied, the amounts of (a) the projected benefit obligation and (b) the fair value of plan assets plus previously recognized unfunded accrued pension cost or less previously recognized prepaid pension cost. The difference between those two amounts, whether it represents an unrecognized net obligation (and loss or cost) or an unrecognized net asset (and gain), shall be amortized on a straight-line basis over the average remaining service period of employees expected to receive benefits under the plan, except that, (a) if the average remaining service period is less than 15 years, the employer may elect to use a 15-year period, and (b) if all or almost all of a plan's participants are inactive, the employer shall use the inactive participants' average remaining life expectancy period. That same amortization shall also be used to recognize any unrecognized net obligation related to a defined contribution plan.

Comments

256. The Board continues to believe that transition is a practical matter and that a major objective of transition is to minimize the cost and to mitigate the disruption involved, to the extent that is possible without unduly compromising the objective of enhancing the ability of financial statements to provide useful information. The transition problem in this Statement is different from some others in several respects. The unrecognized net obligation or net asset described in paragraph 77 is the net total of several components: (a) unrecognized costs of past retroactive plan amendments, (b) unrecognized net gain or loss from previous periods, and (c) the cumulative effect of past use of accounting

principles different from those in this Statement. If those components could be treated separately, it would be consistent with
other provisions of this Statement to treat the last component as
the effect of an accounting change (and to recognize it when this
Statement is first applied), but prospective accounting (or delayed recognition) of the first two components is continued by
this Statement. As a practical matter, the Board is convinced that
it is effectively impossible, at least in many cases, to identify those
components separately. Accordingly, the Board concluded that
the single method of transition required by this Statement should
be used.

Volatility and Delayed Recognition of Gains and Losses: The Rationale for Impacting Current Earnings with Events from the Past

173. Gains and losses, sometimes called actuarial gains and losses,
are changes in either the value of the projected benefit obligation
or the fair value of plan assets arising from changes in assumptions and from experience different from that incorporated in
the assumptions. Gains and losses include actual returns on assets
greater than or less than the expected rate of return.

174. A number of respondents to the Exposure Draft and earlier
documents issued as part of this project expressed concern about
the volatility of an unfunded or overfunded pension obligation
measure and the practical effects of incorporating that volatility
into financial statements. The Board does not believe that reporting volatility per se is undesirable. If a financial measure purports to represent a phenomenon that is volatile, the measure
must show that volatility or it will not be representationally faithful. The Board also notes that the volatility of the unfunded or
overfunded obligation may be less than some expect if the explicit assumptions used in the valuation of the obligation are
changed to reflect fully the changes in interest rate structures
that affect the fair values of plan assets, because changes in the
assets may tend to offset changes in the obligation.

175. However, in the case of pension liabilities, volatility may not
be entirely a faithful representation of changes in the status of
the obligation (the phenomenon represented). It may also reflect
an unavoidable inability to predict accurately the future events
that are anticipated in making period-to-period measurements.
That is, the difference in periodic measures of the pension liability (and therefore the funded status of the plan) results partly
from the inability to predict accurately for a period (or over several periods) compensation levels, length of employee service,
mortality, retirement ages, and other pertinent events. As a re-

sult, actual experience often differs significantly from that which was estimated and that leads to changes in the estimates themselves. Recognizing the effects of revisions in estimates in full in the period in which they occur may result in volatility of the reported amounts that does not reflect actual changes in the funded status of the plan in that period.

176. Some respondents believe that some of the volatility is representationally faithful, for example, gains and losses that result from measuring investments at fair value. They also believe, however, that recognizing those gains and losses, and especially including them in earnings of the current period, would be inconsistent with the present accounting model applicable to employers' financial statements. They argued that such a major departure from the present model should not be made in this project.

177. The Board considered those views and concluded that it should not require that gains and losses be recognized immediately as a component of net periodic pension cost. Accordingly, this Statement provides for recognition of gains and losses prospectively over future periods to the extent they are not offset by subsequent changes. Based on the concerns expressed by many respondents to the Exposure Draft, the Board also concluded that the effects of changes in the fair value of plan assets, including the indirect effect of those changes on the return-on-assets component of net periodic pension cost, should be recognized on a basis that reduces the volatility more effectively than that proposed in the Exposure Draft. The Board believes that both the extent of volatility reduction and the mechanism adopted to effect it are essentially practical issues without conceptual basis. The Board does not believe that the market-related value of assets used in this Statement as a device to reduce the volatility of net periodic pension cost is as relevant as the fair value required for other purposes.

179. This Statement requires use of an assumption, described as the expected long-term rate of return on plan assets, and of a market-related value of assets to calculate the expected return on plan assets. Actual returns greater than or less than the expected return are afforded delayed recognition. The Board anticipates that the expected return on assets defined in this Statement will be less volatile than either the actual return on assets or the return on assets that would have been recognized based on the Exposure Draft. The Board noted, however, that an expected long-term return-on-assets rate significantly below the rate at which the obligations could be settled implies that settlement would be economically advantageous.

180. The Board believes the approach required in this Statement has several advantages. First, it is very similar mechanically to

past practices intended to achieve similar objectives. As a result, it should be easier for those familiar with the details of past practices to understand and apply. Second, it avoids the use of discount rates relevant primarily to the pension obligation as part of a calculation related to plan assets. As a result, it reflects more clearly than did the Exposure Draft the Board's basic conclusion that information about a pension plan is more understandable if asset-related or financial aspects of the arrangement are distinguished from the liability-related and compensation cost aspects.

182. The Board also considered a number of respondents' suggestions that would have further reduced the volatility of net periodic pension cost by using a discount rate that would change less often and less significantly than the rate described in paragraph 44. Those respondents were primarily concerned that the service component of net cost would be volatile because of changes in the discount rate assumption. The Board concluded that the service component is the cost of benefits attributed to service in the current period and should reflect prices of that period. The Board noted that accounting generally recognizes the current prices rather than past or average prices in recording transactions of the current period. The Board also noted that the service component under the provisions of this Statement is essentially the same as net pension cost determined under the provisions of Opinion 8 for a plan that purchases annuities annually for all benefits attributed to service of that year.

Appendix **2**

Employer's Accounting for Postretirement Benefits (Other than Pensions): Financial Accounting Standards Board—Exposure Draft

[At the time of this writing, only the Exposure Draft is available to review the FASB's intended accounting standards for Postretirement Benefits Other Than Pensions. We have excerpted the following material with our comments. While such benefits as non-pension plan-related life insurance and legal services are contemplated, the overwhelming issue is postretirement medical benefits.[1]]

Scope

6. This Statement is applicable to all postretirement benefits expected to be provided by an employer to current and future **retirees** (including those employees deemed to be on a disability retirement), their beneficiaries, and covered dependents, pursuant to the terms of an employer's undertaking to provide those benefits. Postretirement benefits include, but are not limited to, postretirement health care, which is thought to be the most significant in terms of cost and prevalence; life insurance provided to retirees outside a pension plan; and other welfare benefits such as tuition assistance, day care, legal services, and housing subsidies provided after retirement. Often those benefits are in the form of a reimbursement or direct payment to providers for the cost of specified services as the need for those services arises, but they may also include benefits payable as a lump sum, such as death benefits.

[The proposed standards parallel FAS-87 very closely. We therefore concentrate on those aspects of the proposal that differ either in scope

---

[1]Source: Financial Accounting Standards Board. Used with permission. This reprint does not include the appendices to FASB—Exposure Draft. These appendices are an integral part of the document.

or approach from accounting for pensions. The numbered paragraphs are as used in the Exposure Draft.]

The Need for a New Standard

[The need for a new standard rests on these essential arguments:

1. The liabilities are material (very material).

2. Pay-as-you-go accounting is inadequate.

3. ". . . measurement of the obligation and accrual of the cost based on best estimates are superior to implying, by a failure to accrue, that no obligation exists prior to the payment of benefits." (See below.)

In short . . .]

2. Most employers have accounted for postretirement benefits on a pay-as-you-go (cash) basis. As the prevalence and magnitude of employers' promises to provide those benefits have increased, there has been increased concern about the failure of financial reporting to identify the financial effects of those promises.

Summary

This proposed Statement would establish accounting standards for employers' accounting for postretirement benefits other than pensions (hereinafter referred to as postretirement benefits). Although it would apply to all forms of postretirement benefits, this proposed Statement focuses principally on postretirement health care benefits. It would significantly change the prevalent current practice of accounting for postretirement benefits on a pay-as-you-go (cash) basis by requiring accrual, during the years that the employee renders the necessary service, of the expected cost of providing those benefits to an employee and the employee's beneficiaries and covered dependents.

The Board's conclusions in this proposed Statement result from the view that a defined postretirement benefit plan sets forth the terms of an exchange between the employer and the employee. In exchange for services provided by the employee, the employer promises to provide, in addition to current wages and other benefits, health and other welfare benefits during the employee's retirement period. It follows from that view that postretirement benefits are not gratuities but are part of an employee's compensation for services rendered. Since payment is deferred, the benefits are a type of deferred compensation. The employer's obligation for that compensation is incurred as employees rendered the services necessary to earn their post-retirement benefits.

The ability to measure the obligation for postretirement health care benefits and the recognition of that obligation have been the subject of controversy. The Board believes that measurement of the obligation and accrual of the cost based on best estimates are superior to implying, by a failure to accrue, that no obligation exists prior to the payment of benefits. The Board believes that failure to recognize any obligation prior to its payment impairs the usefulness and integrity of the employer's financial statements.

The Board's objectives in issuing this proposed Statement are to improve employers' financial reporting for postretirement benefits in the following manner:

a. To enhance the relevance and representational faithfulness of the employer's reported results of operations by recognizing net periodic postretirement benefit cost as employees render the services necessary to earn their postretirement benefits, pursuant to the terms of the plan

b. To enhance the relevance and representational faithfulness of the employer's statement of financial position by including a measure of the obligation to provide postretirement benefits based on the terms of the underlying plan

c. To enhance the ability of users of the employer's financial statements to understand the extent and effects of the employer's undertaking to provide postretirement benefits to its employees

d. To improve the understandability and comparability of amounts reported by requiring employers with similar plans to use the same method to measure their accumulated postretirement benefit obligation and the related cost of the postretirement benefits.

Footnote Disclosure versus Balance Sheet Recognition: Footnote Status Isn't Good Enough

144. Some agree that better information about the cost of and obligation for postretirement benefits is needed but argue that the information would be just as useful if it were disclosed in the footnotes. In the Board's view, it is important that elements that qualify for recognition be recognized in the basic financial statements. Footnote disclosure is not an adequate substitute for recognition. The argument that the information is equally useful regardless of how it is presented could be applied to any financial statement element, but the usefulness and integrity of financial statements are impaired by each omission of an element that qualifies for recognition. Further, although the "equal useful-

ness" argument may be valid for some sophisticated users, it may not hold for all or even most users. Those who assert that footnote disclosure or recognition would be equally useful, but argue only for disclosure, must believe that recognition would have different consequences.

The Nature of the Exchange

3. The Board views a **postretirement benefit plan** as a deferred compensation arrangement whereby an employer promises to exchange future benefits for employees' current services. Since the obligation to provide benefits arises as employees render the services necessary to earn the benefits pursuant to the terms of the **plan,** the Board believes that the cost of providing the benefits should be recognized over those employee service periods.

The Reliability of Measurement Issue

The Board is sensitive to concerns about the reliability of measurements of the postretirement health care benefit obligation. The Board recognizes that limited historical data about per capita claims cost are available and that actuarial practice in this area is still developing. The Board has taken those factors into consideration in its decisions to delay the effective date for the proposed standard and to emphasize disclosure while phasing in recognition of the transition obligation in an employer's statement of financial position. However, the Board believes that those factors are insufficient reason not to utilize accrual accounting for postretirement benefits in financial reporting. With increased experience, the reliability of measures of the obligation and cost should improve.

124. Some have argued that the uncertainties inherent in quantifying the obligation for postretirement benefits lead to the conclusion that the measurements are not sufficiently reliable for recognition in financial statements. They would prefer to disclose rather than recognize that obligation. The Board does not find those arguments persuasive. The Board concluded that it is possible for employers to produce an estimate of that obligation that is sufficiently reliable and relevant to justify recognition in financial statements as well as disclosure in footnotes. The Board expects that with experience, the reliability of the measurement will be enhanced. The Board concluded that employers' current practice of not recognizing their postretirement benefit obliga-

tions results in less reliable financial statements and impairs the usefulness and integrity of those financial statements.

141. Paragraph 46 of Concepts Statement 6 acknowledges that the effects of economic events are often uncertain and that the existence and amount of items need not be certain for them to qualify as assets and liabilities. Estimates and approximations are commonplace in financial statements. Paragraph 74 of Concepts Statement 5 states that "relevance should be evaluated in the context of the principal objective of financial reporting: providing information that is useful in making rational investment, credit, and similar decisions." Paragraph 59 of Concepts Statement 2 states that the reliability of a measurement of accounting information is dependent on the extent to which users can depend on it to represent the economic conditions or events that it purports to represent. That Concepts Statement acknowledges that this is seldom a clear choice; rather, the issue is whether the accounting information is so relevant that some allowance ought to be made for some lack of reliability because the information provides a better representation of economic conditions than would be portrayed without the information.

The Liability ("Accumulated Postretirement Benefit Obligation")

[Postretirement medical plan provisions ("indenture") are much less clear in providing a basis for accruing costs. The provision focus primarily on eligibility requirements, and the scope of benefits provided at eligibility. Hence the Board has chosen eligibility as the focus rather than retirement age as the benchmark date for liability determination.

Where benefits are pay-related, projected future pay is automatically included in the measurement of *accumulated* obligation. (There is no "projected" obligation in this standard—no counterpart to exclusion and inclusion of future pay as in FAS-87.)]

149. Since the accumulated benefit obligation defined by Statement 87 excludes assumed salary progression, the accumulated benefit obligation for a pay-related pension plan has no counterpart in this Statement. The Board concluded that it would be more confusing to define a fourth measure of a benefit obligation (in addition to the expected, accumulated, and vested postretirement benefit obligations) under this Statement to compare with the accumulated benefit obligation for pay-related plans under Statement 87 than to measure the ac-

cumulated benefit obligation for those plans differently under the two Statements.[1]

[The liability is measured to include only retirees and those active employees currently eligible to receive full postretirement benefits.]

133. Liabilities are defined in paragraph 35 of FASB Concepts Statement No. 6, *Elements of Financial Statements,* as "probable future sacrifices of economic benefits arising from present obligations of a particular entity to transfer assets or provide services to other entities in the future as a result of past transactions or events" (footnote references omitted).

135. An employer that promises to provide postretirement benefits almost certainly has assumed a responsibility to make future payments because at least some of the present employees will receive those benefits in the future. Measurements of the postretirement benefit obligation considers the likelihood that some employees will work to or beyond the date eligibility for some or all of the postretirement benefits is attained, while others will terminate prior to that date and forego any right to postretirement benefits.

136. The second characteristic of a liability is that "the duty or responsibility obligates a particular entity, leaving it little or no discretion to avoid the future sacrifice" (Concepts Statement 6, paragraph 36). Paragraph 36 also states that "...although most liabilities rest generally on a foundation of legal rights and duties, existence of a legally enforceable claim is not a prerequisite for an obligation to qualify as a liability if for other reasons the entity has the duty or responsibility to pay cash, to transfer other assets, or to provide services to another entity." Case law has not been unequivocal concerning the legal enforceability or lack thereof of all promises to provide postretirement benefits, although legal enforceability of certain claims has been demonstrated. However, in accordance with Concepts Statement 6, the Board has looked beyond the legal status of the promise to consider whether the liability is effectively binding on the employer because of past practices, social or moral sanctions, or customs.

137. An entity is not obligated to sacrifice assets in the future if it can avoid the future sacrifice at its discretion without significant penalty. The penalty to the employer need not be in the form of

---

[1]Unlike Statement 87, this Statement includes salary progression in the measurement of the accumulated postretirement benefit obligation of a pay-related plan. Statement 87 refers to the measurement that excludes salary progression as the accumulated benefit obligation and the measurement that includes salary progression as the projected benefit obligation.

another liability but could be in the form of a reduction in the value of assets. Concepts Statement 6, paragraph 203, illustrates that notion as follows: "The example of an entity that binds itself to pay employees vacation pay or year-end bonuses by paying them every year even though it is not contractually bound to do so and has not announced a policy to do so has already been noted. . . . It could refuse to pay only by risking substantial employee-relations problems." The Board concluded that in the absence of evidence to the contrary, an employer is presumed to have accepted responsibility to provide the promised benefits. Thus, for postretirement benefit arrangements, the Board concluded that accounting should be based on the assumption that the plan will continue and that the benefits promised by the employer will be provided.

138. The third characteristic of a liability is that "the transaction or other event obligating the entity has already happened" (Concepts Statement 6, paragraph 36). This characteristic is met when the employee renders service in exchange for the future benefits. The Board concluded that, conceptually, compensation cost should be recognized in the period in which it is earned under the plan—that is, when the employee renders the required service, not when the need for the benefit arises (which is factored into measurement of the obligation). An objective of this Statement is to recognize the compensation cost of an employee's postretirement benefits over the employee's credited service period, even though the complexity of the postretirement benefit arrangement and the uncertainty of the amount and timing of the future payments may preclude complete recognition of the precise postretirement benefit cost and obligation over that period.

Minimum Liability

Findings

55. This Statement requires that an employer's statement of financial position report a liability for postretirement benefits that is the greater of (a) the **accrued postretirement benefit cost** or (b) the accumulated postretirement benefit obligation for fully eligible plan participants in excess of the fair value of the plan assets (minimum liability). That requirement is intended to limit the extent to which the delayed recognition of any transition obligation, prior service cost, and losses can result in omission of a liability for those participants' benefits from an employer's statement of financial position.

Comments

268. The Board concluded that, similar to Statement 87, a minimum liability should be prescribed to limit the extent to which delayed recognition of the transition obligation, plan amendments, and losses can result in omission of liabilities from an employer's statement of financial position. The Board considered defining the minimum liability as the unfunded accumulated postretirement benefit obligation for retirees or for retirees and other fully eligible plan participants. To include other active plan participants in this measurement would have negated most of the delayed balance sheet recognition features of this Statement (except gains and negative prior service cost). Retirees have completed all terms of the contract, including retirement, that entitle them to the benefits. Fully eligible plan participants have completed the necessary age, service, or age and service requirements of the contract to become entitled to the benefits when a specified event occurs or as the need for those benefits arises after retirement; no additional service is required to be rendered for a plan participant to be entitled to receive benefits for which eligibility has been attained.

269. The Board concluded that the minimum liability required by this Statement should be defined as the unfunded accumulated postretirement benefit obligation for retirees and other fully eligible plan participants. The Board concluded that measurement represents a threshold below which the recognized liability would not be sufficiently representationally faithful. The minimum liability defined by this Statement is also consistent with attributing benefits to the date full eligibility for those benefits is attained. For purposes of determining the minimum liability, plan assets are measured at fair value, and all plan assets are attributed to the satisfaction of the accumulated postretirement benefit obligation for retirees and other fully eligible plan participants. This measure of a minimum liability differs from the minimum liability under Statement 87 because this Statement defines the accumulated postretirement benefit obligation differently (as discussed in footnote 8 and in paragraphs 148–150) and because it excludes active plan participants who are not yet fully eligible for benefits from measurement of the minimum liability (as discussed in paragraph 268).

Funding: Assets and Taxes

[The FASB highlighted several "issues that the Board believes are the most significant and on which the Board would like to receive comments." Of particular interest to us was the single issue selected with respect to plan assets. Should they be treated as offsetting reported liabilities and costs or (presumably) reported among other corporate assets and income?]

Plan Assets

> *Issue 11:* Should plan assets be defined and measured in the same way pension plan assets are defined and measured (Statement 87)? Should plan assets be considered to offset the accumulated postretirement benefit obligation for purposes of determining amounts reported in the employer's statement of financial position? Should the return on the investment of those plan assets offset postretirement benefit cost for a period?

Taxes

[The Board recognizes that in the absence of a tax deductible vehicle for funding postretirement medical obligations, that the expected rate of return on plan assets must be net of expected taxes.]

Findings

> 42. For a funded plan, the actual return on plan assets shall be determined based on the **fair value** of plan assets (refer to paragraphs 61 and 62) at the beginning and end of the period, adjusted for contributions and benefit payments. If the plan is a taxable entity, the actual return on plan assets shall reflect the tax expense or benefit for the period determined in accordance with Statement 96. If the return on plan assets is taxable to the employer, no provision for taxes shall be included in the actual return on plan assets.

Comments

> 260. Unlike most pension plans, the return on postretirement benefit plan assets may be subject to income tax because of the lack of tax-exempt vehicles for funding those benefits. Generally, even if postretirement benefit plan assets are restricted and segregated within a trust, the income generated by those assets is taxable. If the plan has taxable income, the assessed tax will reduce the returns available for payment of benefits and reinvestment. The Board concluded that when the plan is taxed as a separate entity on the return on *plan assets* (as defined herein), the expected long-term rate of return should be determined giving consideration to anticipated income taxes under enacted tax law. However, if the tax on income generated by plan assets is not a

liability of the plan, but of the employer, the expected long-term rate of return should not anticipate a tax on those earning since that tax will be reflected in the employer's accounting for income taxes.

Asset Composition and Actual Returns

[Unlike FAS-87, the proposed standard requires disclosure of the composition of assets held and the actual return earned on those assets for the period.]

308. Disclosure of information about the funded status of the postretirement benefit plan is important to an understanding of the economics of the plan. . . . The Board concluded that the information required to measure the vested postretirement benefit obligation should be available and that no significant incremental cost should be associated with providing that disclosure.

309. Management has a stewardship responsibility for efficient use of plan assets just as it does for operating assets. The Board concluded that disclosure of general information about the major types of any plan assets (and nonbenefit liabilities, if any) and the actual amount of return on plan assets for the period is useful in assessing the profitability of investment policies and the degree of risk assumed.

Assumptions

[While on the one hand the Board has found the measurement reliability of postretirement health care obligations sufficient for liability recognition, the points made under assumptions on this issue are daunting: "31. The health cost trend rate assumption . . . shall consider estimates of health care inflation, changes in health care utilization or delivery patterns, technological advances, and changes in the health status of plan participants."

And additionally, there are also to be considered "offsets" for benefits paid by others: "33. Certain medical claims [sic] covered by governmental programs under existing law, or by other providers of health care benefits."

The Board believes: "With increased experience, the reliability of measurement of the obligation and cost should improve."

In addition to the demographic projections required of pension liability and cost measures, postretirement medical benefits accounting requires explicit treatment for:]

- [Assumed per capita claims cost by age]

  29. The **assumed per capita claims cost by age** is the future per capita cost, after **the measurement date,** of providing the postretirement health care benefits at each age from the earliest ages at which plan participants could begin to receive benefits under the plan through their remaining life expectancy or the covered period, if shorter. To determine the assumed per capita claims cost by age, the per capita claims cost by age based on historical claims costs is adjusted for assumed health care cost trend rates and the effects of coverage by Medicare and other providers of health care benefits. The resulting assumed per capita claims cost by age reflects expected future costs and is applied with the plan **demographics** to determine the amount and timing of expected future benefits.

- [Health care cost trend rates including

  Health care price inflation
  Utilization and delivery
  Technological advances
  Changes in health status of participants]

Findings

For purposes of this Statement, a plan that promises to provide retirees a benefit in kind, such as health care benefits, rather than a defined dollar amount of benefit, is considered to be a plan that specifies automatic benefit increases. (The assumed increase in the future cost of providing health care benefits, the assumed health care cost trend rate, is discussed in paragraph 31.) A benefit in kind including the direct rendering of services, the payment directly to others who provide the services, or the reimbursement of the retiree's payment for those services.

31. The health care cost trend rates assumption represents the expected annual changes in the incurred claims cost of health care benefits currently provided by the postretirement benefit plan due to factors other than changes in the demographics of the plan participants. That assumption shall consider estimates of health care inflation, changes in health care utilization or delivery patterns, technological advances, and changes in the health status of plan participants. Differing services, such as hospital care and dental care, may require the use of different health care cost trend rates. It is appropriate to reflect in that assumption the fact that health care cost trend rates change over time.

32. Assumed discount rates include an inflationary element that reflects the expected general rate of inflation. Assumed compensation levels include consideration of future changes attributable to general price levels. Similarly, assumed health care cost trend rates include an element that reflects expected general rates of inflation for the economy overall and for health care costs in particular. To the extent that those assumptions consider similar inflationary effects, the assumptions about those effects shall be consistent.

Comments

171. The assumed health care cost trend rates consider the annual change in per capita claims costs due to factors other than changes in the composition of the plan participants by age or dependency status. Changes in the cost of providing health care benefits are influenced by several factors: changes in the cost of health care services depending on the nature and type of service, changes in the utilization pattern for health care services, changes in the nature of those services as medical practices change and new technology is developed, and the effect of deductibles or copayment provisions on an employer's cost of providing benefits. Thus, in developing the assumed health care cost trend rates, the effects of medical care inflation, changes in medical care utilization or delivery patterns, technological advances, and changes in the health status of the covered population are estimated.

[The proposal requires a measure of sensitivity of the liability to a 1 percent change in the health care cost trend. Such a sensitivity measure for projected wages was excluded from required disclosures under FAS-87.]

313. This Statement also requires disclosure of the effect of a one-percentage-point change (either a one-percentage-point increase or a one-percentage-point decrease) in the health care cost trend rate, holding all other assumptions constant, on measurement of the accumulated benefit obligation for postretirement health care benefits and the related cost. The Board concluded that requiring that sensitivity information will assist users in assessing the comparability of reported information as well as the extent to which future changes in assumptions may affect the measurement of the obligation and cost.

314. Although initially proposed in accounting for pension costs, the Board ultimately decided not to require sensitivity disclosures for pensions because the cost of providing that information was viewed as outweighing the benefits to users. Nevertheless, the Board concluded that the need for sensitivity information is more compelling for postretirement health care benefit measurements because of the subjectivity of the health care cost trend

rate and the significant effect that assumption may have a measurement of the accumulated postretirement health care benefit
obligation. The Board acknowledges that the effects of
percentage-point changes are not linear but concluded that the
significance of the sensitivity disclosure outweighs concerns
about erroneously extrapolating from the amounts disclosed.

- [Medical benefit payments made by others]

33. Certain medical claims may be covered by governmental programs under existing law or by providers of health care benefits.
Benefit coverage by those providers shall be assumed to continue
at the level provided by the present law or plan, absent evidence
to the contrary. Enacted changes in the law or amendments of
plans of other health care providers that will affect the future
level of their benefit coverage shall be considered in current-
period measurements for benefits expected to be provided in future periods. Future changes in the law or future amendments of
benefits provided by others shall not be anticipated.

Accrual versus Cashflow Accounting

[Once again, the Board has stressed the separation of accrual from
cashflow accounting, *and the promise of disclosing cashflow data.* And
once again, the required disclosures omit the relevant cashflows, benefit
payments, and contributions, if any.]

127. This Statement relies on a basic premise of generally accepted accounting principles that accrual accounting provides
more relevant and useful information than cash basis accounting.
The importance of information about cashflows or the funding
of the plan is not ignored. The amount funded or paid is given
accounting recognition as a use of cash, but the Board concluded
that information about cashflows alone is insufficient. Accrual accounting goes beyond cash transactions and attempts to recognize the financial effects on an entity of transactions and other
events and circumstances that have future cash consequences as
those events and transactions occur, rather than only when cash
is received or paid by the entity. Because the Board views the
event obligating the employer as the rendering of employee service in exchange for future (postretirement) benefits, this Statement rejects terminal accrual (accrual at retirement) and cash basis accounting. The Board concluded that for postretirement
benefits, as in other areas, the information resulting from accrual
accounting is more representationally faithful and more relevant

to financial statement users than accounting information prepared solely on the basis of cash transactions.

Disclosures

[Most of the disclosures parallel those of FAS-87 (including the failure to require statement of cashflows and benefit payments, funding contributions, and dividends—interest earned on plan assets). Some have a more technical derivation than need be covered in this book. However, of interest here are three outstanding differences from FAS-87. The first is peculiar to the current tax status of contributions for prefunding postretirement medical benefits. The second and third relate to disclosures that could have applied equally to pension plans, except that the Board is loath to revisit FAS-87.]

   e. The weighted-average assumed discount rate, rate of compensation increase, and health care cost trend rate used to measured the accumulated postretirement benefit obligation and the weighted-average expected long-term rate of return on plan assets and, for taxable plans, the estimated income tax rate included in that rate of return

   f. The effect of a one-percentage-point increase (or decrease) in the weighted-average assumed health care cost trend rate on the net periodic postretirement health care benefit cost and the accumulated postretirement benefit obligation for postretirement health care benefits

   g. The amounts and types of securities of the employer and related parties included in plan assets, and the approximate amount of future annual benefits of plan participants covered by **insurance contracts** issued by the employer and related parties

Transition

[The shift from cash to accrual accounting acknowledges that expenses recognized in the past were an understatement of "true" costs. Hence, current book values are overstated. The alternative "fixes" are to (1) restate past earnings, (2) hit current book values with the cumulative consequences immediately, or (3) create a balance sheet "transition" liability, which is leaked into future earnings over a period of years. The Board finds the first to be impractical and the second politically and economically impossible. We are left then with the distortion of income statements by the assumption of postretirement medical liabilities prior to the adoption date of the new standard for the next 15 years.]

Findings

105. For a defined benefit plan, an employer shall determine as of the measurement date (paragraph 63) for the beginning of the fiscal year in which this Statement is first applied (the transition date), the amounts of (a) the accumulated postretirement benefit obligation and (b) the fair value of plan assets plus any recognized accrued postretirement benefit cost or less any recognized prepaid postretirement benefit cost. Except as required by paragraph 106, the difference between those two amounts, whether it represents an unrecognized transition obligation or an unrecognized transition asset, shall be amortized on a straight-line basis over the average remaining service period of active plan participants, except that (1) if the average remaining service period is less than 15 years, the employer may elect to use a 15-year period, and (2) if all or almost all of the plan participants are inactive, the employer shall use the average remaining life expectancy period of those plan participants. Any unrecognized transition obligation related to a defined contribution plan shall be amortized in the same manner.

Comments

220. The issues of how and when the transition amount should be recognized are sensitive ones to employers who face, for the first time, the prospect of accruing the cost of postretirement benefits exchanged for current service as well as accounting for the cost of those benefits exchanged for prior service. Unlike the effects of most other accounting changes, a transition obligation for postretirement benefits generally reflects, to a considerable extent, the failure to accrue the obligation in the earlier periods in which it arose rather than the effects of a change from one accrual method of accounting to another.

221. A large portion of the transition obligation for postretirement health care benefits represents unrecognized service cost and interest cost for prior periods. That is, an employer changing from the cash basis of accounting for postretirement benefits to the accrual basis required by this Statement has not recognized the cost of the benefits that would have been attributed to the periods of employee service prior to the accounting change—the amount that would have been recognized as the service and interest cost components of net periodic postretirement benefit cost for those earlier periods. In addition, an indeterminate portion of the transition obligation may represent unrecognized prior service cost arising from a plan initiation or amendment or an unrecognized net gain or loss.

Index